In Defense of Neutral Rights

*The University of
North Carolina Press
Chapel Hill*

IN DEFENSE
OF
NEUTRAL RIGHTS

The United States Navy and the Wars of Independence in Chile and Peru

EDWARD BAXTER BILLINGSLEY

Copyright © 1967 by
The University of North Carolina Press
Manufactured in the United States of America
Printed by Heritage Printers, Charlotte, North Carolina
Library of Congress Catalog Card Number 67-23495

Preface

      The major events that have shaped United States history have had a definite east-west orientation—originating in Europe, flowing westward to North America, still westward across the continent to the Pacific seaboard, and finally across the Pacific to the Orient. Consequently, the great continent of South America with its rich, dramatic history and its great significance in relation to the United States has been largely ignored by all but a few North American historians.
  Naval history has followed the same east-to-west movement. With the important exception of studies of the Caribbean and Mexico, areas adjacent to the United States, naval historians have not broken the pattern to examine the relations of the navy with Latin America. Usually, naval activities in South America are dismissed with a few sentences between accounts of operations in the North Atlantic-Mediterranean theaters and the Western Pacific. Even the outstanding naval historian, Alfred Thayer Mahan, seems to have viewed South America more as an inconvenient land mass blocking free access to the Pacific Ocean —making the Panama canal a strategic necessity—than as a major part of the Western Hemisphere. One may look in vain through

his works for more than a casual mention of Latin America south of the Caribbean and Panama. This is all the more surprising when it is learned that Mahan was serving aboard a ship at Callao, Peru, when he received orders to report to the Naval War College to deliver his now famous series of lectures on sea power.

Nevertheless, many officers who gained the plaudits of the nation for their activities in the Mediterranean or the far reaches of the Pacific spent years of their lives off the shores of South America performing equally vital service in the protection of United States interests. During the final phases of the Wars of Independence for Latin America, a succession of outstanding naval officers performed this service in the remote Pacific as well as in the more publicized Atlantic and Caribbean areas. They had little or no direct effect on the gaining of independence by the Latin American countries. Rather, finding themselves enmeshed in problems created by the curious mixture of idealism and self-interest that has always plagued United States foreign relations, they directed all their efforts to the support of United States interests regardless of whether such efforts helped one side or the other in the revolutionary struggle. They loyally supported, and perhaps strengthened, traditional American policies of freedom for neutral trade.

The following study has attempted to ascertain the nature of naval activities off the distant coasts of Chile and Peru in support of American commerce, the resulting relationships of the naval commanders with patriot and royalist officials, the immediate effects on relations of the United States with South American governments, and possible long-range effects on interAmerican relationships.

The writer wishes to acknowledge the guidance and assistance of Professor Harold A. Bierck of the Department of History, The University of North Carolina at Chapel Hill, in the preparation of this study. He also must acknowledge that without the help of his wife Patricia it would never have been finished.

Contents

	Preface	v
I.	*The Strategic Year—1817*	3
II.	*Biddle and the Patriots*	16
III.	*Biddle and the Royalists*	39
IV.	*Biddle and Cochrane*	58
V.	*Captain John Downes versus Paper Blockades*	76
VI.	*Peru, 1820—Downes, Cochrane, Pezuela, and San Martin*	101
VII.	*Ridgely, 1821*	121
VIII.	*Captain Charles Stewart—The Pacific Squadron, 1822–1824*	148
IX.	*Justification by Court-Martial*	174
X.	*The Pacific Squadron Faces West: Conclusion*	194

Abbreviations	211
Notes	213
Bibliography	243
Index	257

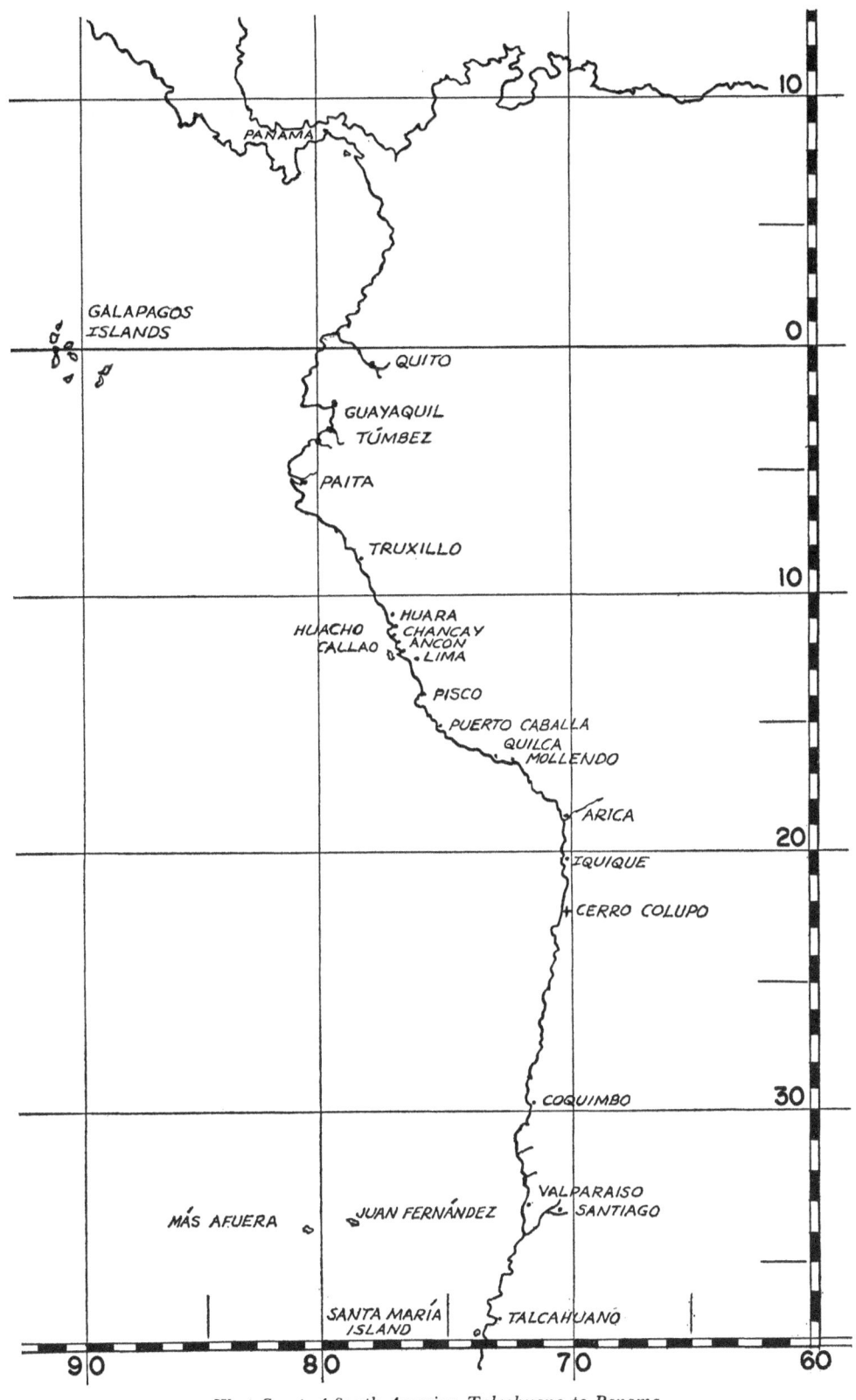

West Coast of South America, Talcahuano to Panama, from an Early Nineteenth-Century Chart.

In Defense of Neutral Rights

Chapter I

The Strategic Year — 1817

Few questions, domestic or foreign, demanded as much time and effort of President James Monroe's administration as those involving the independence of Latin America. Of paramount concern to this administration was the problem of United States relations with Spain and her insurgent colonies. In the Congress and the press as well, such questions as the recognition of the new nations, the maintenance of neutrality toward royalists and patriots, and the protection of United States commerce from both sides occasioned considerable debate. Borderland incidents, such as the establishment of the Republic of Florida by patriot adventurers at Amelia Island, just below the mouth of the Saint Marys River, which formed the boundary between the United States and Spanish Florida, created additional crises in United States-Spanish American relations.[1] It was our burgeoning commerce with Spanish America, however, that became the most important single factor in inter-American relations.[2]

The protection of this commerce became the responsibility of the United States Navy. In his inaugural address of 1817 Monroe enjoined the navy to "aid in maintaining the neutrality of the United States with dignity in the wars of other powers and in saving the property of their citizens from spoliation."[3] The previous year a special squadron had been organized for the protection of American commerce in the Caribbean and the Gulf of Mexico from pirates and privateers.[4] During 1817 other naval forces were deployed on the Atlantic coast of South America. Late in that year the sloop of war *Ontario* was ordered to the Pacific Ocean for the purpose of reclaiming the Columbia River territory from the British, but with the additional mission of observing conditions on the west coast of South America and checking on the welfare of American commerce and shipping in that area.[5] Thereafter, until the termination of the Wars of Independence, with the exception of a few months in 1819, one or more warships were stationed on the west coast of South America to protect United States interests.[6] It is with the affairs of these vessels and their commanders that this study is concerned.

The year 1817 marked the beginning of the end of Spanish supremacy in South America. During the year two great revolutionary leaders, Simón Bolívar in the north and José de San Martín in the south, began the military campaigns that eventually terminated in Peru, the last stronghold of the royalists on the continent. At the beginning of the year, however, royalist forces were in secure control of all Spanish America with the exception of the greater part of the old viceroyalty of La Plata and segments of Venezuela. In La Plata the Congress of Tucumán in 1816 had formally declared the independence of the United Provinces of Río de la Plata and named Juan Martín Pueyrredón as supreme director. In Mexico and New Granada the fires of revolution were banked if not entirely extinguished. Central America and Peru had not yet been disturbed to any great degree by revolutionary unrest.

On the southwest coast the former captaincy general of Chile had enjoyed a brief period of self-government between 1811 and 1814, known to Chilean historians as the *patria vieja*. Unfortunately the splitting of the patriots into two warring factions, one under José Miguel Carrera and the other under Bernardo O'Higgins, made it relatively easy for the royalist troops under General Mariano Osorio to reconquer Chile.[7] After the battle of Rancagua in October, 1814, remnants of the defeated patriots fled across the Andes, where many, under the command of O'Higgins, were incorporated in the Argentine Army being organized by San Martín. That general, while in command of the Argentine Army of the North, had clearly perceived that the independence of Spanish America could not be permanent until the royalists were ousted from their stronghold in Peru. Despairing of reaching the royalists through the Andes, he conceived the plan of attacking lower Peru from the sea by way of Chile. To execute this plan he secured an appointment as governor of Cuyo and began to organize and equip an army at Mendoza.[8]

In February, 1817, after two years of preparations, San Martín led the Army of the Andes through the treacherous mountain passes between the independent United Provinces and royalist-held Chile. A crushing defeat of the royalists at Chacabuco on February 12 marked the beginning of liberation for Chile. Four days later a *cabildo abierto* in Santiago chose O'Higgins as supreme director with dictatorial powers after San Martín had refused the post. The patriot forces quickly occupied the important ports of Valparaiso and Coquimbo while the royalists withdrew below the Bío-Bío River and clung tenaciously to the port of Talcahuano near the mouth of that river, where they planned to launch a counterattack.[9]

San Martín remained in command of the patriot army and, supported by O'Higgins, began preparations for the implementation of his master plan to conquer Peru from the sea. A superior naval force being essential for the success of this audacious undertaking, the two leaders set about building a navy that would eventually drive the Spanish fleet under the protecting guns of the forts of Callao and Guayaquil.[10] In 1817, however, the Spanish still were in command of the southeastern Pacific.

In the United States, events in Latin America were watched with interest, but there was no abrupt change of policy toward the Spanish American revolutions with the change of administration in March. As president, Monroe continued the policies he had helped formulate as Madison's secretary of state. Alejandro Álvarez, Chilean diplomatic historian, has summarized the policy of the United States toward the Latin Americans during this period as interested inquiry into the state of the struggle for independence and the maintenance of neutrality toward it.[11] United States historians describe the policy as one of benevolent neutrality, somewhat favoring the rebellious colonies.[12]

Monroe was personally sympathetic toward the insurgents and sought to convince them of the friendliness of the United States to their cause without compromising the publicly avowed neutrality. Until the arrival of John Quincy Adams as secretary of state in September, 1817, the members of the Cabinet shared the benign views of the president toward the patriots.[13] After he joined the Cabinet Adams supported the policy of neutrality but questioned the competency of the South Americans to establish democratic institutions of government. To him the patriots appeared to be more interested in achieving political freedom than in establishing true civil liberty.[14] He expressed doubts as to the expediency of recognizing the new Spanish American states or taking action in that direction before seeking more information on actual conditions in the new republics and ascertaining the attitudes of the European powers.[15]

There was a fraternal sympathy in the United States for any attempts by colonial peoples to break away from the domination of European monarchs as the North American English colonies had done in 1776—an instinctive approval of any nation claiming the blessings of democracy and liberty. In the case of the Spanish American states these blessings were enhanced by the opportunity of increased commerce as the new republics cast aside Spanish restrictions and opened their ports to all comers. American merchants and shippers had experienced a taste of Spanish American commerce when Spain was forced to abandon her centuries-old monopoly during the early stages of the Napoleonic Wars. Their activities temporarily curtailed during the War of 1812 with Great Britain, North Americans eagerly sought to recapture a share of the newly opened markets in South America after the Treaty of Ghent. By the end of 1817 there was a brisk trade with both the royalists and patriots, in the Pacific as well as the Atlantic.

Except for the four-year period of the *patria vieja*, most of the trade with the west coast had been of a clandestine nature before the liberation of Chile by San Martín, since the Royal Decree of 1797 lifting restrictions on neutral trade with the Spanish colonies had not applied to Pacific ports.[16] Thus, Chilean and Peruvian settlements were not regularly scheduled ports of call; but frequently, American ships bound for the Pacific Northwest and the Orient, taking advantage of the provisions of the Treaty of 1795 with Spain, would slip into Valparaiso or one of the other ports under the guise of taking on water, repairing damage sustained during the hazardous trip around the Horn, or seeking medical aid. Most of them carried a *carta de amistad* from Juan or Tomás Stoughton, Spanish vice-consuls at Boston and New York, which assured a friendly welcome if they were forced into one of His Catholic Majesty's ports by "bad weather or other misadventure." Many, incidentally, engaged in amicable smuggling. West coast ports also became an important source for the specie demanded by the China trade.[17]

Another important commercial link with the southeast Pacific was the ubiquitous New England whaling fleet. They, too, engaged in smuggling activities in addition to their legitimate pursuits.[18] The whalers were the first North Americans to return to the area after the War of 1812. In June, 1816, Monroe reported to Madison that no fewer than twenty-five vessels "had turned Cape Horn to take fish in the Pacific."[19] As the patriots threw open the ports of Chile, the whalers were joined by trading vessels from the great mercantile houses of New York, Boston, and Baltimore. Many of the merchantmen carried arms, ammunition, and other contraband, in addition to their regular merchandise. Thus, John Jacob Astor's ship *Beaver* from New York and the brig *Canton* from Salem carried munitions in addition to their normal cargoes. Both of these vessels were seized and condemned by the royalists at Talcahuano in the summer and autumn of 1817 for having on board contraband of war allegedly destined for the patriots.[20]

Not all of the trade was with the patriots. After the defeat of his army at Chacabuco, the viceroy of Peru, Joaquín de Pezuela, unable to get support from Spain, was obliged to seek replacements for the lost arms and equipment from the United States. The Spanish minister to the United States, the Chevalier Luis de Onís, acted as purchasing agent in North America and arranged for shipment of the arms in American bottoms. Often these ships would make one or more trading voyages along the coast before returning to their home ports. For example, the schooner *Governor Shelby* delivered a cargo of arms to Callao in May, 1818, at the order of Onís and, with the approval of the viceroy, made at least one trading voyage to Panama before returning to the United States.[21]

As contacts with the South Americans increased there was a corresponding increase of public interest in the United States in their affairs. If the administration pursued a policy of benevolent neutrality no such reticence was displayed by the public. Encouraged by a corps of skilled propagandists and a vociferously republican press, the public overwhelmingly favored the patriots and clamored for recognition if not outright military assistance to the rebels. During 1817 a number of pamphlets appeared in the United States favoring the South American Revolutions. Many widely read newspapers featured laudatory articles about the Spanish-Americans.[22] The Kentucky legislature adopted a resolution recommending that the United States recognize the independence of those Latin American countries that had declared themselves independent and had shown a reasonable ability to maintain their independence.[23] Sentiment was not confined to mere pronouncements in favor of the patriots. Some advocated open assistance; others indicated their feelings by harrassment of Spanish representatives in the United States. Onís complained to Adams that local authorities in New Orleans refused to take action against persons who had beaten the acting vice-consul there. The Spanish minister's own house had been assaulted, windows broken, and the lamps before the house smashed. One night the household had been awakened to find a dead fowl hanging from the bell rope.[24]

Public clamor in favor of the South American republics was

reflected in the Congress. Leader of the congressional faction favoring the insurgents was Henry Clay, speaker of the House of Representatives, who from that position of power sought to force the administration into recognition of the South American states. Honestly convinced of the integrity of South American republicanism and with a genuine respect for the rebels, Clay led many debates favoring a more positive attitude toward them. In January, 1817, in a debate on proposals to strengthen the neutrality acts, he made a masterful speech refuting the old charges that South Americans were incapable of self-government because of superstition and ignorance.[25] His most spectacular demand for recognition came in March, 1818, when he attempted to amend the general appropriation bill to provide $18,000 for the expenses of a minister to be sent to the United Provinces of Río de la Plata. His motion brought on the first full-scale debate in Congress on the question of recognition. The administration's policy of neutrality and watchful waiting prevailed, and the amendment was defeated by a vote of 115 to 45.[26]

The one-sided vote against Clay's move for recognition was not alone the result of pressure from the administration. A great many substantial citizens had genuine doubts as to the stability of the emerging republics. During 1817 the increasing lack of respect by patriot privateers for the flag of the United States magnified these doubts in the minds of many merchants and shipowners, particularly in the New England states. The seizure of Amelia Island by patriot forces bearing commissions of the Spanish American governments shocked many patriotic Americans who had long anticipated that Florida in due time would become the territory of the United States. Citizens of the slave-holding states were most sensitive to the northward advance of the doctrines of emancipation advocated by South American rebels.[27]

There was mounting pressure on the president for action of one type or another during 1817. Not all of it came from the advocates of recognition. A considerable amount came from shipowners who demanded protection for their vessels against Spaniard and patriot alike. These demands were not new. For example, in June, 1816, Monroe, then secretary of state, had dealt with the case of an American whaling ship that had been detained by the royalist officials of Lima because she had no sea letter. The owners of other ships in the Pacific, fearing that the same fate would befall their vessels, valued at around half a million dollars, banded together and deputized a Mr. Gardner of Nantucket to plead their case for protection in Washington. Not only did Gardner request that the government make strong protests to the Spanish, but he confidentially stated to Monroe that the sending of a frigate and a suitable agent to the South Pacific would be welcome to the shipowners. The suggestion was given serious consideration, but no action was taken during 1816 because of lack of funds in the Navy Department.[28]

Monroe and his advisers were acutely aware that their deliberations on South American problems were severely handicapped for lack of complete, accurate, and unbiased information on conditions in the Southern Hemisphere. There was only one United States representative in all of South America with the dignity of a fully accredited diplomatic agent—the minister to the Portuguese court in Rio de Janeiro. In Spanish America a few scattered agents for commerce and seamen performed consular duties but had no diplomatic powers. These agents were, for the most part, businessmen who performed consular duties for the fees involved or to further their own commercial ventures. For this reason full confidence could not be placed in their reports to Washington.[29] Throughout 1817 there was no United States representative on the west coast of South America. To remedy this deficiency, William G. D. Worthington was appointed special agent to Buenos Aires, Chile, and Peru but did not arrive on station in Santiago until February, 1818.[30] Jeremy Robinson was appointed agent for commerce and seamen at Lima by Acting Secretary of State Richard Rush in March, 1817, but the appointment was revoked by Adams the following November before Robinson had left the United States.[31]

Obviously, unbiased accounts of conditions could not be expected from the patriot agents assigned to the United States. Indeed, it was often hard to determine just exactly who or what some of the patriot agents represented. Commodore David Porter wrote unofficially to his friend, José Miguel Carrera, that this

The Strategic Year — 1817

fact was one of the reasons the United States was slow to recognize the new nations. He told Carrera it was soon discovered that the South American agents were not representatives of governments so much as of a faction or party.[32]

Extraordinary measures were taken during 1817 to determine the true state of affairs in Spanish America. In April, Joel R. Poinsett, former consul general to Buenos Aires and Peru, was offered a new appointment as special agent to Buenos Aires and the La Plata area, but he declined the post.[33] Concurrently, Rush, at the direction of the president, initiated action to obtain reliable information concerning the Spanish Main. Captain Charles Morris in the frigate *Congress* was instructed to visit that area "to obtain as much and as precise information as possible on conditions there."[34]

After Poinsett's refusal to return to South America, it was decided to send a special commission of three prominent citizens to observe the situation in the La Plata area. Throughout the summer, Rush labored industriously to recruit suitable commissioners, prepare instructions, and arrange for transportation. There was a sense of urgency in the efforts of the harried statesman to get the commission organized and on its way.[35] The Navy Department was requested to provide transportation. While Rush struggled with the organization of the mission, Secretary of the Navy Benjamin Crowninshield and the Navy Board were busy getting a ship ready. Captain James Biddle was ordered to take command of the sloop *Ontario* and prepare her to receive three "respectable gentlemen" who were expected to embark before July 4.[36] By midsummer two commissioners, Caesar A. Rodney and John Graham, and a secretary, Henry M. Brackenridge, had been chosen. Rush, still working under pressure, believed the commissioners would soon depart. He issued instructions for their guidance on July 18 and optimistically reported to Monroe that he might now consider them "as finally got off."[37] Sailing orders for the *Ontario* were issued by the Navy Department on July 21, and by the end of the month Biddle reported her ready to put to sea the "minute his passengers embarked."[38]

Believing arrangements for the commission to Buenos Aires completed, Rush turned his attention to another area about which little or nothing was known, the west coast of South America. To correct this deficiency, Judge John B. Prevost was appointed special agent to Chile and Peru with general supervision over other United States agents in the area, including Worthington and Robinson. Biddle was directed to take Prevost on the *Ontario* as far as Buenos Aires, where the agent was to disembark and proceed overland to Chile.[39]

For one reason or another the departure of the South American Commission was delayed. In August, Midshipman John Rodney, a son of the senior member and attached to the *Ontario*, contracted fever and died in New York. On receipt of this unhappy news in Washington, the mission was temporarily suspended out of consideration of the elder Rodney.[40] It was merely delayed, not cancelled. Eventually, in December, augmented by a new member, Judge Theodorick Bland of Baltimore, the commission sailed for Buenos Aires aboard the frigate *Congress*, now commanded by Captain Arthur Sinclair.[41]

In the meantime, Adams, who had now assumed the duties of secretary of state, was anxious to get Prevost on station in the Pacific, not only to perform the duties of agent but also to reassert the claim of the United States to the Columbia River territory, which still remained in possession of the British. This action had been urged by John Jacob Astor since the end of the War of 1812.[42] Adams decided to take advantage of the ready state of the *Ontario* and send her with Prevost on board directly to the Pacific. Accordingly, new instructions were issued to Prevost and the commander of the *Ontario*. After consultation with Secretary of the Treasury William R. Crawford, Adams, in his duplicate instructions to Biddle, associated the naval officer with Prevost in "the ceremony of taking possession, in the name and on behalf of the United States, of the territory at the mouth of the River Columbia."[43]

Adams' instructions were also incorporated in the secretary of the navy's new sailing orders to Biddle. These orders directed him to proceed around Cape Horn in the *Ontario* with Prevost as passenger. In the Pacific the ship was to put into Valparaiso for a limited visit to take on provisions, effect any repairs required as a result of the trip around the Horn, and make prepara-

The Strategic Year — 1817

tions for the onward voyage to the Columbia. En route to the Northwest a brief stop was to be made at Lima. The duration of the stay in each port was to be determined after consultation with Prevost. At the Columbia the claim of sovereignty of the United States was to be asserted "by some symbolical or appropriate mode adapted to the occasion." From the Northwest the *Ontario* was to return to the United States, stopping at Lima or Valparaiso only long enough to disembark Prevost. With Prevost on board, the *Ontario* sailed for the Pacific in October.[44]

Spanish American problems continued to plague the administration. On October 30 the Cabinet was assembled to discuss a series of questions submitted for consideration by the president. At this session, which lasted three and a half hours, it was decided to proceed with the special commission to South America.[45] It was also determined to break up the patriot establishments at Amelia Island and Galveston, using force if necessary. The Navy Department was requested to provide the additional vessels needed to implement these decisions. As a result, John Henley, captain of the *John Adams*, was ordered to take charge of a nondescript force of smaller vessels and occupy Amelia Island in co-operation with the army. Subsequently, a joint army-navy force under Henley and Major James Bankhead occupied Amelia on December 23, 1817.[46]

By December, 1817, the navy was heavily committed in virtually all Spanish American waters as a result of the Wars of Independence. The frigate *Congress* was en route to Buenos Aires with the South American Commission; the *John Adams* with a force of smaller vessels was busy evicting the "patriot" government of the Republic of Florida from Amelia Island; at New Orleans, Captain Daniel F. Patterson was directing the operations of a fleet of small vessels against the pirates and privateers in the Gulf of Mexico; and the *Ontario* was rounding Cape Horn on her way to the Pacific.

It is doubtful if many naval officers had strong convictions concerning the Spanish American Wars of Independence until after 1814, for the simple reason that they were too preoccupied with their own battle with Great Britain. It is reasonable to assume that they followed the popular attitude of the public and the press in approval of the revolutions as being in the best republican tradition. There were a few outspoken advocates of the patriots on the navy rolls. Among them were Commodores Sinclair and Porter. The latter was especially active in espousing the patriot cause, having operated off the coast of Chile in the famous cruise of the *Essex* during the War of 1812. That cruise had coincided with the first period of Chilean independence, the *patria vieja*.[47]

Other prominent naval officers were not so favorably disposed to the patriot cause. As the naval forces of the new Spanish American states began to expand and the tempo of the war at sea quickened after 1816, carelessly commissioned privateers became excessively active. Frequently they were more concerned with the taking of prizes, regardless of flag or cargo, than with coming to grips with the enemy. North American naval officers in direct contact with the patriot naval forces began to have doubts as to the purity of their motives. Adverse reports began to trickle into Washington from the Gulf of Mexico and the Caribbean, the points of maximum contact with the rebel forces. Early critics were Captain Morris, in command of United States forces in the Gulf and Caribbean in 1816 and 1817, and Captain Patterson, commanding officer at New Orleans. They were joined in their criticism by Captain Henley and Master Commandant John H. Elton, who were responsible for observing and curbing the unlawful acts of the patriot forces at Amelia Island.[48] Their reports undoubtedly had a strong effect on the thinking of the administration. Morris was in Washington during September and October when many of the important decisions of 1817 were made. He was interviewed by Adams just ten days after the latter took over as secretary of state, and the new secretary found his report sufficiently interesting to forward to the president. Benjamin Homans, chief clerk of the Navy Department, in the absence of Secretary Crowninshield, suggested the "propriety of [Morris'] calling on the President at his residence" to brief him on the Spanish-Americans. The administration had the naval officer's report printed unofficially in the *National Intelligencer*.[49]

The publication of Morris' report was indicative of the administration's concern with the mounting interest and tension throughout the country on the Spanish American question and perhaps an attempt to justify the actions initiated during 1817. In a congratulatory letter to Monroe on his annual message, read to Congress on December 2, Nicholas Biddle, Philadelphia tycoon and confidant of the president, correctly pinpointed Spanish American relations as the greatest problem facing the government: "With regard to the affairs of South America there exists a very strong excitement. This is indeed the great question of your administration; and for your sake, for the sake of our country & for the great cause of free government, I feel a feverish anxiety that our course may be so fair and manly and liberal as to leave no room for reproach or even for suspicion."[50]

Nearly one-fourth of the entire text of Monroe's first annual message was devoted to Spanish and Spanish American affairs. It clearly defined the problems created for the United States by the revolutions in South America, the actions taken or planned to meet such problems, and the official attitude of this country toward the new governments. In that portion of his message announcing the special commission to South America, the president linked the navy with his civilian representatives: "To obtain correct information on every subject in which the United States are interested; to inspire just sentiments in all persons in authority on either side, of our friendly disposition so far as it may comport with an impartial neutrality, and to secure proper respect to our commerce in every port and from every flag, it has been thought proper to send a ship of war with three distinguished citizens along the southern coast with instructions to touch at such ports as they may find most expedient for these purposes...."[51]

For some reason Monroe made no mention in his annual message of the *Ontario*'s voyage to the Pacific. Although her primary mission was the repossession of the Columbia River territory for the United States, her exuberant commander soon became involved in the death struggle between the patriots of Chile and the royalists of Peru through his efforts to protect American merchantmen in the Pacific ports. He was the first of a succession of naval commanders charged with enforcement in the Pacific of the commander in chief's dictum "to secure proper respect to our commerce in every port and from every flag."

Chapter II

Biddle and the Patriots

When the decision was made to send the *Ontario* into the Pacific without waiting for the dilatory South American Commission, both the State and Navy Departments had to revise their instructions on short notice. In the ensuing exchange of orders, Prevost received instructions to report for transportation aboard the *Ontario* before Captain Biddle himself was officially notified of the new assignment. Thus, when Prevost reported on October 2 expecting to proceed at once, Biddle informed him that the ship was still under orders to take the commissioners to Buenos Aires and that he had no authority to proceed without them.[1] This incident presaged the touchy relationship that later developed between the two men. New sailing orders for the *Ontario* were received the next day, and Prevost returned on board late that evening. The ship was underway for the Pacific the next morning, October 4.[2]

The change in destination also created new logistic problems for the navy. One of these was the procurement of adequate navi-

Biddle and the Patriots

gational charts of the Pacific. There were none in the Navy Department, and none were to be had in the New York book shops. Finally, a set of Vancouver's *Voyages* and Cook's *Voyages* with accompanying chart folios were found in the New York Library. These were loaned to the navy on Biddle's promise that they would be replaced with similar editions from London.[3]

The procurement of suitable stores for a diplomatic mission of this importance posed no problem since the Department of State had ordered an impressive array of delicacies at New York for the South American Commission. These were transferred to Prevost and Biddle for their use on the Pacific cruise. An extensive wine list included fifteen gallons of cognac, ten gallons of Jamaica rum, twenty dozen bottles of first quality claret, and twenty dozen of second quality claret. Among other items were one thousand pickled oysters, one hundred pounds of bourbon coffee, fifty pounds of fresh butter put up in small stone crocks and covered with saltpeter, and fifty dozen fresh eggs packed in sand after having been dipped in hot oil.[4]

The dispatch of the *Ontario* to the Pacific was unique not only because of her special mission to the Columbia River but also because she was the second United States man-of-war to round the Horn and the first to make the passage while the country was at peace. Her predecessor, the frigate *Essex*, had made the voyage in 1813 under Captain David Porter in order to elude British forces in the Atlantic.[5]

The *Ontario*, unlike the *Essex*, was bound on a peaceful mission. She was in competent hands. Her commander had been selected originally as host to the South American Commission as much for his background and diplomatic capabilities as for his naval record. Biddle was a member of a distinguished Philadelphia family; his uncle, Captain Nicholas Biddle, had served in the Continental Navy, and his brother, another Nicholas Biddle, was a financier and intimate of President Monroe. Before entering the navy he had studied at the University of Pennsylvania, where he was interested in literature. His naval career was distinguished. Appointed midshipman in 1800 he served in the Mediterranean, where he was captured in the *Philadelphia* by the Tripolitans and kept prisoner in Tripoli for nineteen months.

His family offered to ransom him but he refused, preferring to share the lot of his shipmates. He was treated better, however, than most prisoners of the bashaw, for he had letters of introduction to Sir Alexander Ball, governor of Malta, who supplied him with food and clothing and directed the British consul at Tripoli to watch over his welfare. During the War of 1812 he was a lieutenant on board the *Wasp* when she captured the *Frolic* and commanded the *Hornet* at the capture of the *Penguin*. For these exploits he was honored with a medal by Congress and promoted to captain.[6]

Biddle was typical of the naval officer of the period—an expert seaman, a strict disciplinarian, bold, proud, sometimes arrogant, consciously aware of his own worth, and determined to uphold his personal honor at all costs. In common with his brother officers, he was sensitive of his responsibility to uphold the rights and honor of the young United States on the high seas and in foreign ports. Indeed, the naval officers instinctively equated their own honor with that of the nation. Hence, they were quick to resent any indication of slight to themselves or their country and insisted on the measured observance of protocol, which in international usage is the mark of respect. Nor was the navy alone in this attitude; the people and the press applauded the nationalism of its officers. The press took delight in publishing letters from naval officers abroad and usually added a few patriotic observations of its own. *Niles' Weekly Register* in reporting excerpts from letters of officers of the Mediterranean Squadron took occasion to praise the character of the officers themselves, who presented "the happiest unions of *mind*, with valor and skill." The editor believed that they "speak a language also of a singular character—we *can* do this, we *will* do that, we HAVE DONE another thing; it is the language of men who suppose themselves invincible, on anything like equality of terms—and *they are so*...."[7]

At the public dinners honoring the heroes of the War of 1812, patriotic speeches and belligerent toasts were common fare. Laudatory poems and mawkish songs of praise were features of the program. One such song in honor of Biddle was sung at a dinner for him in New York. Entitled "Columbia's Naval Heroes" a portion of it ran:

> Columbia can boast, of her heroes a host,
> The foremost at Duty's and Danger's proud post,
> Who full often have won upon Ocean's rough wave,
> The brightest leav'd laurel that e'er deck'd the brave.
>
> The world with one voice bids their Country rejoice,
> As with blushes it owns that these sons of her choice
> For valor and feeling have gain'd the rich prize,
> And stand first midst the first that live under the skies.[8]

It is small wonder that such public acclaim bestowed on men accustomed to the authority of the quarterdeck and the absolute obedience accruing to ship command should develop a corps of naval officers with supreme confidence in their ability to serve the best interest of their fellow citizens. Nor was this attitude centered solely in their own egos; they also cherished an unquestioning faith in their nation and the virtue of its institutions. It was this combination of confidence in themselves and faith in their country that could permit Stephen Decatur, in all sincerity, to propose his famous toast at a dinner in his honor: "Our country! In her intercourse with foreign nations may she always be in the right; but our country, right or wrong."[9] It was with these sentiments that Biddle approached his duties in Latin America.

The first lieutenant of the *Ontario*, David Conner, was assigned at the special request of Captain Biddle.[10] As second senior officer on the *Ontario*, one of his duties was to supervise the preparation of the ship's log and a journal of the cruise. Conner also kept a private journal, which is more detailed in some respects than the official records. Fragments of it have been preserved and provide interesting commentaries on events and customs in South America in 1818.

Their passenger, John B. Prevost, had a distinguished public career and influential connections. A stepson of Aaron Burr, he had been secretary to Monroe when the latter was minister to

France. He was thought to be a prime favorite of the president and to have considerable influence in the White House.[11]

The voyage of the *Ontario* from New York to Valparaiso was unexceptional. After a brief stop at Rio de Janeiro, where Prevost conferred with Thomas Sumter, Jr., United States minister to the Portuguese court, she continued on to the Pacific. The Horn was negotiated with no great difficulty, and the *Ontario* arrived off Valparaiso on a pleasant summer day, January 25, 1818.[12]

Off Valparaiso the North Americans made their first contact with one of the combatant forces in the Pacific. Cruising before the port was a blockading squadron of two ships and a brig under the command of Spanish Capitán de Navío Tomás Blanco Cabrera. The entire province of Chile had been ordered blockaded by Viceroy Joaquín de la Pezuela in February, 1817, immediately after receipt of news of the Battle of Chacabuco in Lima. Under United States interpretation of international law the blockade was not legal, inasmuch as the Spanish did not have sufficient naval ships to keep an effective watch on the entire Chilean coast and did not maintain ships continuously on station off the blockaded ports. Indeed, the haphazard maintenance of the blockade before Valparaiso by his naval commanders was a source of major concern to the viceroy himself.[13]

Regardless of the legality of the blockade, three Spanish ships were present to enforce it at Valparaiso when the *Ontario* set course to enter the harbor. She was hailed from the flagship *Venganza*, ordered to back her sails with head off shore, and send a boat to the flagship. To Biddle's reply that the *Ontario* was a public vessel of the United States bound for the Northwest Coast with orders to touch at Valparaiso for provisions, Cabrera sent a boarding officer to inform him that the ports of Chile were under a strict blockade to men-of-war as well as to merchantmen and offered to provide any needed stores at Callao or from his own ships. There then followed a game of bluff, which Biddle won. He informed Cabrera's boarding officer that his orders made it mandatory for him to "touch" at Valparaiso. The Spanish officer replied, truthfully, that his orders from the viceroy allowed no exceptions. Finally, to break the impasse, Biddle sent Conner to Cabrera to ask him bluntly if he intended to use force to prohibit the entry of the *Ontario* to Valparaiso. Cabrera replied he would not resort to force but requested that Biddle give him a statement in writing that he had been warned of the blockade.[14]

Biddle supplied the requested statement with great relief. A year later in his official report of the cruise, he stated that he would not have forced his way into Valparaiso. His reasoning in this respect coincided with the Spanish contention regarding the status of the colony. Biddle's report said: "Considering Valparaiso, not in the light of a foreign port in respect to Spain, but as a Spanish port and in a state of revolt against its own government, I was of opinion that Spain had a right to interdict the entrance to it of even Men-of-war."[15]

Having made his point Biddle kept the *Ontario* offshore until the following morning when she stood into the harbor and anchored. Present were five North American and three British merchantmen, held in port by the blockading force. The British man-of-war *Amphion*, under command of Commodore William Bowles, was also in port. Having anchored at Valparaiso the day before the blockading squadron arrived on station, the *Amphion* had escaped an argument over her right to enter.[16]

Prevost and Biddle busied themselves in learning all they could about their countrymen's affairs and extending to them such aid as appeared practicable. A few days after their arrival Prevost went up to Santiago to confer with officials of the Chilean government. Before leaving the coast for the capital he learned that upwards of twenty North American ships had visited Valparaiso in the past twelve months and that an estimated forty whalers from New Bedford and Nantucket were operating off the shores of Chile and Peru. The cargoes of the United States ships at anchor in Valparaiso were valued at a million dollars. Five more ships were reported at anchor at Coquimbo up the coast. First reports of the seizure and condemnation of the *Beaver* and *Canton* by the royalists at Talcahuano were received. Impressed by the magnitude of the United States commercial interests in the area, Prevost recommended a permanent naval force in the Southeast Pacific, citing in his report the activity of the British Navy in support of English shipping.[17]

In Santiago, Prevost learned that Chile had made no changes in the old Spanish laws governing commerce. Her revenue was derived primarily from import and export taxes—30 per cent on imports and 10 per cent on exports. Alluding to the prevalence of *mordida* ("bite") in the customs service, he wrote that the import tax was not nearly as onerous as it appeared since the value of imports was determined by an appraiser "whose judgement is mostly swayed in favor of the importer by application of a secret and irresistible influence always within his means."[18]

While Prevost was in Santiago, Biddle gave his attention to the problems of the North American merchantmen in the harbor. He found them beleaguered by both royalists and patriots. They had been caught in port by the arrival of the blockading squadron in January and could not leave without danger of being seized for violation of the Laws of the Indies. Meanwhile, their crews were being seduced by the patriot privateers with promises of higher wages, rapid promotion, and rich prize money. Since the Chileans had no merchant shipping of their own, they were almost entirely dependent on "volunteers" from English and North American ships. Some of the merchantmen had lost so many crewmen to the patriots that they could not get underway with safety. It was useless for the ships' officers to appeal to the Chilean officials since even the governor connived with the deserters. Reporting their plight to Biddle the masters asked help in putting a stop to future desertions and in recovering crewmen already lost.[19]

Accordingly, Biddle wrote to San Martín asking him to put a stop to the enticement of the crewmen. The general evaded the issue, claiming that his authority extended only to military affairs, and suggested the matter be referred to the supreme director at Santiago.[20] Nonetheless, the day after his written rejection of Biddle's request, San Martín was a guest aboard the *Ontario* and promised to issue the necessary orders to stop the suborning of American seamen. Appeals were also made to the supreme director, the commandant of the fort, and the governor of Valparaiso, with some degree of success. Although very few of the absentees were returned, open incitement to desertion ceased, at least as long as the *Ontario* remained in port.[21]

Biddle's relations with the Chilean authorities during this visit were, for the most part, harmonious. The usual amenities were exchanged. For San Martín's visit to the *Ontario* on February 2, 1818, the yards were manned and a salute of fifteen guns was fired in his honor. The acting supreme director, Luis de la Cruz, was given the same honors when he came on board February 19. Both he and Tomás Guido, representative of the supreme director of the United Provinces of Río de la Plata to Chile, sent warm letters of welcome to the warship of a sister republic. The latter remarked on the "natural relations" existing between the revolutions of North and South America and the similarity of objectives of the two peoples.[22]

Friendly relations were easy to maintain with higher officials in the relatively remote capital, but friction soon developed with those at the working level in Valparaiso. Biddle became so angry with the governor of Valparaiso, Francisco Calderón, that for a while he refused to have any type of intercourse with him. Part of the American's ill humor was caused by a misunderstanding over the exchange of salutes.

When the *Ontario* first arrived in port and official calls were exchanged, Biddle had proposed to fire a salute to the Chilean flag provided it was returned gun for gun. The governor accepted this proposition but requested that the exchange be deferred until the following day so that troops in the vicinity could be notified, lest unscheduled firing cause them to go to battle stations. He was to have notified the ship commander when he was ready to return the salute. The following day the *Ontario*'s gunners stood by their batteries all day expecting to fire the promised salute. No word came from the governor. The punctilious Biddle came to the conclusion that his proposal had been rejected and characteristically construed it as an affront to himself and his country.[23]

The misunderstanding between Biddle and Calderón was heightened by the un-co-operative attitude of the latter toward returning merchant seamen to their ships and reached the breaking point when he refused to surrender promptly some sailors apprehended trying to desert from Biddle's own command. On the night of February 6, six men from the *Ontario* commandeered one of the ship's boats and attempted to reach shore, with the intention of signing up with the patriots. They were discovered pulling away from the ship and were fired on by the sentries. The firing attracted the attention of a Chilean patrol boat, which took them into custody and escorted them ashore. Biddle naturally assumed the defectors would be returned to his ship and sent one of his junior lieutenants to bring them back. The Chilean authorities refused to surrender the men to this officer, whereupon the first lieutenant was sent ashore to fetch them. When Conner too was rebuffed Biddle sent him back to Calderón with a written note demanding return of the men, whereupon the latter gave assurances that the men would be sent out at eight o'clock the following morning after an official examination. By nine o'clock the men had not been returned. Once more the first lieutenant was sent ashore, this time with a harsh note inquiring as to the governor's ultimate intention and accusing him of insulting the United States flag. Conner met Calderón as the latter was returning from the British frigate *Amphion*, where he had gone to consult with Commodore Bowles. The British commander had advised return of the men to their own command without delay. This was done, but Calderón had the bad taste, as the impatient Biddle considered it, to suggest that the deserters not be punished because they had wanted to join the service of Chile.[24]

Biddle was so exasperated over the affair of the *Ontario*'s deserters that he determined to have no further intercourse with the governor and proposed to shun the shore until he could go on to Lima.[25] A projected trip to Santiago was cancelled, and the acting supreme director was advised that circumstances transpiring in Valparaiso imposed on the commander the necessity of remaining aboard his ship.[26]

De la Cruz apparently knew the details of the quarrel. A few days later he was in Valparaiso and visited the *Ontario*. When he was piped aboard he remarked in a jocular vein that he had come to settle the differences between the ship commander and the governor and to take the naval officer back to the capital on a visit. Biddle refused to be mollified. He frankly told the acting supreme director that he considered the governor's conduct insulting and would so report it to Washington unless some satisfactory explanation was given. De la Cruz assured him that no disrespect was intended by Calderón but failed to come up with an acceptable explanation of the governor's conduct. Biddle declined the new invitation to visit Santiago, stating that the explanations he had received did not justify abandonment of his determination not to leave his ship in the patriot port.

Biddle was disgusted with Valparaiso and wished to go on to Lima as soon as possible. On the twentieth he sent Conner to Santiago to request Prevost's concurrence in departing earlier than they had previously planned. At the same time he prepared a full account of the events that had transpired in Valparaiso in a report to the secretary of the navy. Unfortunately for Biddle's later defense of his activities in Chile this report was never "posted." It was sent to Santiago for Prevost's information, and was then to be delivered to a gentleman departing for Buenos Aires. Prevost took exception to the last paragraph, which he considered derogatory to the Chilean government and requested its deletion. As a result the letter missed the prospective courier and was never sent, amended or otherwise. The paragraph to which Prevost objected read: "I incline to believe that in the present state of this Country, there is not a disposition on the part of the Government, to do upon such occasions, that which is required no less by a just regard to their own honor, than a due respect to the rights of foreigners visiting their ports."[27]

Lieutenant Conner recorded details of the courier trip to Santiago in his journal. The party left Valparaiso between 8:00 and 9:00 P.M. on February 20 and arrived in Santiago at about the same time the next evening with a few hours stop at a farm house for sleep enroute. The trip was made on government post horses hired through the director of the port. For twelve and a half cents a league the service provided the necessary horses, pack animals, and a postillion. The horses were changed at frequent intervals—usually every three leagues and never more than six; they covered about ten miles an hour.

Like most nineteenth-century travelers fresh from the cold, perilous passage around the Horn, Conner was enthusiastic about the beauty, climate, and natural resources of Chile. Concerning the land and its products he was rhapsodic. Corn, wine, and oil were plentiful. The excellent and extensive variety of fruit "exceeded all belief." Concerning the livestock: "Animals not only multiply but improve in this delightful climate." An ox could be bought for ten dollars and a horse for twenty. There were no beasts of prey nor venomous insects. Valuable mines of gold, silver, and copper abounded.

About the people he was less enthusiastic: "But all these blessings are rendered vain by the indolence of the people. . . . Its mines are unwrought and its fields are uncultivated." This lack of ambition and progress was attributed to the repression of Spanish rule for the past three centuries. Like most North Americans, Conner had faith in the benefits of republicanism and a free commerce. He approved of the Chilean revolution and predicted the people would soon overcome the handicap of centuries. "Active commerce" and the subsequent intercourse with other countries would "soon raise this country to that elevated station it is entitled to fill among the nations of the world," he wrote, and added: "This great change is rapidly taking place. . . ." These comments were made soon after the arrival of the *Ontario*.

By March he was less certain that the Chileans could overcome their heritage of "ignorance, prejudice and bigotry." The immediate cause of this observation was a picturesque Easter festival in Valparaiso harbor, which was described in detail in his journal: "March 21st—at 10 this morning a salute was fired from the patriotic batteries and shipping to commemorate the resurrection of our Savior, at the same time Judas (His betrayer) was exhibited hanging from the yardarms and bowsprits of the different vessels, from which he was plunged into the water where to make his disgrace complete, boats filled with boys and men were ready to beat this effigy with their oars and pelt him with stones." This rather pagan ceremony led to some somber reflections on the readiness of the people for liberty:

Is it possible for a people who suppose this absurd custom is acceptable to the deity, and in the performance of which, they are taught to believe this fulfills the most sacred obligation of their religion—can it be possible I say for such a people to appreciate the blessings of liberty which in all human probability they are about to atchieve [sic]—no! ignorance, prejudice and Liberty are incompatible—they may change their masters—but Freedom will never deign to make that house his abode; ... whose sons are chilled by the iron grip of ignorance, *prejudice & bigotory [sic]*.

The young officer shared the prevailing Anglo-American Protestant's distaste for the Catholic clergy and what he considered the superstitious religious festivals of the church. He noted that hospitals were without physicians but that churches were attended by numerous priests "some of whom" he had "seen intoxicated in scandalous company."

The naval officer was more sympathetic toward family groups and described the houses and living conditions in some detail. His attitude toward the females varied, but on the whole was most complimentary. On one occasion they were described as sitting in Turkish fashion and entertaining their visitors "with bad music and worse singing to the guittar [sic]." Yet their flashing black eyes, it seems, were irresistible. There is a hint of romance in the entry, "In this delightful region, the Angel Woman fulfills her destiny!"[28]

Young Isaac Coffin of the brig *Canton* had much the same impression of the land and inhabitants of royalist-held Chile. In his *diario* he wrote: "In regard to beauty and salubrity of climate, fertility of the soil, as well as landscape and variety of products, there is no region in the world which surpasses it. Its mountains are sublime and at the same time picturesque beyond belief, its fields wide and fertile, its rivers broad and deep, its stock beautiful and noble: all with the exception of its sovereign, man, who, unaware of these natural beauties and conditions, goes about buried in contemplation of earthy things."[29] Coffin was struck somewhat unfavorably by the trading propensities of the

Chilean *campesino*: "On a small scale they are traders, as their time is passed in dealing and haggling. Characteristically, nothing is permanent in their homes or on their persons, and there is nothing, either, which they have or can buy that they would not be ready to sell at any time, if it gained them a profit, however small...."[30]

Prior to Conner's courier trip to Santiago the United States merchantmen in Valparaiso, apprehensive of being caught in the patriot port in the event of a royalist victory and desirous of getting their valuable ships and cargoes as well as their crewmen out of the reach of both belligerents, had appealed to Biddle, through Prevost, for convoy through the royalist blockade under the protection of the *Ontario*. Biddle considered that his instructions did not cover such a heavy responsibility and refused to break the blockade. Furthermore, he was dubious of the legal position of the merchantmen since there was no doubt that they had engaged in trade with the patriots in a former Spanish port in violation of existing Spanish laws.[31]

He agreed, however, to approach the blockade commander with the request that they be allowed to depart peacefully from Valparaiso and to continue their voyages unmolested on the grounds that they had entered the port without previous knowledge of the blockade and before an effective force had actually been stationed off the city. On February 14 the *Ontario* put to sea to parley with the blockade commander. The better part of the day was spent in conferences and exchanges of viewpoints between the North American and Spanish commanders. Biddle was politely and correctly received but pleaded for the merchantmen's free departure in vain. Pleas for release of the *Beaver* and *Canton* on similar grounds were also rejected.

Cabrera wasted little time defending the technical aspects of the blockade, although he reminded the North American that it had been in effect nearly a year. He based his right to seize foreign vessels entering or leaving a Spanish colonial port on the Laws of the Indies, which forbade foreign vessels from trading in such ports without authority from the crown. Regardless of their claimed independence, Valparaiso and other Chilean ports were still Spanish and subject to Spanish law in the eyes of the blockade commander. He announced that he would continue to consider any foreign ships leaving as well as entering the Chilean ports as fair prizes.

As for the *Beaver* and *Canton*, Cabrera said the same laws applied at Talcahuano as at any other Spanish colonial port. He made no attempt to refute the contention that they had put in there from necessity, merely stating that ships of his squadron had taken them in custody on suspicion of violating the Laws of the Indies and their cases had been decided by legitimate tribunals ashore. In the case of the *Beaver* he had personal knowledge that she carried arms, munitions, and other contraband. He was not familiar with details of the *Canton*'s case but was confident that proceedings were in accordance with Spanish law.[32]

Biddle, uncertain of the true facts in the cases of the *Beaver* and *Canton* and of their legal status, realized there was no point in further argument with the Spanish commander. He decided that the best way to help them was to appeal to the viceroy during his approaching visit to Callao. The liberation of these vessels became one of his prime objectives during the remainder of his cruise in the Pacific.

The stories of the *Beaver* and *Canton* are typical of those of many merchantmen on the west coast of South America during the Wars of Independence. The *Beaver* belonged to John Jacob Astor, who in 1817 loaded her with a cargo valued at $140,000 and placed her in charge of Captain Richard J. Cleveland for a trading voyage to Chile, although her papers stated that she was bound for Canton and the Northwest. Part of her cargo consisted of arms and munitions. She blundered into Talcahuano in search of wood and water in the mistaken belief that it was a patriot port. The royalists promptly seized her and confiscated the cargo on the grounds that she was illegally attempting to trade with the patriots.[33] The *Canton* from Salem had similar misfortunes.

The two ships were stripped of their cargoes, which were turned over to the hard-pressed royalist armies. Some of the officers and crewmen took events quite philosophically, among them young Isaac Coffin of the *Canton*, who kept a diary of his experiences in royalist Chile. Because of the royalists' straitened circumstances, he viewed their seizure of the *Can-*

ton's cargo as much a matter of necessity as of law and recorded in his diary that if they had not found a law to justify the confiscation they would have invented one.[34] Others were less complacent. Francisco Ribas, second supercargo of the *Beaver*, and several other crewmen made good their escape to patriot territory. Ribas cast his lot with the patriots and became an ardent supporter of the revolutionary regime. It was he who alerted Biddle to the seizure of the *Beaver* when the *Ontario* pulled into Valparaiso.[35]

Captain Cleveland had hoped that the *Ontario* might help him recover his ship. This hope, however, did not deter him from taking aggressive action on his own. When the *Beaver* and *Canton* were sent to Callao, Cleveland gained the confidence of the viceroy and with his concurrence engaged in trading expeditions between Peru and the patriot coast, utilizing chartered ships. In effect, he became a partisan of the royalists. With true "Yankee" ingenuity he improved his fortunes to such an extent that by 1820 he could boast he was part owner in five vessels or their cargoes trading out of Peru.[36]

Another mission that Biddle undertook for his countrymen was the collection of a claim on behalf of the ship *Enterprise*, another of Astor's ships. The *Enterprise* had contracted with the Chilean government to repatriate the patriot exiles from Juan Fernández Island for a fee of five to six thousand dollars. She had been paid only one thousand dollars before leaving Chile. Biddle had met her master in Rio de Janeiro and agreed to undertake collection of the unpaid balance. He pressed the claim with his usual vigor. A favorable opportunity presented itself when the acting supreme director requested that a printer attached to the *Ontario* be allowed to join the patriot forces. It so happened that the man in question was one of those who had attempted to desert in February. Biddle would have preferred to send the would-be deserter home in irons rather than allow him to join the patriots but in the interest of diplomacy allowed him to join the Chileans. In the letter announcing the sacrifice to the acting supreme director, Biddle shrewdly brought up the question of the *Enterprise*. Claiming to be an intimate friend of the owners, he pressed for payment as an indication of the Chilean government's interest in repaying its just debts. The minister of state, Miguel Zañartu, suavely replied for the government that Biddle's friendship for the owners was sure to bring favorable consideration and the claim would be speedily settled with W. G. D. Worthington, who had recently reported to Santiago as special agent of the United States.[37]

Events prolonged the visit of the North Americans to Valparaiso. The arrival of the *Ontario* came at a critical time in Chile's war for independence. Only eight days previously nine transports from Peru, escorted by the frigate *Esmeralda*, had landed an expeditionary force of some thirty-six hundred men at Talcahuano.[38] Under the command of General Mariano Osorio this force raised the patriot siege of that port and advanced toward Santiago. Between the royalists and the capital, patriot armies estimated at ten thousand, under San Martín and O'Higgins, were confidently awaiting the assault. O'Higgins had turned over the civilian duties of the supreme directorship to De la Cruz in order to take the field. The future of Chile, and with it that of Peru, depended on the outcome of the impending battle. Shortly after Prevost's arrival in Santiago he had sent back word to Biddle at Valparaiso that they should postpone their departure for at least a month. Biddle agreed to this proposal.[39]

Near the end of February, Prevost returned to Valparaiso, and March 3 was fixed as the date of departure. On the evening of March 1 an officer from the staff of San Martín came on board and requested that they defer sailing until after the issue between the patriots and the advancing royalists was decided. He gave as the reason that San Martín was certain of victory and hoped the *Ontario* would carry the news to Lima, whereupon he expected the people of Peru to rise in revolt. The American citizens of the area provided a more convincing reason for remaining when they requested that departure of the warship be deferred until the impending battle was decided. At that time the opposing armies were reported in sight of each other.[40]

The next two weeks were marked by much unrest. Many unfounded reports of action reached Valparaiso.[41] On March 5 the British East Indiaman *Windham*, mounting thirty-four guns, evaded the blockading force and entered the harbor. She had been sent out from England by José Álvarez Condarco for sale to the Chilean government.⁴² A special commission, of which Guido was the leading member, came down from Santiago to negotiate the purchase. The uncertain military situation ashore and a difference of $20,000 in the bid and asked prices temporarily interrupted the negotiations. The commission offered $180,000, while the owners held out for $200,000. The commission returned to Santiago, but one of them, a Mr. Campbell, remained in Valparaiso. This gentleman informed Conner that purchase of the *Windham* was really a private speculation with interested merchants putting up the bulk of the money and the government the remainder. The merchants expected to be paid back from the capture of the royalist flagship *Venganza*.⁴³

Meanwhile, Chilean fortunes took a turn for the worse. The battle of Cancha Rayada, near Talca, occurred on March 19. News of the disastrous defeat reached Valparaiso on the twenty-second. Wild rumors circulated through the city—it was said that O'Higgins was mortally wounded and that San Martín was probably dead. The patriot troops were reported in utter disorder. The patriots began preparations to leave Valparaiso, while the royalist sympathizers made ready to come out into the open. The officers of the *Ontario* believed their presence prevented open warfare between the patriots and the royalist partisans since patriot garrison troops had been withdrawn immediately after the battle.⁴⁴

News of the disaster created an unexpected and serious problem for Biddle. With the patriot army defeated it was only a matter of time until the royalists occupied Valparaiso. The least the North Americans in the port could expect would be confiscation of their ships and property. The blockading squadron offshore prevented their free departure. To make matters worse, Osorio threatened to execute every American and Englishman who fell into his hands. Although Biddle considered the threat was made more to discourage the foreigners from assisting the patriots than with any real intention of carrying it out, he could not ignore it and determined to do all he could to protect the lives and property of his countrymen. The British frigate *Amphion* having left Valparaiso, the master of the *Windham* offered to place his ship and its crew of a hundred men under the American's command although it was still British-owned. By this time the blockading squadron had been reduced to one frigate and two smaller vessels so that the combination of the *Ontario* and the *Windham* had a good chance of defeating them in an open fight. Therefore, Biddle decided to convoy the American and other vessels through the blockade, using force if necessary. Orders were issued to the merchantmen present to get underway and proceed out of the harbor when signaled by the *Ontario*. In case of trouble between the armed ships and the Spanish squadron they were to scatter and proceed as best they could.[45]

On March 23 Worthington arrived from Santiago and confirmed previous reports of the patriot defeat. He announced that the capital was being evacuated. It was decided to sail with the merchantmen the next day, but the following morning the movement was postponed because the merchantmen were not ready. That afternoon, the twenty-fourth, a message was received from San Martín announcing that the patriot army was reassembling in good order and expected to defeat the enemy. The confidence of the commander in chief inspired Valparaiso. The citizens went from despair to joy, and that night the city was illuminated and salutes were fired as if a victory already had been won.[46]

In the meantime another frigate joined the blockading squadron. This made a drastic difference in Biddle's plans to oppose the Spanish with force. The odds against the *Ontario* and the *Windham* were now too great to risk an open battle. Not only was it possible that the effort would fail, but it would almost certainly have far greater consequences than the immediate safety of the merchantmen. The American commander decided to remain at anchor, keeping the *Ontario* ready for eventualities and hoping that her physical presence would provide some measure of protection for his countrymen if, and when, the royalists occupied Valparaiso. There was also a chance that the blockading force might again be reduced, permitting a return to the original plan.[47]

Interest in Biddle's probable line of action was not confined to the harbor of Valparaiso. In Concepción and Talcahuano there was much speculation among the royalists and the crews of the *Beaver* and *Canton* as to what would happen to the American ships anchored in the patriot port after Osorio's expected victory. They were curious as to how far Captain Biddle would go to defend them.[48]

The naval commander faced a grave responsibility. Balanced against his duty to protect United States citizens and property was the risk of involving his country in war with Spain. He was prepared to take that risk as long as there was a chance of success but prudently declined to take precipitate action that would more likely lead to disaster than to the liberation of the merchantmen. The dilemma was resolved by the patriot victory at Maipú. Biddle made no pretense of hiding his relief and satisfaction when he wrote his brother Nicholas of the events in Chile:

> Osorio invaded [the] country with the determination, it is believed, of putting to death every American and every Englishman that fell into his hands. The belief of this rendered my situation extremely embarrassing and painful as the English and Americans all expected me to defend their persons and their property agt. the common enemy by land and by sea. The magnitude of responsibility which circumstances might have induced me to take made me wait with fear and anxiety the event of the battle; and the victory, relieving me from all my embarrassments, has given me a most lively joy; more lively perhaps than I should have felt solely from my love of justice and of the sacredness of the cause of the victors. The truth is, as you perceive, my interest as well as my feelings were enlisted on the side of the patriots.[49]

At that time Biddle was convinced that the patriots represented the sacred cause of republicanism against the tyrannical forces of monarchy. In the dark days between Cancha Rayada and Maipú his enthusiasm for the republican cause was expressed in more than words. Biddle reported that no request of the patriots that was not definitely unneutral and that was within his power to grant went unheeded.[50] Indeed, at times the rules of neutrality were stretched beyond recognition.

There is evidence that Biddle intervened to hasten the purchase of the *Windham*. On March 31 Calderón relayed word to San Martín from the captain of the *Ontario* that it was absolutely necessary to buy the East Indiaman or she would sail within three days for Lima. Calderón recommended making all sacrifices to acquire the ship.[51] Biddle's motive for this message is not clear. He was most anxious to have as much support as possible for any clash with the Spanish blockade squadron and thus may have wanted to be sure of keeping her around; or he may have been trying to help the captain of the *Windham*, who had generously agreed to take his commands, to make a profitable sale.

Guido returned to Valparaiso and resumed negotiations to buy the *Windham*. He was invited to live aboard the *Ontario* but declined, lest it be thought that he was afraid of the royalists. He deemed it prudent, however, to deposit a large sum of money to be applied to the purchase of the East Indiaman on the United States man-of-war for safekeeping.[52]

The purchase of the *Windham* was completed on April 5, 1818, the date of the battle of Maipú. She was renamed *Lautaro* and work began immediately to arm her as a warship. Biddle gave freely of his advice and assistance in this task. Carpenters and armorers from the *Ontario* helped in the conversion from merchantman to man-of-war.[53] For his assistance Biddle received a warm note of thanks from San Martín.[54] Guido gave both Biddle and Prevost much credit for the acquisition and conversion of the ship, and was reported to have been annoyed at the Chilean government for not publishing acknowledgement of their assistance.[55]

The conversion of the *Lautaro* to a warship mounting forty-six guns was continued at a rapid pace. Toward the end of April, after the *Ontario* had left the harbor, she was almost ready for action, but changing her rigging and armament proved easier than finding an experienced crew. With no United States warship present to prevent it, the Chilean officers once more began to raid the helpless merchantmen in the harbor. The governor even resorted to force to take men.[56] In an affidavit executed before the United States vice-consul at Valparaiso, Solomon Townsend and Shubal Burr, master and mate of the ship *Lion* from Providence, described the methods used to draft their crewmen.[57] The *Lion* had arrived in Valparaiso in October, 1817, and had been unable to get away since that time because of a combination of the blockade, a shortage of men, and patriot embargoes. Some of the crew had deserted before the arrival of the *Ontario*, but the Chilean officials had taken no action on the master's protests. The desertions stopped while the *Ontario* was in port, but things changed as soon as the warship left the harbor. On April 20 one man of the *Lion* deserted to the *Lautaro*. Appeals to the governor and to the captain of the converted man-of-war were fruitless. Indeed, the latter stated that he would receive and protect any sailor joining his ship; he would release them only on an order from the supreme director himself. As a last resort, Townsend, with other masters, sent a special messenger to Santiago to request the intervention of Worthington with the supreme director.

On the morning of April 23 all masters of ships in the harbor were directed to report to the governor's house at ten o'clock. When they arrived they found present Guido, the governor, Charles Denegal, and Henry Hill. The last two were agents for the *Lautaro*. Hill was also the United States consul, recently appointed. Guido took the floor and advised the masters that the object of the meeting was to consult on methods of raising men for the *Lautaro*. He proposed that each merchant captain allow a part of his crew to volunteer for that service. Apparently this was intended only for a single action against the *Venganza* since Hill seconded the proposal and explained that any men lost to the Spanish in the action could be replaced by inexperienced *chilenos*. He hinted that in the absence of volunteer assistance the government might use the same methods it had used with the *Rambler*, a Providence ship that had been forcibly taken and employed as a patriot cruiser the previous year. The captains of the merchantmen were not impressed by these arguments and withheld co-operation.

The next day two of the *Lautaro*'s officers and a port official of Valparaiso came aboard the *Lion* and ordered a muster of the crew. Paying no attention to the ship's officers they offered a ten dollar bonus and shares of prize money to men volunteering for duty on the Chilean warship. Five of the *Lion*'s crew agreed to sign up. Later in the day when a custom's house boat came alongside and demanded the men, the master refused to allow them to leave the ship. Still later an Englishman in the Chilean service

Biddle and the Patriots 37

came alongside and stated that he had orders to board every ship in the harbor and take four men from each of their crews.

Armed with a note from Worthington to the effect that the supreme director was ordering the previous deserters sent back to their ships, Townsend, accompanied by Hill, called on the governor to request return of his men. The governor, after listening to their plea, said he would not give up a single man, "even to an order to that effect from General Saint Martin or God Almighty himself."

Other ship masters experienced the same treatment. Charles S. Carey, master of the *Levant* of Boston, made a similar affidavit. Carey was bitter about his treatment because he had loaned his ship's carpenter to the *Lautaro* and had been told by the warship's captain that none of his men would be drafted. He accused the governor of treating "with contempt" the order of the supreme director to restore the shanghaied seamen to their normal ships.[58]

After the battle of Maipú there had been no apparent reason for the *Ontario* to remain in Chile and the interrupted voyage to the Columbia River was resumed. Before sailing Prevost forwarded a report of recent events in which he recommended early recognition of Chile and praised the good effect produced by the *Ontario*. An enclosure to his report was a memorial from ten masters and supercargoes of vessels at Valparaiso, plus Henry Hill the consul, thanking Biddle for his efforts in their behalf and crediting him with protecting them from ships of the Spanish blockade; preventing the seduction of their seamen by the patriots; furnishing aid necessary to the safety of the ships; and saving nearly a million dollars of American property from condemnation and many American citizens from oppressive imprisonment.[59]

Biddle, prior to sailing, wrote a detailed account of conditions in Chile to his brother. In it he was very critical of his countrymen who had come out to join the Chilean army. There could not be a sorrier lot, he said; some of them "succeeded only in getting in jail."[60] With regard to Chile's chances of conquering Peru he considered an overland attack impossible; naval ascendancy was a necessity. If the Chileans could land an army the conquest of Peru, he believed, was certain. He thought the news of Osorio's defeat would produce a revolution in Peru and would strengthen his own hand in dealing with the viceroy when he arrived at Lima.

As for acknowledgement of the independence of Chile, Biddle wrote:

> It is certain we might secure great commercial advantages by being before hand with the British in coming out in favor of this people, especially if we had an intelligent, discreet agent on the spot, but, unfortunately, when our ship sails, W. G. Worthington will be our public agent & he, by his folly and misconduct, has lost the confidence of the Chile government. But there is a strong sentiment of sympathy and kindness toward our government here & in all classes of people, & we are in fact greatly preferred before all other foreign nations. This sentiment, I can flatter myself has not been weakened by the presence of this ship.[61]

This letter was received in the States in September, 1818, and Nicholas Biddle considered it of sufficient importance to forward to President Monroe for his information.[62]

When the ship got underway for Callao on April 12, 1818, the blockading squadron was sighted off Valparaiso but no messages were exchanged. None of the merchantmen accompanied the *Ontario* because the day before she weighed anchor the patriots declared an embargo on merchant ship sailings in order to prevent news of the *Lautaro*'s preparations from reaching the Spanish squadron. The embargo, a favorite device of both royalists and patriots, was supposed to remain in effect until the republic's new ship could get to sea in an effort to break the blockade.[63]

Chapter III

Biddle and the Royalists

After an easy nine-day voyage along the route to Peru, called the "Ladies' Passage" by the Spanish because it was so pleasant, the *Ontario* arrived in Callao on April 21. But the calm of the benign Pacific had found no counterpart in the cabin country of the warship. During the passage the captain and his passenger had a misunderstanding that has never been fully explained.

By the time they reached Callao, Biddle and Prevost were hardly on speaking terms.[1] The underlying cause of the quarrel was undoubtedly the division of authority between two strong-willed men. It appears that the civilian agent attempted to interfere in the operations of the naval officer's command. Biddle confided to Jeremy Robinson that Prevost had attempted to dictate to him who should be received on board the *Ontario* at Valparaiso, and later at Callao had insisted that the ship should be anchored beyond the range of the guns of the forts.[2] This last statement is symptomatic of a more serious cause of conflict between the two men—disagreement over the policy to be adopted toward the patriots and royalists—a difference that was intensified by the visit to Callao and subsequent events.

During the visit to Valparaiso, Biddle's enthusiasm for the patriots had waned. It cannot be said that there was a corresponding conversion to royalist ideology, but he did find it much more comfortable to deal with Viceroy Pezuela than with the somewhat demanding and unpredictable patriots. There grew up a mutual respect and trust between him and the royalist official that was not achieved in his relations with the patriot officers. On the other hand, Prevost's sympathy for the patriots increased, and he never overcame the mistrust of the royalists evidenced by his unwillingness to put himself within range of the shore batteries of Callao. He believed, with some reason, that the unexpectedly friendly reception accorded them on their arrival at Callao by the viceroy was due wholly to the unfavorable situation that official found himself in as a result of the defeat at Maipú.[3]

The arrival of the *Ontario* at Callao had been expected. Onís, the Spanish minister at Washington, had forewarned Pezuela that the ship was bound for the Pacific, ostensibly to protect commerce. On the basis of the original orders to the *Ontario*, he had mistakenly warned that her real purpose was to bring three commissioners to observe conditions in Lima, Chile, and Buenos Aires, and to treat with the insurgents for recognition of their independence. When Pezuela first met Prevost he identified the latter with the commissioners against whom he had been warned and immediately took a great dislike to the United States agent.[4] He reserved judgment on Biddle.

Regardless of their personal differences, Biddle and Prevost each pursued the same goals in seeking to secure better treatment for United States ships and citizens on the South American coast. They both sought the relaxation of the Valparaiso blockade, the release of the *Beaver* and *Canton*, permission for whalers to obtain wood, water, and provisions on the mainland without risk of seizure, and the release of United States citizens imprisoned as a result of the war.[5]

The North Americans brought the first news to Lima of the Spanish defeat at Maipú and gave the viceroy a very gloomy account of the loss of his army in Chile. He was also informed of the arming of the *Lautaro* and the patriots' plans to attack the Spanish blockade squadron, after which a strong expedition against the coasts of Peru was expected. The commander of the *Ontario* gave the viceroy to understand that his ship had been diverted from its trip to the Columbia River for the sole purpose of bringing news of the battle of Maipú in order that preparations could be made for defense of the Peruvian coast against a surprise attack.[6] By exposing the vulnerability of the viceroyalty while emphasizing the friendship of the United States, the Americans hoped to gain concessions from the viceroy to the advantage of United States shipping and commerce.

Pezuela was convinced of the basic truth of his visitors' accounts and quietly began preparations for the defense of Peru. In order to prevent disorders among patriot sympathizers in Lima he encouraged doubts as to the truth of the accounts brought by Biddle and Prevost, professing to believe them improbable so soon after the smashing royalist victory at Cancha Rayada. This attitude created much public hostility toward the visitors, especially after the *Venganza* entered port and her commander refused to confirm the report of Maipú, having himself had no news later than Cancha Rayada of Osorio's actions.

The strategy of Biddle and Prevost worked. Pezuela had stripped Peru in order to assemble the expedition for the reconquest of Chile. Realizing that he needed time to rebuild his defenses, he determined to utilize the *Ontario* to delay the expected patriot assault.[7] He was prepared to make concessions to secure the co-operation of Biddle and Prevost.

The first move was made through a confidential agent, who was sent to Prevost to ask whether it would be possible for the *Ontario* to return to Valparaiso with a royalist minister on board to effect an exchange of prisoners and a cessation of hostilities. It was explained that the viceroy could not make a direct approach to the Chileans since he had previously refused to treat with a patriot emissary on the same subject—hence the desire to utilize a neutral. Prevost was given to understand that as evidence of his sincerity the viceroy was willing to order his blockading squadron to refrain from molesting United States merchantmen not carrying arms. Whaling vessels would be permitted to visit the mainland to receive supplies. Prevost considered the proposal as being in consonance with his mission to the Pacific and recommended to Biddle that it be accepted, agreeing to take the responsibility for delaying the voyage to the Columbia River. Biddle gave his assent.[8]

The confidential agent who talked with Prevost was probably Félix de Ochavarriague y Blanco, factor of the Philippine Company, who contacted Biddle on the same subject, either concurrently or shortly after Prevost had indicated approval of the project. From the time of Biddle's agreement to take the *Ontario* back to Valparaiso, Prevost seems to have been bypassed in the negotiations—a fact that he reported to Adams with obvious distaste. For his part the viceroy preferred dealing with the naval officer rather than the agent. Pezuela wrote: "It was necessary that in my critical situation I should secure some advantage from the commander of the *Ontario*, Mr. Biddle, of whom I had formed as good opinion as I had unfavorable of his passenger, Prevost."[9] Biddle had studiously avoided making any inquiries about troops, arms, or public opinion, or making any comments on the conflict between the patriots and royalists. He carefully avoided association with any persons suspected by the royalists. This circumspection was noted with approval by the viceroy and sharply contrasted with Prevost's open preference for the insurgents.[10]

Biddle was approached by Ochavarriague, who urged him to take the *Ontario* back to Valparaiso on the humanitarian mission. The American seized the opportunity to seek concessions from the viceroy. He asked for relaxation of the Valparaiso blockade and release of the *Beaver* and *Canton*, as well as release of any United States citizens held in Lima's prisons. Ochavarriague had no authority to make such concessions but suggested that Biddle seek an interview with Pezuela, at which such matters could be discussed. Biddle was given to understand that if the interview was satisfactory to him he then would be expected to initiate an offer to carry a commissioner to Valparaiso to arrange an exchange of prisoners.[11]

The resulting interview proved satisfactory. On April 27

Pezuela graciously replied to an earlier letter of Biddle's protesting the Spanish blockade.[12] The viceroy stated that he would give orders to the blockading squadron at Valparaiso permitting United States ships to depart provided they carried no insurgent property. Future vessels approaching the port, whalers or cargo ships, would be warned of the blockade and would not be seized unless they attempted to violate the blockade after such warning or carried contraband, in which cases they would be considered fair prizes. The viceroy made it clear that this action was taken in the interest of Spanish-United States amity. He stated positively that international law, to which Biddle had appealed, had no force in the present situation and that Spain maintained her right to interdict trade with her colonial ports under her own general laws—such laws had been effective for centuries and were well known to all nations.

Although the viceroy had written Prevost that he knew of no Americans imprisoned at Lima, Biddle learned that there were several so confined. On his visit to the viceroy he asked for them by name. The viceroy released them to him. Two of them, Abel Bacon and Reuben Cash, had been convicted of coining false money. Four others, Thomas Pearle, George Lake, George Brown, and Michael Wharton, had been crewmen of a Buenos Aires privateer. None of these men had a clear claim to the protection of the American flag, but Biddle took them on board the *Ontario*. The men did not appear to have suffered or to have been harshly treated in prison. Concerning the viceroy's prisons, Biddle wrote: "the severe and rigorous imprisonment, which it has been said, our Countrymen unjustly suffer from the Spanish royalists, however true it may be with respect to other parts of South America is not true with respect to Peru."[13]

The American ship commander also aided British subjects. One John Amory, surgeon of a British whale ship, wrote for assistance in getting out of prison. He had been left in Pisco because of illness and was being held by the Spanish because he had no passport. Biddle requested the Englishman's release and promised to take him out of Peru. The viceroy readily agreed and the surgeon was taken to Valparaiso aboard the *Ontario*.

Pezuela provided a ready excuse for Biddle to return to Valparaiso. He announced that he had no means of immediately communicating his new orders to the blockade commander and probably would not be able to send a ship to the south for some time. In order to save the American merchant ships inconvenience should they wish to leave Valparaiso in the interim, Pezuela suggested that Biddle himself carry the order south. Biddle, in his turn, replied that he would be happy to undertake the delivery of an order so important to his compatriots. Then, noting that many prisoners were held by both sides with no organization for their exchange, he offered his mediation and good offices toward effecting that result. This offer was accepted by the viceroy with alacrity.[14]

Thus the mission to negotiate a cartel and possibly an armistice between the royalists and patriots was arranged. Ochavarriague was appointed by Pezuela as his emissary because the businessman and San Martín had served together in the Spanish army in their youth. A British-born merchant of Lima, Thomas Crompton, was sent along as secretary to the commissioner. To make the mission more acceptable to the Chileans, four patriot officers held as prisoners by the royalists were put aboard the *Ontario*. Pezuela's offer to send back to Chile all patriot prisoners he held at Lima—some eighty—was declined for lack of room aboard the warship. Ten thousand pesos in coin and one hundred ounces in bar silver were put on board for the welfare of the Spanish prisoners, the money being entrusted to Biddle.[15]

The viceroy did not mitigate His Catholic Majesty's laws for nothing. Although he was genuinely anxious to effect an exchange of prisoners, he had other motives as well. Biddle's offer made it possible, with all safety, to send an agent on the *Ontario* with orders to purchase ten thousand guns that it was understood were for sale in the foreign ships at Valparaiso and to have them sent to Callao. Orders were also given to Ochavarriague to return immediately with any information of insurgent plans for invasion of Peru.[16] Pezuela's secret agent was probably Crompton, the secretary of the cartel mission. His presence on the mission aroused the suspicions of the Chileans and subsequently caused comment among the foreign colony in Santiago.[17] That the exchange of prisoners was a secondary consideration to

Pezuela is attested by his own statement: "I sent them [Ochavarriague and Crompton] under the pretext of continuing the exchange of prisoners begun at the request of San Martín."[18]

Just how much of this plan was known to Biddle is not clear. In his *memoria*, Pezuela indicates that the naval officer was privy to the scheme but does not differentiate between what he, Pezuela, expected to gain and what Biddle, the middleman, offered in sponsoring the mission. It is unlikely that an officer with Biddle's high sense of personal integrity and conscious pride as guardian of his country's honor would knowingly countenance traffic in contraband or spying activities on a project that he had sponsored in his official capacity. At a later date, when he was accused by the patriot foreign minister of carrying Ochavarriague to Chile as a spy, he indignantly denied that the mission had any other purpose than the exchange of prisoners.[19]

There is nothing in either Biddle's or Conner's accounts of the *Ontario*'s cruise to indicate that Biddle encouraged illegal trade, but it is certain that he encouraged the viceroy to open the channels of legitimate trade to his countrymen. Throughout the cruise he did everything in his power to promote such trade with both belligerents. It should be remembered that this was before the era of "total" war. Traffic in foodstuffs and other noncontraband goods with belligerent countries, even between the countries at war, was entirely in accord with international law as understood by the United States. The right to carry on such commerce was one of the cornerstones of this country's foreign policy. During the South American Wars of Independence, trade in foodstuffs between belligerents, such as Chile and Peru, was common. Biddle actively and openly participated in the arrangements for the American ship *Two Catherines* to carry a cargo of wheat from Valparaiso to Callao when he returned to the latter port in June. He proudly reported to the secretary of the navy that the *Two Catherines* "made a great voyage," meaning that she netted a handsome profit.[20]

On May 8 Ochavarriague and the other passengers boarded the *Ontario* at Callao. That evening she weighed anchor for Valparaiso[21] and after an uneventful voyage arrived at the Chilean port on May 29, 1818. One reason for the voyage had been eliminated by the time she arrived—there were no Spanish warships off the harbor, the blockade having been broken by the *Lautaro* on April 26. On that date the new Chilean warship had left Valparaiso with the deliberate intention of joining action with the frigate *Esmeralda* and the brig *Pezuela*, which were then maintaining the blockade. The resulting battle was indecisive, but the *Esmeralda* was damaged so severely that she withdrew to Talcahuano for repairs, taking with her the brig. Thus, the *Lautaro* accomplished the most important part of her mission, the breaking of the blockade. Returning to Valparaiso she captured the richly laden Spanish brigantine *San Miguel*. The proceeds from this vessel enabled the Chilean government to pay off the merchants who held shares in the *Lautaro*, and she became a regular man-of-war, wholly owned by the government.[22]

Of the American ships that had been left embargoed in Valparaiso in April, only one, the ship *Two Catherines*, remained. Although shorthanded as a result of patriot recruiting methods, the others had sailed as soon as they possibly could after the *Lautaro-Esmeralda* engagement. Biddle was annoyed at the reported treatment of the American masters by the Chilean officers in recruiting a crew for the *Lautaro* but made no official protest.[23] He was too concerned with the cartel negotiations to make an issue of the matter.

Immediately on anchoring Biddle dispatched a letter to the supreme director explaining the unscheduled return to Chile and his part in the proposed negotiations for exchange of prisoners. Permission was requested for the viceroy's emissary to proceed to Santiago with his secretary to begin negotiations. Authority to expend the ten thousand pesos for the welfare of Spanish prisoners was also asked. Biddle indicated his desire to accompany the minister and offered his services to further the aims of the mission. He was very much concerned that the royalists should be well received and made it clear that he considered himself responsible for their safety and well-being. In this regard he wrote:

As this gentleman [Ochavarriague] with his secretary, Don Thomas Crompton, have come hither in this ship and under my protection, I request your Excellency permission for them to land and proceed to Santiago, and I also request that your Excellency will be pleased to give me assurances that they shall be respected during their stay and be allowed freely to embark on their return at any moment they may desire—upon receiving this permission and these assurances from your Excellency, I shall myself accompany Don Felix to Santiago & I shall be very happy to contribute all my endeavours to produce between the two countries such an arrangement with respect to prisoners as may alleviate the evils of the war which at present unhappily exists.[24]

Biddle's letter was welcomed by the patriots not only because of the opportunity to establish a cartel for exchange of prisoners but also because it was believed the negotiations constituted a step toward recognition of Chile's status as an independent nation by the viceroy. The minister of state, Antonio José de Irisarri, immediately replied, welcoming the commission and giving assurance that the passengers would be received in Santiago with generosity and decency and might leave whenever they had completed their charge, or before if they wished. Biddle was profusely thanked for his efforts and advised that a lodging was being prepared for his personal use in Santiago by order of the supreme director.[25]

Biddle was pleased with the prospects for exchange of prisoners. His letter to the supreme director proposing the mission and Irisarri's reply were given prominent space in the *Gaceta ministerial*, official journal of the Chilean government. Biddle and his passengers, Ochavarriague and Crompton, were escorted to Santiago by an officer and a guard of soldiers. In the capital the naval commander was received with every mark of respect and friendship by O'Higgins. On June 5 the supreme director gave a fiesta in his honor. One of the guests was Theodorick Bland, a member of President Monroe's Special Commission, who had come overland to Chile from Buenos Aires the previous month.[26]

Biddle's passengers did not fare as well in Santiago. With good reason, they were treated as suspect by the patriots. Ochavarriague was placed with an officer of the government and kept under surveillance throughout his stay. Biddle said he was in the "custody" of the Chileans. The secretary was kept under what amounted to close confinement.[27]

The suspicions of the patriots turned to rage when they learned that Ochavarriague's credentials as the viceroy's emissary were addressed to General San Martín as an individual and not in his official capacity as general in chief of the Army of Chile. The viceroy had been unwilling to go that far in recognizing the belligerent status of Chile. General Antonio Gonzales Balcarce, acting as commander in chief of the army in San Martín's absence, refused to treat with Ochavarriague under such credentials, and the negotiations came to an abrupt end. The patriots pointed to George Washington's refusal to treat with a British general under similar circumstances as precedence for their action.[28] At the time, no official blame was attached to Biddle for the failure of the mission. Guido, in reply to the former's enquiry as to the cause of the breakdown of the negotiations, assured him of the patriots' appreciation of his humanitarian efforts. On the day before Biddle left the capital the supreme director himself paid the American a formal visit and expressed his friendship "in the strongest language."[29]

In the meantime, patriot resentment against Ochavarriague took the form of insults and actual threats against his life. Biddle's report stated: "The officer in whose custody he was had insulted him very grossly, telling him among other things that the government of Chile would not permit him to go away in the *Ontario*, and that if he had any influence he would have him hanged." When Ochavarriague told Biddle of the threats, the naval officer assured him of continued protection since the Peruvian had come to Santiago under his security. Biddle proposed to make an immediate complaint to the supreme director of the inhospitable treatment of the envoy, but Ochavarriague dissuaded him, fearing that too much fuss might incite the Chileans to action rather than words.[30]

While these activities were in progress there were no less than five persons in the Chilean capital who were considered as representing the United States. Omitting mention of his own commanding officer, Conner noted this plethora of representatives: "Judge Prevost included[,] the U. S. had at this moment no less than four special agents in Chile viz Worthington, Bland and Robinson. . . ." Lack of agreement among his countrymen was evident. "It would appear from this that the President is very anxious to acquire exact information of the state of this country," wrote Conner, "but I am disposed to think his very means will defeat the object required, as I am convinced no two of these gentlemen will agree in opinion respecting this country."[31] Disagreement between Bland and Prevost extended to virtually all questions concerning Chile. Bland opposed recognition of Chile while Prevost advocated it. Bland favored the Carerras while Prevost favored O'Higgins. Regarding the mission from Peru, Robinson stated: "Judge Bland disapproved of the proceedings of the *Ontario*—Judge Prevost said it was a matter of humanity to negotiate the exchange of prisoners." Robinson, who always favored the official with the highest rank or the greatest ability to promote his personal interests, had a very poor opinion of Prevost and Worthington, and a great admiration for Bland. Concerning the three men he wrote: "Mr. Prevost will attempt to overreach Judge Bland—Mr. Worthington will play off and perhaps into the hands of Mr. Prevost—Mr. B[land] is honest and good—the rest are Jesucitical [sic] politicians—or avaricious ambitious men."[32] Robinson had no official standing although it was generally understood at the time that he held some kind of commission from the United States government.

After Balcarce refused to receive Ochavarriague there was nothing to do but return to Lima. Accordingly, the Peruvian envoy and his secretary, accompanied by Biddle, left Santiago on June 10, escorted by a Chilean officer. Prevost remained in Santiago. He did not again go on board the *Ontario*, reporting to Adams: "Some subjects of collision having latterly occurred[,] I could not consent to place myself at the discretion of Capt. Biddle...."[33] Robinson was deputized to go to Peru to represent the United States in appeals for release of the *Canton* and *Beaver*, and Biddle was asked to undertake the repatriation of the Columbia River territory alone.

Freed of any responsibility for the cartel mission other than the safety of the Peruvian personnel, Biddle turned his attention to assisting American merchantmen, an activity in which he always took a lively interest. Before he left Santiago he discussed with the supreme director the claim of the *Enterprise*, which had not been settled in spite of Zañartu's previous assurances. O'Higgins admitted the claim was just and promised payment on return of the *Ontario* from the Columbia River, candidly stating that there was no money in the treasury to pay it at that time. When Biddle requested return of documents he had submitted in the case he was disgusted to learn that they had been "lost."[34]

The *Ontario*'s commander learned that the *Two Catherines* would be ready to go to sea shortly after his own expected date of departure, whereupon he informed Ochavarriague that he would delay sailing in order to accompany the merchantman unless the envoy would give her a passport protecting her from seizure by Spanish ships. Ochavarriague not only issued the passport but assured the master of the *Two Catherines* that if she carried a load of wheat to Peru she would be welcome to enter Callao harbor to sell it. The *Two Catherines* did, in fact, carry a load of wheat to Callao to her profit. Biddle augmented her shorthanded crew by sending over the prisoners he had rescued in Peru. Unable to contact the Spanish naval forces at Talcahuano himself, he turned the viceroy's order modifying the royalist blockade over to one of the British warships in Valparaiso for future delivery to the Spanish commander.[35]

In the harbor during the *Ontario*'s visit there were two British men-of-war, the frigate *Andromache* under Captain William Henry Shirreff and the sloop of war *Blossom* under Captain James Hickey. Throughout his cruise in the Pacific, Biddle enjoyed good relations with his British counterparts and extended assistance freely to British ships whenever it was practicable to do so. Most of his contacts with the British Navy were with Shirreff of the *Andromache* and Commodore Bowles, His Britannic Majesty's senior officer on the Pacific station. The American had a high regard for these officers and reported to President Monroe that he "associated with them upon frank and intimate terms. . . ." Anglo-American co-operation in the Pacific was attested by the statement that "Captain Sherriff [sic] personally and Commodore Bowles by letter, expressed to me thanks for services I had rendered some British merchantmen & assured me they would seek opportunity of returning them to my countrymen who might be in need."[36]

Assisted by boats of the *Andromache* and *Blossom*, the *On-*

tario was towed clear of Valparaiso harbor and set sail for Callao on June 14. She carried more passengers away from Chile than she had brought in. Jeremy Robinson took Prevost's place. Besides Ochavarriague, his secretary, and four royalist officers exchanged for the four Chileans, there were a royalist naval officer, a Spanish lady with three children, and three Spanish merchants. The extra passengers were taken on board at the specific request of officials of the Chilean government.[37]

After a gloomy voyage that belied expectations of the "Ladies Passage" the ship arrived at Callao on June 28. Two American vessels were at anchor in the harbor—the *Canton*, which had been brought by a Spanish crew from Talcahuano for new condemnation proceedings, and the schooner *Governor Shelby* of New York. According to the log of the *Ontario*, the schooner was laden with "warlike" stores. Cleveland and Francis Coffin, captain and supercargo respectively of the *Beaver* and *Canton*, had come as passengers on the *Canton* to press their claims in the new hearings on their vessels that had been directed by the viceroy.[38]

The merchantmen asked Biddle to stop at Callao on his return from the Columbia and suggested that he let it be known publicly that he intended to do so. They believed this would influence the Lima court to make a favorable decision in their cases. Biddle concurred and in a lengthy letter to the viceroy dwelt on his personal acquaintance with Astor, the owner of the *Beaver*; and the latter's importance in the United States. He emphasized the concern in the United States about the fate of the two ships and ended by announcing that the *Ontario* would touch at Lima on the way home in order to obtain the latest news concerning them to take back to the United States.[39]

The presence of the *Ontario* and Biddle's interest in the *Beaver* led Cleveland to hope for a speedy trial and restoration of the ship. Optimistically he wrote Astor that their chances were much improved. He appreciated the efforts of Prevost and Robinson but placed more reliance in the practical effect of a man-of-war. To Astor he wrote:

The mission of Messrs. Provost [*sic*] and Robinson may have had a beneficial influence on our affairs, inasmuch as it evinces a watchfulness and determination on the part of our government to protect the commerce of its citizens; but I am fully convinced that, with this government, one such vessel as the *Ontario* is of more utility than a host of negotiators, nor do I believe that the united powers of a Demosthenes and a Cicero, with truth and justice on their side, would be in any degree so efficacious as the silent eloquence of one of our formidable frigates.[40]

Robinson, too, was struck by the "silent eloquence" of a man-of-war. After the *Ontario* left Callao he detected a definite change in attitude among the officials. He wrote Adams: "Although there was probably no change of disposition on the part of the Government yet a change of deportment was manifested immediately after her departure."[41]

Ochavarriague wasted no time in reporting the failure of his mission to the viceroy. The envoy dwelt at length on his distressing personal experiences in Santiago and gave Biddle credit for his safe return. With some exaggeration he told the viceroy that if the naval officer had not extended the protection of the United States flag with firmness and even with threats, he might not have been allowed to return at all.[42]

The viceroy, wishing to show his appreciation, invited the *Ontario*'s commander to dine with him the day before the warship sailed for the Northwest. Biddle, having business to attend to in Callao, declined but paid a short courtesy visit to the palace that afternoon. He was graciously received by the viceroy, who was profuse in his thanks for the American officer's services in the abortive cartel mission. At the end of the interview Pezuela impulsively directed one of his aides to fetch his personal sword, which was presented to the naval officer as a token of friendship and appreciation. This gesture was made in the presence of the viceroy's family and personal staff. There was nothing Biddle could do but accept the sword in the spirit it was presented. The sword had been a gift to the viceroy from a friend and, as Biddle later learned, was quite valuable, having a scabbard of gold and a diamond-studded hilt. When he returned to the United States, Biddle forwarded the sword to the secretary of state for deposit in accordance with custom in such instances.[43] This action, however, did not protect him from congressional accusations of receiving favors from royalty.[44]

The following day, June 30, the *Ontario* departed Callao for the Northwest Coast. She was away from South American waters for nearly four months. At Cape Disappointment on August 19, 1818, Biddle executed the original mission of the expedition into the Pacific. In the presence of some fifty officers and men from the ship and a few curious Indians, he turned over a sod of earth and took possession, "in the name and on the behalf of the United States, of both shores of the River Columbia."⁴⁵

The *Ontario* did not tarry long in the Northwest but hastened back to the troubled coast of South America. On the way south she stopped at Monterey to obtain wood, water, and fresh provisions. The governor of Upper California, Pablo Vicente Sola, gave them every courtesy, as much because of his innate hospitality as because Biddle carried a letter from Viceroy Pezuela directing the governor of any Spanish port where they might anchor to supply their needs. In Monterey was the Russian ship *Kutusoff*, whose commander assured Biddle that reports carried in British newspapers of the establishment by Russia of a fortified post in the Sandwich Islands were false.⁴⁶

Arriving back in Lima on October 22, Biddle found the affairs of the *Beaver* and *Canton* in much the same state as he had left them four months previously. Once more he brought pressure to bear on the viceroy to have their hearings conducted as soon as possible. The Spanish tribunal eventually heard the cases and in November restored the ships to their owners. Restitution was not made for damages, loss of time, nor the confiscated cargoes, but the way was left open for claims for these items to be made to the Spanish government. Biddle attributed the restoration of the *Beaver* and *Canton* to the presence of a public vessel of the United States, whereas Robinson attributed the favorable decisions in the *Beaver* and *Canton* cases only in part to the presence of the *Ontario* and fear of an unfavorable reaction in the United States. In an analysis of concurrent factors he assigned much credit to the effect of adverse criticism of the seizure of the two ships that had appeared in the British ministerial press and to the presence of the British frigate *Andromache* as well as the *Ontario* during the hearings.⁴⁷

The *Andromache* arrived in Callao from Valparaiso on November 11. One of her passengers was the ubiquitous Cleveland, who had been to Valparaiso on a confidential errand for the viceroy. In his memoirs, Cleveland gave Biddle much credit for restoration of his ship. He did not believe the latter's efforts were decisive, however. Cleveland's son, in a biography of his father some years later, implied that the *Beaver* was returned to the elder Cleveland because he undertook to go to Valparaiso on a secret mission to purchase a sixty-four gun East Indiaman for the Spanish government rather than let her go to the patriots. The plan failed because the ship had already been sold when Cleveland reached Valparaiso. The captain of the *Beaver* was of the opinion that Biddle's greatest service was in providing crew members for his ship, including a first officer, Midshipman Alexander B. Pinkham, and in helping recondition her for sea after a year's occupation by the Spanish. He stated that without the *Ontario*'s assistance it would have been impossible to have gotten the *Beaver* under sail again.[48]

The *Beaver*'s captain received assistance from all sides. The commander of the *Andromache* lent his artificers to help those of the *Ontario* refurbish the ship. The viceroy, perhaps in return for services rendered, allowed Cleveland to select ten or fifteen of the prisoners in the Castle of Callao to augment his crew before she sailed. These men were from the patriot privateer *Maipú*, which had been captured a short time before. They were all so anxious to serve on the *Beaver* that the captain found it advisable to let the jailer make the selection.[49] Their release under such conditions tends to confirm Cleveland's claim that he had a private understanding with the viceroy.

More than thirty of the prisoners were United States citizens. Among them was Midshipman George D. Dods of the United States Navy, who had been third lieutenant of the privateer. He had requested a furlough in July, 1817, to attend to "some business of importance" that required his "immediate attention." There were also four deserters from the *Ontario*. The captives arrived in Callao on November 21 while the *Ontario* was still in port, and Biddle immediately appealed to the viceroy for their release, not as a right, since they had forfeited any right to protection by joining a foreign privateer, but as an act of generosity.

Pezuela refused but intimated that in a few months he might reconsider his decision. In the meantime he offered to let Biddle have a few men whom he might specifically request. In this way seven men were surrendered. They included the four deserters from the *Ontario*, who no doubt would just as soon have remained in the Spanish prison. Among the others was a seaman named Miles, who had been a prisoner with Biddle in Tripoli. Biddle sought to obtain Dods' release on the grounds that he was a deserter from the United States Navy but was unsuccessful.[50]

Pezuela was most anxious to retain the good will of the Americans. He was acutely aware of his isolated position and growing dependence on foreign shipping to keep open his line of supply. In July a plot to start a revolution in the royalist stronghold of Callao was uncovered. One step of the rebels' plan was the assassination of the viceroy. In October he was advised that a serious uprising in the district of Aymaraes in Upper Peru had been suppressed. The viceroy watched with dismay the growth of Chile's navy and compared it with some misgivings with his own naval forces. At a council of war on August 25, Osorio presented a pessimistic evaluation of the royalist position in Talcahuano. A written report from Capitán de Fragata Luis Coig, in command of naval forces off southern Chile, indicated possible loss of his squadron to a numerically superior rebel force unless reinforcements were sent from Callao. On October 4 the American merchantman *Macedonian* brought news that one of a fleet of twelve transports enroute from Cadiz to Peru, escorted by the frigate *María Isabel*, had gone over to the patriots at Buenos Aires.[51]

On November 6 Pezuela held a grand review of royal troops on the public promenade of Callao. His object was twofold: to instill respect in the rebellious elements of Callao and to impress the English and Americans of the good state of his armed forces. He was particularly anxious to impress the personnel of the *Ontario* since he knew that ship would soon visit Valparaiso. He hoped they would carry word there of his state of readiness and thus cause additional delay in San Martín's projected invasion of Peru.[52]

When several midshipmen of the *Ontario* on shore leave in

Callao were roughly treated by a party of Spanish soldiers, who attempted to rob them, Biddle demanded that the culprits be arrested and punished. Two men were arrested and sent in irons to the *Ontario* by the governor of Callao for punishment by her commander. They were then to be returned to shore for trial by a Spanish court-martial. Biddle learned that this action had caused much indignation among the officers of the garrison, who were not only resentful that Spanish soldiers should be subjected to summary punishment by a foreigner but also assumed that the punishment would be unnecessarily severe. He prudently declined to punish the men on board the *Ontario*, and after they had apologized to the offended officers before the assembled crew, they were returned to their own command with the request that no further action be taken against them.[53]

On his leave-taking visit to the viceroy, Biddle tried to explain that he had striven to maintain an attitude of strict impartiality toward the warring parties in South America. During the interview Pezuela took from his desk a letter that he had been writing to his home government and read a portion of it to his visitor. The letter praised Biddle for presenting the claims of the United States in a polite, correct manner, free of the rashness that had been observed in other representatives of his country. The viceroy had written: "And so it is that whatever demands Biddle has made of this government, were granted, because they were all just."[54]

One other incident illustrates the viceroy's willingness to consider any reasonable complaint of the American representative. On December 5, the day the *Ontario* was scheduled to sail for Valparaiso, the whale ship *Eliza Barker* anchored in Callao harbor. Her captain went at once on board the man-of-war and reported that his ship had been stopped on the high seas by the Spanish cruiser *Velos* and plundered of some twelve hundred dollars worth of provisions and supplies. Biddle delayed his sailing to present the *Eliza Barker*'s complaint to the viceroy. The latter promised to have the case thoroughly investigated when the *Velos* returned to port and to make full indemnification if the whale ship had been wronged.[55]

Satisfied that justice would be done in the case of the *Eliza*

Barker, Biddle sailed for Valparaiso the following day. He had good reason to be satisfied with his sojourn in the viceroyalty of Peru. An understanding based on mutual respect had been established with the viceroy. In his dealings with the latter, Biddle had not hesitated to clothe himself in the authority and power of the country he so proudly represented, nor had he shrunk from taking full advantage of Pezuela's precarious position in relation to the patriots. But he had carefully refrained from making unreasonable or exaggerated claims that would denigrate the authority of the viceroy or the dignity of his sovereign. On his part, Pezuela, recognizing in the naval officer a man of reason and integrity, was willing to concede any requests that could be justified under international usage and were not contrary to Spanish laws. Thus, Biddle gained significant concessions on behalf of his countrymen.

Chapter IV

Biddle and Cochrane

Biddle's successes in Peru became known to the patriots and, together with his sponsorship of the Ochavarriague mission, clouded his already shaky relations with the officials at Valparaiso. When the *Ontario* arrived at that port on December 27, the Americans encountered an atmosphere of suspicion and distrust. Biddle soon became embroiled with Lord Cochrane, the new commander in chief of the Chilean Navy, in a quarrel that was resolved by a rather ignominious departure from the patriot harbor.

During 1818, an amazing change had occurred in Chilean sea power. When the *Ontario* first visited Valparaiso in January, the patriot government had only one small warship, the brig *Aguila*, and the Chilean coast was under blockade by a Spanish squadron. By December the blockade had been broken and the patriots could send to sea a fleet of seven ships, mounting two hundred and thirty-six guns. Two additional frigates were en route from the United States.[1] The patriots were ready to challenge the royalists for control of the Southeast Pacific.

The creation of an effective naval force was one of the most remarkable achievements of the patriots, the more so as Chile had no ships, no shipyards, and no seafaring tradition. O'Higgins once told Bland that "there was not a sailor to be found among all the people of Chile."[2] Credit for assembling the fleet in the face of great odds belongs to San Martín and O'Higgins. Immediately after Chacabuco, San Martín, with the loyal backing of O'Higgins and the support of the Buenos Aires government, had set in motion the machinery for acquiring the ships, arms, and men needed to create a navy. Manuel Hermenegildo Aguirre, an agent of the Buenos Aires government to the United States, was given a commission to purchase two frigates and two smaller vessels for the Chilean government. A similar commission was given to José Antonio Álvarez Condarco in London. Aguirre, because of a shortage of funds, was able to contract for only two frigates in New York. He ran afoul of the United States neutrality laws and had considerable legal difficulty before he got his ships to sea.[3] Part of his expenditures were covered by bills of exchange that were eventually turned over for collection to United States naval commanders bound for Chile.[4]

Álvarez Condarco was much more successful than Aguirre. It was through his efforts that the two East Indiamen that became the *San Martín* and *Lautaro* were sent to Chile. But his greatest contribution to the new fleet was the recruiting of one of the most colorful and capable naval officers in Europe to head the Chilean navy. This officer was Lord Thomas Cochrane, who had served with distinction in the British Royal Navy during the Napoleonic Wars but had been dismissed in 1814 for complicity in a "sordid scheme of conspiracy and fraud" to rig the London stock market. For this he was imprisoned, fined, and deprived of his naval rank, his Knighthood of the Bath, and his seat in Parliament. In 1818 he accepted an invitation to command the new Chilean fleet. Admiral Manuel Blanco Encalada, who had been in command of the fleet, stood down and Cochrane became "Vice Admiral of Chile, and Commander in Chief of the Naval forces of the Republic."[5]

Cochrane, accompanied by his young wife, Lady Katherine, arrived in Valparaiso on November 28, 1818, and immediately began to reorganize the patriot fleet. At his insistence equipment was overhauled, deficiencies were corrected, drills were instituted, and above all discipline was introduced and enforced. The going was tough in the face of scant funds, inexperienced crews, and jealousy in the officer corps, composed largely of British and a few other foreigners. His task was made easier, however, by the fact that under his predecessor, Blanco Encalada, the young fleet had won a brilliant victory the previous month in taking the Spanish frigate *Maria Isabel* at Talcahuano. Seven of the transports she was supposed to be convoying from Spain to Peru fell into patriot hands either by capture or by defection. This victory inflamed the pride of the Chileans and they gave full support to the tiny navy from which they expected great results.[6]

The jealousy that existed in the officers' corps also extended to the ranks, but there it was caused by differences in pay and treatment between the native Chileans and the foreigners. An anonymous observer of the period, describing difficulties in manning the fleet, wrote: "The English and North American sailors, who were the only ones valued as intelligent, . . . taking advantage of the circumstances, placed their pretensions very high & lent their volunteered services at a very dear rate." There was keen competition between the privateers and the regular navy for seamen just as there had been during the North American Revolution. The Chilean government ordered general impressment of Chilean coastal dwellers and fishermen. The anonymous writer contrasted the two elements in the naval crews: the natives, "violent and ignorant of the duties of the sea"; and the foreigners, "without discipline, whom it was not easy to make content." The customs of each group "obliged them to establish odious distinctions between them, which was the origin of rivalry and rancour. The foreign seamen were better paid & had a ration of spirits, cocoa & other things of which those of the nation were deprived."[7]

Lord Cochrane and his officers placed the stamp of Britain on the new navy, in custom, tactics, and language. "The language of the squadron was English, in English the orders of routine on shipboard were given. In English the notes and communications were issued, in English the Commanders and subalterns conversed."[8] Cochrane brought a knowledge of maritime law and custom based on years in the British service. He was well versed in international law and insisted on its full observance in connection with Chilean rights.[9] Quite naturally, his concept of international law stemmed from British interpretation, particularly as interpreted by Britain during the recent Napoleonic Wars. It is not surprising, therefore, that some differences should arise between him and the United States naval commanders in the Southeast Pacific in regard to blockades and the rights of neutrals.

In spite of his many outstanding qualities there were some personal characteristics that detracted from Cochrane's ultimate effectiveness as a commander. The British historian F. A. Kirkpatrick compared him to Nelson in skill, insight, and dash, but concluded that his effectiveness as a commander was marred "by an impracticable violence of temper and an intrusion of personal aims which produced constant quarrels and undignified recrimination."[10] Henry Hill, who, as United States vice-consul at Valparaiso, had an opportunity to become acquainted with Cochrane, described him thus: "He was almost always in hot water, being impulsive, headstrong, persevering, determined to have his way, and meeting others who were determined to have their way. He was brave, industrious, restless, perhaps, and had a good deal of talent; but his mind was not balanced. His appearance was not prepossessing. He was not a brawny Scotchman, but tall, lank, stooping, awkward, with sandy hair, and freckled. . . ."[11]

To completely grasp the complex character of Cochrane is impossible, but some comprehension is essential to understand events in the Southeast Pacific. When the trident of sea power passed from the royalists to the patriots, the commander of the Chilean navy became the dominant figure in the maritime phases of the War for Independence in that area. Whatever their opinions of Lord Cochrane, United States naval commanders in the Pacific had to reckon with his powerful personality from the day he assumed command of the patriot navy in November, 1818, to his resignation in 1823.

And so it was with Biddle in Valparaiso, a place that seemed always to create quarrels and disappointments for the naval commander. Shortly after arrival on his third visit he became embroiled in an acrimonious dispute with Cochrane over the exchange of salutes, a question which had helped to cloud his relations with Governor Calderón eleven months previously. On the day of arrival in port, the American commander made the usual courtesy calls on De la Cruz, who had now replaced Calderón as governor of Valparaiso, and on Admiral Cochrane, aboard his flagship, the *San Martin*. The governor in accordance with protocol returned the call the following day and it was expected that Cochrane would do the same. A few hours after Biddle left the *San Martin*, however, Cochrane sent a note over to remind the American "that Ships of War of a foreign Nation on arriving in friendly ports, have ever been in the habit of publicly saluting that flag." Cochrane pointedly alluded to an incident that was supposed to have happened in Gibraltar in 1802, when Commodore Bainbridge had refused to salute the flag of the British admiral, Lord Keith, and as a consequence was ordered out of Gibraltar. The implication was plain—either salute or get out of Valparaiso! Biddle replied in moderate language, explaining that he had offered to salute on his first visit to Valparaiso in January, provided it would be returned gun for gun, but the offer had been refused. Therefore, he declined to salute at the present time.[12]

There followed an exchange of notes in which veiled threats and insults were couched in polite language. Cochrane offered to return a salute "gun for gun" if Biddle would give him assurance that such was the "uniform practice of the American Commanders in chief . . ." The *Ontario*'s commander refused to discuss the issue of relative number of guns and informed Cochrane that his preceding letter "was intended to decline saluting altogether . . ." The American could not allow the Briton's aspersions against a brother officer to go unchallenged. The admiral must have been "misinformed," he avowed, since "I am persuaded, that my friend Captain Bainbridge who commanded the Essex in 1802, would not have permitted himself to be ordered out of port in the manner stated by your Lordship." Cochrane's parting retort was: "I plainly see the awkward situation in which you are placed. You cannot, yourself regret them [the circumstances] more than I do. It will deprive me of what (previous to the receipt of your last letter) I should have deemed a pleasure, namely, of paying my respects to you, which now consistently I cannot do, without such an explanation as shall reconcile the seeming contradictions of your public letters."[13]

Biddle did not answer this letter but sent a message to the supreme director explaining events and informing him that in the exchange with the admiral there had been no intention to be disrespectful to the Chilean nation or its officials. His quarrel had been only with Lord Cochrane and would be so reported to his own government.[14]

Regardless of the personal feelings of the two commanders it is likely that they would have reached an understanding on the salute if there had not been other factors involved. The truth was that Biddle was open to charges of violation of the obligations of neutrality in the Chilean port. On board the *Ontario* was $201,000 in specie carried on the account of merchants of Lima to correspondents in Rio de Janeiro and New York, and five Spanish passengers bound from Lima to Rio.[15]

Biddle could justify the carrying of specie on the basis of custom and regulations. The British Navy carried large quantities of specie, and it was covered by regulations from which those of the United States Navy were derived. The "Act for the better government of the Navy of the United States," enacted in April, 1800, prohibited the carrying of "goods or merchandise" in naval vessels but made an exception of "gold, silver, or jewels." New regulations promulgated in 1818 did not change the basic law of 1800; they neither authorized nor prohibited transportation of specie. The Navy Department officially sanctioned the practice in October, 1818, when acting secretary of the navy John C. Calhoun gave Commodore Daniel F. Patterson of the New Orleans station permission for ships of his command to transport specie belonging to United States merchants. Prior to that time, as a matter of policy, it had denied requests for such authority if approached directly. There seems, however, to have been no strong action to discourage the practice when it was not a direct issue. Charles Morris, speaking of the advantages to be gained by his projected cruise to the Pacific in 1816, said: "It was supposed also that some pecuniary advantages would accrue to me by participating in the safekeeping and transportation of the precious metals, which had hitherto been monopolized by English vessels of war."[16] The authority granted to Patterson in the Gulf of Mexico was subsequently extended to other naval commanders bound to South America.[17]

Biddle could justify the specie far easier than he could explain his passengers. Four of them were civilians—two merchants and a woman with her child—and the status of these might have been justified on humanitarian grounds. But the fifth was an officer in the Spanish army, one Colonel Olarria, nephew of the viceroy of Peru. There was no way the American could justify bringing an enemy officer into the Chilean port under cover of his neutral flag. The character of the *Ontario* as a public vessel of the United States made it all the more important that the rules of neutrality be scrupulously observed. Biddle was vulnerable and he knew it.

Olarria was not sent into Valparaiso as a spy. His presence there was purely incidental to the visit of the *Ontario*. His primary mission was to get to Spain via Rio de Janeiro and make a complete report to King Ferdinand of the deteriorating military situation of the royal forces in the Pacific. He was to urge immediate dispatch of a ship and a frigate to Callao to restore Spanish naval power in the area. Pezuela considered his message so vital that General Osorio was given the same mission via other transportation.[18]

Biddle, of course, knew nothing of Olarria's real mission, but he realized that he had placed himself and the United States in an anomalous position when he agreed to take the viceroy's nephew on board as a passenger since he had known that he would stop at Valparaiso en route. He had reluctantly agreed when the viceroy made the request during the negotiations over release of the *Beaver* and *Canton*. His justification for acceding to the viceroy's solicitation was that to have refused would have jeopardized the restoration of those ships to their owners. His report to the secretary of the navy stated: "As this was solicitated of me at the time I was most pressing with the Vice King upon the subject of the Beaver and Canton I did not doubt, but that upon my compliance with the desire of the Vice King depended the acquittal of these vessels. I regretted very much that such a request should be made since I felt reluctant to comply with it lest the government of Chile should complain of it as a breach of impartiality."[19]

It is not clear whether or not Biddle informed any Chilean officials of his passengers. He had intended to visit Santiago and explain the situation to the supreme director, but the unfortunate dispute with the admiral over the salutes caused the cancellation of the trip. Obviously he did not discuss the matter with Cochrane, who wrote the supreme director that he had learned of the Spanish passengers from deserters from the *Ontario*. In any event, it was not long before the presence of the money and the Spaniards was known in Valparaiso. The facts about the specie were greatly exaggerated. Gossip placed the amount at a million dollars. Rumors were current that the *Ontario* would be stopped and searched if she attempted to leave the port.[20]

These rumors reached the *Ontario* as well as reports that the Senate of Chile had determined that monies taken aboard the *Andromache* and the *Ontario* at Lima would be removed from them, presumably by force, if brought into the port of Valparaiso. John Higginson, an American at Valparaiso, came on board and partially confirmed the latter report. He informed the officers that such a procedure had been discussed by the Senate and sanctioned by the supreme director and San Martín in the case of the *Andromache* but not in the case of the *Ontario*, as it was not believed the American ship had enough money on board to make the risk worth while.[21]

The misunderstanding with Lord Cochrane, the uncomfortable circumstance of having the Spanish colonel on board, and the rumors reported by Higginson convinced Biddle that he should not prolong his stay in Valparaiso. He hastily took on provisions and water and prepared to sail on December 30, notifying the governor and Cochrane of his intentions. When Cochrane heard this plan he asked the American to delay getting under way until after the Chilean squadron, which was about to sail to attack Callao, could get to sea. De la Cruz also asked Biddle to delay departure. On being assured that the Chilean sortie would be completed the following day, December 31, Biddle agreed to postpone his own sailing twenty-four hours.[22]

That evening the *San Martin* and *Chacabuco* shifted berths, anchoring in positions Biddle considered as threatening to his ship, the *San Martin* to seaward, and the *Chacabuco* so close aboard that there was danger of fouling the *Ontario*. These maneuvers could very well have been in preparation for the scheduled sortie of the Chilean squadron, but Biddle, connecting them with the reports he had heard, concluded there was an intention either to attack the *Ontario* if she attempted to go to sea, or to intimidate her from sailing. He "did not choose to be deterred from sailing, whichever was the intention" and decided to take his ship to sea as soon as possible.[23]

The following morning, the *Ontario* got safely to sea although for a while it appeared to the Americans that Cochrane's fleet intended to interfere as shown by entries from the log for December 31, 1818:

At daylight hove up to the Starboard anchor and laid by the Kedge. The Chacabuco that had anchored close to us in the night also weighed and loosed her topsails—At 9 a.m. we perceived the San Martin of 62 guns getting underweigh and firing signal guns.... At 10 we made all sail, as did the San Martin although her anchor was *uncatted* and she had a boat towing astern—We passed within half cannon shot of that ship ready to repel any insult she might have afforded to our flag and in a few hours she was 3 or 4 miles astern and about noon we saw her & the Chacabuco tack and thus for the port. This circumstance confirmed our suspicions—[24]

Did Biddle save his ship from the indignity of search by Chilean forces, or was his action unnecessarily precipitous? It is not likely that the patriots would have taken the drastic step of searching the warship of a friendly power whatever provocation they might have believed to exist. Joaquin de Echeverría, minister of state and foreign relations of Chile, indicated in a complaint to Prevost that such an action was considered and rejected. Jeremy Robinson told Adams: "The Government . . . disavow[s] all intention to have incommoded the *Ontario* notwithstanding that both before and after her arrival it was intimated that a search was intended." But Antonio Álvarez Jonte, judge advocate and secretary-general of the Chilean squadron, wrote San Martín that the *Ontario* should have been detained and her "cargo" condemned. He suggested that San Martín should warn the Buenos Aires government to take that action if the *Ontario* touched at Buenos Aires.[25]

Under the circumstances Biddle's action was wise. To have remained in Valparaiso in the face of growing resentment was inviting possible violence. By leaving the harbor, Biddle eliminated the possibility of an ugly incident that might well have involved the governments of the United States and Chile in open hostilities. Once the ship, her crew, passengers, and contents were out of the physical reach of the patriots, the incident could be reduced to its true perspective—the indiscretions of an individual officer.

The Chileans appreciated this point of view and publicly attributed Biddle's precipitous departure to the dispute over exchange of salutes with Cochrane. The correspondence between the two men was published in the *Gaceta ministerial* under the following lead: "The frigate of the United States *Ontario*, commanded by Mr. Biddle, left Valparaiso suddenly the thirty-first of last month; and this having given rise to various rumors circulated among the public over this affair, we publish here, for the satisfaction of all, the literal translation of the correspondence between the Vice Admiral of the naval forces of Chile and Mr. Biddle."[26]

The hasty departure caused mixed reactions in Santiago and Valparaiso. Among the Chileans there was a combination of concern and resentment. The British colony's reaction was one of smug satisfaction at the apparent discomfiture of their American rivals. The American merchants were angry because they were deprived of an opportunity to take passage home or to remit money. Some were concerned because the *Ontario*'s departure meant that there was no United States warship left on the coast to protect their interests.[27]

Worthington, who was about to leave Chile, made a special effort to ascertain what had really happened and to soothe the injured sensibilities of the patriots. In response to his enquiries, Echeverría replied: "The Government knew very well that on board the *Ontario* were European Passengers, proceeding from Lima, and enemies [sic] property; but notwithstanding the prejudice which this conduct occasioned us it never was thought of to search by force or otherwise a Neutral ship. . . ."[28] Cochrane professed to treat the matter lightly, jesting with Worthington: "the winds seem to blow pretty strong off the land against your ships of War in this port." Worthington did not find out if Cochrane had intended to search the *Ontario*. The closest he came was Cochrane's jocular remark, "I had intended if I had been authorized to have made your countryman Wooster—search the British Frigate Andromache."[29]

Prevost, Robinson, and Worthington were unanimous in their opinion that the affair had been harmful to the relations of the United States with Chile. Worthington called the affair of the salute "the unkindest cut of all." He was most concerned about the waning popularity of the United States and the increasingly favorable position of the British. In a previous letter to Adams regarding the non-delivery of the two ships Aguirre had contracted for in New York, he had noted the weakening "partiality to us" and had said: "Nothing is more true than that 'hope long deferred makes the Heart sick,' for they always, that is the Nation, expected so much from us, & now getting Ships, Sailors, Goods &c of the British, visited by their Ships of War two or three at a time,—feasted and treated on board of them—& a hundred et ceteras which I could mention, and our falling so far short of their anticipations, produces a recoil upon us, of a very disadvantageous Case—."[30]

Two and a half months after Biddle's departure, Echeverría filed a complaint about Biddle's actions with Prevost, who had hurried from Lima to Valparaiso when he heard of the quarrel between Biddle and Cochrane and the flight of the former from Valparaiso against the wishes of the Chilean officials. Prevost forwarded the complaint to Adams with comments that left no doubt that he considered Biddle's conduct censurable. He expressed the hope that whatever other action the president took he would put a stop to the practice of warships carrying monies and properties of foreigners, particularly of belligerents. To Echeverría he was more restrained, merely acknowledging his letter and expressing regret that any misunderstanding had occurred.[31]

Echeverría's complaints were not confined to the events of December 27–31 but covered the American's previous visits to Valparaiso as well. The Chilean sought to emphasize that his government attributed the actions to Biddle as an individual, not to the United States government. His accusations may be summarized under five headings: carrying property of the enemies of Chile; providing a precedent for British ships to transport enemy goods, specifically the *Andromache*, which had carried a "considerable number of articles from Lima for England" shortly after Biddle's visit; introducing Ochavarriague y Blanco into Chile as a spy; receiving a valuable gift, a sword, from the viceroy of Peru for his services; and refusing to salute Chile's flag.[32]

In the meantime, the *Ontario* arrived at Annapolis in April, 1819, after brief pauses in Rio de Janeiro and Pernambuco. In Rio the Spanish passengers and $160,000 in specie were landed. An additional $15,000 in silver consigned to John Jacob Astor and Son of New York was utilized by Biddle to buy provisions and pay the officers in Brazil.[33]

As soon as the *Ontario* arrived in the Chesapeake, Biddle forwarded "a memorandum of the proceedings in detail" of the ship under his command "during the late absence from the United States."[34] He anticipated that this would be the final report of the Pacific cruise and looked forward to a pleasant tour of shore duty in his home city. In this expectation he was sadly mistaken. As reports began to trickle back to Washington of events of the past year on the coasts of South America, the commander of the *Ontario*, either voluntarily or on orders of the secretary of the navy, was obliged to submit at least four supplemental reports in defense of his actions in the Pacific.

The first occasion was in reply to anonymous attacks appearing in the press concerning his spat with Lord Cochrane. This affair was widely discussed and comment passed from paper to paper. Some of the interpretations, notably in the pro-patriot press, were unflattering. Biddle, at the insistence of friends, published a statement of his differences with Lord Cochrane in an open letter to his friend Commodore Bainbridge. At the same time he forwarded to the secretary of the navy an amplification of the report contained in his journal. This "supplemental" report contained copies of his correspondence with the patriot officials and Pezuela. He detailed the problems he had faced with each and compared the difficulty of doing business with the former with the satisfaction he had received from the Spanish viceroy in the protection of United States interest and honor.[35]

In spite of his own unfavorable comparison of the actions of the patriots and the royalists, Biddle publicly professed to be on the side of the patriots. Perhaps unconsciously he was reflecting the popular American belief that any democratic organization was *per se* better than any monarchical institution. He was willing to condemn the personnel but not the ideal. When James and Thomas H. Perkins publicly thanked him for his services in saving their ship *Levant* from capture by the Spanish blockading squadron off Valparaiso, he told them he had only done his duty and then showed his sensitivity to public criticism by adding: "I am very sensible to your kind and flattering expressions; particularly at this moment when my character is assailed in some of the newspapers, for a conduct which I had trusted would not have incurred any public reproach; for, however much my wishes were on the side of the Patriots of South America, I felt it incumbent upon me, in my official conduct, not to comprimit [compromise], in my intercourse with them, the reputation of the flag under which I serve."[36]

Echeverría's charges arrived in Washington in August. Biddle either was in Washington when they were received or was summoned from Philadelphia to give his account of the events. He went over the accusations point by point with Secretary of the Navy Smith Thompson, who requested him to submit his version in writing to the president. Biddle's lengthy statement to the president is here summarized.[37]

He claimed that the only property carried on the *Ontario* was specie from Lima valued at $201,000, all of it private property. $11,000 was consigned to a shipowner of Boston, $15,000 to Astor of New York, $15,000 to a Mr. Gracie of New York, and the remainder to individual merchants in Rio de Janeiro. He claimed the transportation of specie was sanctioned by law and custom.

As for providing a precedent for the British Navy, he pointed out that English ships in the Pacific had been carrying specie long before the arrival of the *Ontario.*

Regarding the accusation that Ochavarriague y Blanco was carried as a spy to Chile, Biddle stated that so far as he knew the mission to exchange prisoners was no more than a humanitarian effort to alleviate the hardships of war. It had been openly announced to the patriots and welcomed by them. After its failure the supreme director and other officials expressed their gratitude to Biddle in the warmest terms.

The sword had been accepted from the viceroy as a token of his friendship and gratitude for attempting to arrange the exchange of prisoners and for Biddle's protection of the viceroy's representative against patriot threats and insults. To have refused it would have been an affront to the viceroy.

Biddle felt himself on solid ground on the question of salutes at Valparaiso, believing that salutes were not obligatory in a foreign port after the first visit but were a matter of discretion with the officer concerned. He had made a previous report of his reasons for refusing to salute on his third visit to Valparaiso. He had learned from Jeremy Robinson by letter dated February 1, 1819, that the supreme director agreed with Biddle's interpretation that salutes were a matter of discretion and in this case it was a question of etiquette to be settled between the officers concerned. The supreme director had disapproved of Cochrane's conduct.[38]

As a result of faulty translation of the Spanish minister's letter the naval officer made two minor errors in his refutation. He spent some time answering Echeverría's supposed statement that in consequence of his having brought Ochavarriague to Chile as a spy the government had prohibited his entrance to Chilean ports. Actually, Echeverría had made no such statement but had stated that the government had "refused to prohibit" Biddle's entry into their ports.

Biddle's second error was due to the date on Echeverría's translated letter. Biddle invited attention to the fact that it was written some four months after his own departure from Valparaiso and after Prevost's return to that city from the Northwest. The

Spanish version enclosed with Prevost's letter of March 20 was dated March 16, 1819, but a careless translator had copied the date as May 16. Hence, Biddle connected the detested agent with the accusations.

Benjamin Homans, chief clerk of the Navy Department, appended several comments to Biddle's letter that did much to relieve the *Ontario*'s commander from censure by the president or the secretary of the navy. Among Homans' comments were:

> ... I cannot see cause of accusation against Capt. Biddle, his conduct as Commander of a ship of the U.S. Navy cannot be impeached. Although it is apparent that he took occasion to make himself conspicuous and of extra consequence among the authorities in Chile & Lima, yet his own explanations may be considered valid unless contradicted.
> Captain Biddle has violated no law or regulation of the Navy...[39]

In additional notes Homans states that "some of Capt. Biddle's assertions are incorrect." This had reference to statements that ships in the Caribbean made a regular practice of transporting specie. Homans denied that it had been the practice to allow ships to carry specie until November, 1818, when Patterson had been granted such authority.

No official reply was made to the Chilean government's complaint against Biddle until July, 1820, when a new agent to South America, John M. Forbes, was given copies of the papers bearing on the case and directed to make an answer to the Chileans that would "justify the conduct of Captain Biddle" and at the same time manifest a friendly disposition of the president towards Chile. As Forbes did not go beyond Buenos Aires, the papers and instructions were given to Prevost, who had, to him, the unpleasant task of "justifying" the actions he had condemned.[40]

Biddle was not without friends or influence. When he was defending himself against the Chilean government's accusations, his brother Nicholas submitted the documents involved to Robert Walsh of the *National Gazette*, who promptly volunteered his editorial aid. Walsh's letter returning the documents read: "I have read the documents, and see nothing in them but what is creditable to Captain Biddle, although much that is pitiful and dishonorable on the part of the Government of Chile in its denunciation."[41]

In November, 1819, the monotony of criticism was broken by a letter from the Spanish legation on behalf of His Catholic Majesty expressing appreciation for Biddle's conduct and mentioning the polite attention, the harmony, prudence and discernment with which he conducted himself while in Peru. The letter continued: "His majesty, pleased with conduct so exalted and gallant, orders . . . thanks to you in his royal name."[42]

It was inevitable that the valuable sword, received from the hand of a vice-king, should become the central theme of mounting attacks on Biddle in and out of Congress by the leaders of the group that wished immediate recognition of the South American states by the United States. Biddle and his sword were sarcastically mentioned by Clay in a speech of March 20, 1820, advocating recognition of the patriot governments.

On March 31 the House of Representatives, in a resolution that showed a remarkable knowledge of what had occurred during the *Ontario*'s cruise in the Pacific, directed the secretary of the navy to submit information on Biddle's actions in the Pacific and "whether any and what, instructions have been given by the Department of the Navy respecting the transportation in public ships of the United States of passengers, money or effects."[43]

In response to this resolution the secretary of the navy invited Biddle to submit any new material he might have pertinent to the investigation. There was little in his new report that Biddle had not previously covered. He revealed that he received a freight of 2½ per cent on monies transported and went into detail about the passengers carried. Of these, only one, the Spanish Colonel Olarria, troubled his conscience, and he indicated that his agreement to carry that officer was made to secure the release of a number of his countrymen from Lima prisons and restoration of the *Beaver* and *Canton* to their owners. He contended that he carried passengers impartially for the patriots and the royalists. In this connection he said: "It was my fortune to pass between two parties in a civil war, embittered against each other and one at least of them prejudiced against the U. States." He had tried to render humane services to all parties consistent with duty to his own country. Transportation of persons between ports not otherwise open to transportation had been one service he considered reasonable. "I therefore apprized the government of both Chile and of Lima, that as I was unwilling to refuse a passage to all those who applied, I would give the preference to such as the respective governments felt a desire to oblige; and accordingly it will be seen that all the persons named were connected with the relations or friends of the respective governments."[44]

Biddle had the backing of the administration. After forwarding all reports and correspondence pertinent to the enquiry to the House of Representatives, the secretary of the navy sent a supplemental report enclosing extracts from Biddle's journal, the memorial to Biddle from the ship masters and supercargoes of American ships in Valparaiso, and portions of letters from Worthington tending to show the high regard the supreme director of Chile had for the naval officer. Thompson requested that the new material be appended to the record, "as showing more distinctly the benefit which has resulted in our trade, and the protection afforded by our public ships in the Pacific ocean, and, also, the estimation in which Captain Biddle was held for the services rendered."[45]

The cruise of the *Ontario* became a political question. The House of Representatives passed a bill to prevent officers in the naval service from "accepting of any present or emolument, of any kind whatever, from any King, Prince, or foreign state, and for other purposes." The bill died in the Senate Committee on Naval Affairs. With tongue in cheek, Henry Clay introduced a resolution in the House that would have requested the president to present to "the most worthy and distinguished" general in the patriot service "the sword which was given by the Viceroy of Lima to Captain Biddle, of the *Ontario*, during her late cruise in the Pacific, and which is now in the office of the Department of State." He withdrew the resolution in favor of a more serious one calling for provision of an outfit and salary for a minister or ministers "to any of the Governments of South America, which have established and are maintaining their independence on Spain."[46]

Brother Nicholas attributed the attacks to partisan politics and so informed Monroe in a letter dated June 14, 1821, soliciting sea duty for James as evidence of approval of his conduct. Nicholas told the chief executive that James's enemies in Congress were trying to discredit both the naval officer and the administration and suggested that the best way to show confidence was to give his brother a command at sea.[47] His brother was ordered to command of the frigate *Macedonian* and in March, 1822, was ordered to the Caribbean to take charge of United States forces there in the protection of commerce and the suppression of piracy.[48]

In comparing the effectiveness of Biddle and Prevost in guarding the welfare of their countrymen, John Quincy Adams had this to say:

Biddle's conduct was perhaps indiscreet, and not entirely disinterested. But he turned it at least to the account of his countrymen, for whom he saved and rescued property to a very large amount. He obtained also the release of many citizens of the United States who were prisoners. Prevost has never saved a dollar nor obtained the release of a man. . . . There is something disheartening in all our correspondence and transactions relating to South America. We have done everything possible in their favor, and have received from them little less than injury in return. No satisfaction has been obtained from them upon any complaint, and they have been constantly endeavoring to entangle us with them and their cause.[49]

Chapter V

Captain John Downes versus Paper Blockades

While Biddle was in the Pacific, the relations of the United States with Spain and her rebellious colonies continued to be the major problem of the administration. In April, 1818, Andrew Jackson marched into Florida and occupied Pensacola. This action caused rumors of war to spread to Europe and South America. Commodore Charles Stewart, commander of the United States naval forces in Europe, made plans to strike at Spain in the Mediterranean in the event of any hostile move on the part of King Ferdinand. In case of co-operation between Spain and England, he planned to withdraw from the Mediterranean altogether.[1]

In Chile it was reported that the United States and Spain were already at war, leading the patriots to hope for early recognition and material help in their struggle with Spain.[2] But the United States government was not yet ready to take a decisive stand and clung to the policy of neutrality. In April a greatly strengthened neutrality act was passed by Congress at the insistence of the administration.

Adams was deeply interested in the intentions of the European allies toward the conflict in South America. He knew that Spain was maneuvering to get the Holy Alliance to intervene in order to save her colonies. Quite by chance the South American Commission learned in Rio de Janeiro that a move was underway to have Great Britain mediate the conflict. Neither possibility caused Adams very much concern. He believed the European powers would not "deem it advisable to interpose in this conflict by any application of force." As for Britain's mediation, the secretary was too familiar with that nation's penchant for trade to believe she would take any actions that might endanger her new and valuable commerce with the South American provinces. "She admits all the pretensions of legitimacy until they come in contact with her own interest; and then she becomes the patroness of liberal principles and colonial emancipation," he wrote of England.[3]

Adams was willing to co-operate with Europe in bringing peace to South America, but only on the basis of total independence, political and commercial, for the colonies. The United States was no more willing than Britain to see the lucrative trade of the colonies return to the monopoly of Spain. The secretary of state revealed an attitude toward the colonies not far different from that he attributed to Britain when he wrote Albert Gallatin: "The situation of these countries has thrown them open to commercial intercourse with other nations, and among the rest with these United States. This state of things has existed several years, and cannot now be changed without materially affecting our interest."[4]

The military position of Spain steadily worsened during 1818. In the spring she received eight ships from Russia, which were intended to bolster her naval forces but which proved to be almost a total loss because of their rotten condition. After great effort, an expeditionary force of 2,500 men in twelve transports, escorted by the frigate *María Isabel*, left Cádiz on May 21 for

Chile and Peru. Only five of the twelve ships reached Callao. The remainder fell into patriot hands, some by capture and others through defection of the ships' crews and troops.[5]

In July the frigate *Congress* returned to Hampton Roads with all the members of the South American Commission except Bland, who had remained behind to visit Chile.[6] The commissioners were unanimous on only one point: the resubjugation of the colonies by Spain was impossible. But on the internal condition of the new nations and their recommendations on recognition they were so hopelessly divided that each made a separate report.[7]

During 1818 American shipping in the Southeast Pacific increased. In August, Robinson reported between sixty and seventy United States whalers operating off Peru and Chile and about forty merchant vessels trading on the coast. Captain Joseph Allen of the whale ship *Maro* provided Robinson with a list of forty-six vessels and their captains employed in the "Whale fishery" of the Pacific Ocean, most of them out of Nantucket.[8] Robinson urged a strong naval force in the Pacific to protect the "interests and personal rights of our citizens amid the violence of revolution and the frequent fluctuation of power...."[9] He noted that English ships received much better treatment than the Americans because the English kept a "respectable" naval force on the coast at all times. Prevost, in his first report to Adams from Chile, recommended additional ships be sent with specific instructions to protect United States commerce.[10] A few weeks later Worthington passed along Prevost's request to press the "necessity of our always having vessels of war in the waters of these Provinces" and seconded the appeal.[11]

These pleas for a permanent naval force in the Pacific coincided with similar representations from commercial interests in the United States. On May 13 the Honorable Samuel Smith, an influential member of the House of Representatives from Maryland, wrote the secretary of the navy that there was a strong feeling in Philadelphia that the government should send a frigate to the "China Sea." The Philadelphians, according to Smith, "had alarmed themselves lest the Patriot Privateers, or Pirates sailing under their flag may intercept our specie ships." Smith himself had no such apprehension but thought a frigate there would be a good idea, since "we are the second trading people in the world and ought to give respectability to our trade by showing a naval force in every sea." Not only would this be salutary for trade, but it would "increase the knowledge of our officers and employ our seamen."[12]

On the same date as Smith's letter, a Cabinet meeting was held to discuss a number of questions on foreign affairs submitted by the president. One of them was: "Whether an armed force shall be sent to visit both sides of the coast of South America for the protection of our commerce, and to countenance the patriots?" To this was added, "Whether a frigate should also be sent into the India Seas?"[13] Adams, who recorded the meeting in his memoirs, does not give the details on the discussion of these questions, but on May 30, 1818, no doubt as a result of the Cabinet deliberations, orders went out to Commodore William Bainbridge, commanding officer at Boston, to prepare the U.S.S. *Macedonian* for a cruise to the Pacific Ocean without delay.[14]

Captain John Downes was selected to command the *Macedonian*, a small frigate that had been captured from the British in the War of 1812 and recommissioned a man-of-war under the United States ensign. The orders appointing him to command directed that the ship be ready to proceed some time in August.[15] Having been second in command of the famous expedition of the *Essex* under Porter in 1813–14, Downes was thoroughly familiar with the Southeastern Pacific—from Guayaquil to Cape Horn and westward to the Marquesas. Porter had given him command of the *Essex Junior*, a prize converted to a warship, and in her, Downes had scoured the Pacific whaling grounds in search of British shipping. He had gained an intimate knowledge of the operations of the whaling fleets and merchantmen operating along the western South American coast. As Porter's representative, he had taken captured British prizes into Valparaiso for disposition. There he had become acquainted with some of the leading figures and the politics of the *patria vieja*.[16] A better choice than Downes could not have been made for the Pacific duty.

Henry Hill, who became an intimate friend of the naval officer, described Downes's temperament in these words: "He was quick in action, kind, gentle, but impulsive and passionate; yet the gust was soon over, and he was lion and lamb at the same moment." Once, when Downes saw a sailor kick a dog aboard ship, he knocked the sailor into the scuppers with one blow of his fist. He was immediately contrite and explained to Hill, who was present: "A man can take care of himself, but I cannot bear to see a brute abused." Hill attempted to tone down the naval officer's salty language. Downes admitted that he swore and was ashamed of it. "No one despises the habit more than I," he told Hill. "It is vulgar and ungentlemanly; but I have been so much among sailors. I never swear when I am in the company of ladies."[17]

By the end of summer the frigate was ready for sea. Downes had been given carte blanche in the selection of his officers, and there were many to choose from. When it became known in the fleet and on shore stations that the *Macedonian* was bound for the Pacific, the Navy Department was swamped with eager applicants for duty on board. Of the seven lieutenants assigned, all but two were requested personally by the new commander. An old shipmate, Lieutenant John M. Maury, became his first lieutenant. Others whose names will be recognized by naval historians were Hiram Paulding and Josiah Tattnall. Bainbridge, with his knowledge of Boston, secured a chaplain, Azariah Wilson, who came "highly recommended to him by the President of the University of Cambridge." Another alumnus of Harvard who "went out" in the *Macedonian* "in the capacity of surgeon's mate for scientifick [sic] reasons" was John Locke, specifically appointed to do botanical research along the Pacific Coast.[18]

Sailing orders for the *Macedonian* were issued by the secretary of the navy on September 2, 1818. Since they served as a model for future expeditions to the Pacific they will be given in some detail. The *Macedonian* was to shape course for the Brazil coast, and after stops at Pernambuco and Rio de Janeiro she was to proceed to the Río Plata to await favorable weather for rounding the Horn. After passing the Cape and in pursuing his course through the "South Sea," Downes was directed to ascertain "whether any interruption" had been given "to our Whale Fishery or Merchant Ships in that quarter." He was to endeavor to assist such ships whenever possible and, if necessary, convoy them to friendly ports. Every mark of respect was to be shown to "the existing governments of the several places you may visit"— a phrase that neatly allowed for rapid political changes incident to the revolution. The usual salutes and courtesies to ships of war of friendly nations were to be rendered.[19]

The orders were broad in scope and left much to the commanding officer's discretion. "One of the principal objects of the expedition of this ship," they read, "is to afford to the persons and property of the citizens of the United States protection and security, consistently with the laws of nations, and the respect due to all existing authorities, wherever and whenever such protection may be needed, and can be afforded."[20]

"By order of the President of the United States," supplemental instructions were sent to Downes by the chief clerk of the Navy Department. These directed that the ship should be "displayed" so as to "produce impressions favorable to the United States," enjoining the captain to guard "sedulously . . . against any act that might compromise the United States in any manner, except under the necessity of urging such just claims as may arise out of the detention or interruption of the whaling ships, or others carrying on lawful commerce in that quarter." The supplemental instructions concluded: "In all difficult cases, you will advise and consult with John B. Prevost, Esqr. United States Agent at Lima."[21]

The *Macedonian* sailed from Boston on September 20, 1818, but encountered a devastating gale on the twenty-sixth that dismasted and all but sank her. By heroic efforts and superb seamanship the frigate managed to make Norfolk, where new masts were stepped and other repairs effected.[22] During the period in the yard the *Macedonian* lost her botanical researcher. The one brief, hazardous voyage was enough to send Surgeon's Mate Locke back to land. He submitted his resignation, which was promptly accepted by the Navy Department.[23] His place was partially filled by Charles Gauntt, one of the junior lieutenants, who kept a journal in which he recorded navigational data, miscellaneous observations on places visited, and a day-by-day account of the events of the voyage. Charles J. Deblois, the captain's clerk, also maintained a daily record of events in a private journal. Gauntt and Deblois have provided many details of the *Macedonian*'s voyage in the Pacific of a livelier nature than the bare facts recorded in the ship's official log.

Because of the unexpected delay, supplementary instructions were sent to Downes at Norfolk. These directed him to proceed directly around Cape Horn to the South Pacific. Enclosed in the new instructions were three bills of exchange amounting to $10,100. They were drawn by Aguirre, the "Authorized Agent of the present Government of Chile," and the naval officer was directed to present them to the Chilean government for payment.[24]

Emergency repairs completed, the *Macedonian* resumed her voyage. As she passed Norfolk on her way to sea she "received three hearty cheers from the inhabitants, which was cheerfully returned by a like number from the ship."[25] Eighty days after clearing the Virginia capes, the *Macedonian* anchored in Valparaiso harbor on January 28, 1819.[26]

Henry Hill went on board the man-of-war at once. No doubt the vice-consul briefed Downes on Biddle's difficulties the month before. Although the patriot fleet was at sea, the *Macedonian* fired a salute of fifteen guns, which was returned by the Valparaiso forts gun for gun. The commander made an official call on Governor de la Cruz, who received him cordially and appeared most anxious to be friendly. Throughout his visit in Chile, Downes tried to make friends with the officials and people with whom he had contacts. With his outgoing nature and the instinctive sociability of the Chileans this proved an easy matter.[27]

In Valparaiso, Henry Hill and Downes soon formed a friendship that lasted the rest of their lives. Hill introduced Downes and his officers to the leading Chilean personalities and members of the foreign colony of the city. The arrival of the *Macedonian* was the occasion for a round of social activity. Nearly every night there was a ball or dinner for the visitors, which was reciprocated by the captain and his officers. Visitors were cordially received on board the *Macedonian* and every effort was made to make them feel welcome. An accommodation ladder was manufactured and rigged to make it easier for ladies to come on board. On Sundays members of the American and British colonies came aboard to attend divine services conducted by Chaplain Wilson.[28]

Downes was presented to the beautiful Lady Katherine Cochrane, wife of the commander of the Chilean naval forces. Henry Hill described her as "young, genial, a bold rider, fond of picnics, parties, music and dancing."[29] The American naval officer was captivated by her ladyship and spent much time in her company at social affairs.[30] Six or eight men of the carpenter's gang and the painter, under the supervision of a midshipman, were sent ashore to do repair work on the Cochrane quarters.[31] This may have been the reason why some of the ship's company thought their commander was seeing entirely too much of her ladyship.

The captain's clerk was one who thought so. "Our Captain pays her great attention, he rides, walks, and spends most of his time with her," he wrote. "She appears greatly attached to him." Deblois himself appears to have been fascinated by the vivacious Lady Katherine. He looked upon her as a Jezebel attempting to weave evil spells around his beloved captain. He described her as "horrid ugly, her face entirely covered with rouge," but conceded that "her form is very good" and she "appeared to understand riding perfectly." To his puritanical eyes she was "an abandoned profligate & ought to be treated as such." He recorded with relish the report, "believed by many inhabitants," that Lady Cochrane "was still a kept mistress" of his lordship. Whether or not the gossip was true he thought his captain should "be less frequent in his visits to the mansion of my lady C."[32]

The New England-bred clerk apparently looked upon any form of pleasure with a suspicious eye. Some of his mental processes can be understood better when it is learned that he disapproved of grog and gave up his navy ration in order to increase his pay $21.90 a year. He refused to go to a ball given in honor of the *Macedonian*'s officers in Valparaiso because he did not have the proper clothes and disapproved of borrowing. He admired the Chilean ladies but was uncomfortable in their presence. "I should like them very much if they kept their Boosoms [sic] covered," he wrote. "I believe it is the custom here to go uncovered, the most respectable of the female class goes this way"—which in Deblois' opinion was "not only indecent but unladylike."[33]

Deblois also had a low opinion of Lord Cochrane, whom he characterized as an adventurer seeking to re-establish his lost character and reputation in England by a brilliant performance in South America. The American grudgingly admitted that "the Patriots almost idolize him."[34]

Social activity continued. On Washington's Birthday the officers of the *Macedonian* gave a "Handsome Ball to the Ladies and Gentlemen of Valparaiso at which all the Americans and English of respectability were invited." No effort was spared to make the event an international success. The upper decks were lavishly decorated with flags and bunting, with the flags of the United States and Chile prominently displayed. Modern marines will blanch at the thought of using muskets as candalabras by stacking them in circles and forcing sperm candles into the muzzles. Dancing lasted until four o'clock in the morning when the company went to the "dining room" on the gun deck for supper. Democracy was praised and many toasts to inter-American friendship were proposed and drunk. If it was observed that the Chileans "found it difficult to preserve their equilibrium" it was equally true that "the officers too carried a heavy press of sails."[35]

The cruise was off to an excellent start. After their long voyage the officers and men of the *Macedonian* were enchanted with Chile and their hosts. It was not long, however, before the less glamorous aspects of their mission became apparent. Thrown into direct contact with the diverse and restless elements of a revolutionary port city, the lower ranks and ratings were the first to become aware of the differences between theory and practice in a revolutionary society. Deblois was appalled at the poverty, lawlessness, and low morality that existed in Valparaiso. Food of excellent quality was abundant but was beyond the reach of the poorer classes, who were "miserable" and "dirty." He concluded that the poor of Valparaiso subsisted solely on fish and fruit. These wretches lived in hovels that looked like dens of "thieves and assassins." Compared to the mass of the populace, mechanics did well in Valparaiso. Carpenters, riggers, blacksmiths, painters, and similar artisans drew $2.50 a day. Seamen could demand $35.00 a month and there was much competition for their services.

Lawlessness was rampant. Numerous cases of robbery and banditry occurred. In many cases the victims were personnel of the *Macedonian* or other foreigners. Chilean military personnel who were responsible for maintenance of law and order made little effort to stop such outrages. Indeed, the soldiers were often guilty of robbery and mayhem themselves. Conditions were so bad that it was not safe to go ashore after dark. The *Macedonian*'s first lieutenant issued an order that every officer going ashore should go well armed. Deblois wrote: "Robberies and murders are very common here, almost every night either one or the other is perpetrated. The Chileans, the soldiers particularly are a most consummate set of villains, they would do any thing for *cash & clothes*—they are wretchedly poor, they are not half clothed, very seldom get any money on a/c of their pay."[36]

Deblois correctly pinpointed poverty and misery among the populace and the soldiery as the cause of most of the banditry, but there seems to have been an element of nationalism involved as well. There was resentment at the comparative affluence and better treatment of the foreigners in the military services, particularly the crewmen of the warships and privateers.[37] One night two English crewmen of the patriot warship *Galvarino* were robbed and murdered. The following night a brawl occurred between the crew of the warship and soldiers of the Valparaiso garrison. A number of the soldiers were wounded and it was reported that the "soldiers and many of the low class of inhabitants" of Valparaiso swore "vengeance against the English & Americans." The same night a mob attacked and sacked a tavern run by three United States citizens, stabbing one of them. Following these outrages the captain's clerk once more exploded: "There is no Laws, any one can do as he likes, D——d such a Government."[38]

Not even the most exalted were immune from robbery and personal attacks. In February thieves entered Lady Cochrane's boudoir and made off with watches, jewels, and trinkets valued at five hundred guineas. John Spry, the English captain of the

Galvarino, was "slightly" stabbed one night on the streets of Valparaiso shortly before the brawl between his crewmen and the soldiers. As a result of these disorders a curfew was declared after 9:00 P.M. Soldiers found in the streets were to be imprisoned and given fifty lashes. Foreigners were to be held overnight and fined $5.00 apiece.[39]

The hospital was unattended. Deblois, as had Conner of the *Ontario* before him, noted the lack of doctors. One lone, elderly friar tried to administer to the needs of the sick. Venereal disease was widespread and virulent—many of the friar's patients at the hospital were English, Spanish, and Americans undergoing treatment for the disease. The surgeons of the *Macedonian* spent much time in the hospital helping the overworked friar.[40]

Shortly after the arrival of the *Macedonian* on station, the captain went to Santiago to meet the political leaders and to present the Aguirre bills of exchange to the government for payment. He also claimed on behalf of Porter and the United States government the money received by the Chilean government from sale of the former British whaler *Montezuma*, a prize taken by Porter and left in Valparaiso after the defeat of the *Essex*. The prize had been sold in the name of the Chilean government, which pocketed the money.[41]

The trip to Santiago was a success as far as social relations with the patriot officials went, but Downes got exactly nowhere with the patriot officials on the Aguirre bills and the *Montezuma* claim. He returned to Valparaiso empty-handed although government officials agreed to pay the Aguirre bills if they had not been paid in Buenos Aires, where the former envoy was supposed to reside.[42]

Downes was always conscious of his instructions to look out for United States whaling vessels and merchantmen. When the *Macedonian* first arrived at Valparaiso, two American whale ships, the *Independence* and the *Planter*, were cruising hungrily off the port. They would have been welcomed by the patriots but did not dare to enter for fear that later they would be seized by the royalists for trading with the rebels. An even greater deterrent to entering the harbor was the fear of losing their crews by desertion in Valparaiso. Consequently, the whalers remained offshore and transacted any business they might have, such as purchase of provisions, by small boat. As soon as the warship anchored, the captains of the whale ships manned their boats and boarded the *Macedonian* to pay their respects to her commander. They spent the better part of the day aboard getting news from the States and briefing Downes on United States shipping in the area. When the naval officer learned that the *Planter* was shorthanded he discharged two men from his crew and sent them out to the whaler.[43]

Downes had no wish to interfere in Chilean affairs but whenever events occurred which threatened the safety and welfare of his own crew or of the American merchantmen, his sense of duty and honor obliged taking official action. One such event took place in March, when an unusual attack was made on John Percival, second lieutenant of the *Macedonian*. The details are contained in the following letter of Downes to the governor, demanding punishment of perpetrators of "insults" to his officers:

Sir,
I have to represent to your excellency that last Evening while the Second Lieutenant of my Ship was passing through Almandral on horseback, he was met by a guard of Soldiers, one of them immediately left his ranks, and approached the Lieutenant who not supposing for a moment that so great an outrage was intended, did not put himself on his guard, the Soldier charged bayonet & killed the horse on which he was mounted—I have to request that you will be pleased to order the circumstances investigated, that the offender may receive the punishment merited by so flagrant an outrage, several of my officers have before been insulted by the Soldiery, but as the particular men who offered the insult could not be designated no representation was made to your Excellency—I however in this case shall expect ample justice—I can with confidence assure you that the attack on my second Lt. and insults offered to other officers of my Ship, have been unprovoked and wanton in the extreme. I hope the punishment inflicted on the offender will be such as to convince me that our good feelings toward the people of the Country are reciprocated.[44]

The man accused of this irrational act was brought to trial by the governor and condemned to be shot! De la Cruz and his successor were also much more co-operative in helping to run down and return deserters from United States ships, both naval and commercial, than Calderón had been with Biddle. When it was heard that a deserter from the *Macedonian* was being secreted aboard the privateer *Andes*, an order was obtained from the governor to search her. Percival and two boatloads of men went to the *Andes* and searched her, although the first lieutenant of the privateer swore the man was not on board. The unhappy culprit was found secreted under floor boards in one of the holds and returned to the *Macedonian*, where he was confined in double irons. It was rumored he would be made to run the gauntlet as punishment.[45]

The Chileans continued to try to entice seamen away from the foreign ships but with diminishing success, thanks to the efforts of United States and British warships and the inability of the Chileans to make good their exaggerated promises. Many members of the patriot armed forces went for months without pay. Deblois learned that Vice-Consul Hill had to assist a number of United States citizens in the army who had not been paid and he himself met several who had served for twelve to eighteen months and were willing to sell all the back wages due them for as little as $20.00. "The Chilians makes great and fair promises," commented the captain's clerk, "but very seldom conforms with them."[46]

Downes assumed responsibility for the discipline of all English and American merchantmen in the harbor. In the absence of a British man-of-war, eleven mutinous seamen from the British brigs *Thomas* and *Rebecca* were confined aboard the *Macedonian* at the request of their masters. When the *Andromache* arrived in Valparaiso from Lima on March 7, the Britishers were turned over to Captain Shirreff for final disciplinary action. Downes continued Biddle's policy of co-operation with the British Navy, and the American and British commanders made a reciprocal agreement to receive on board the *Andromache* or *Macedonian*, whichever might be in port, any mutinous merchant seamen of either nation.[47]

The men from the *Thomas* were taken on board at the request of her master, John Murphy. It seems that they had been ashore and there had met Captain Spry of the *Galvarino*, who gave them $5.00 apiece and offered to enlist them for his ship.

When they returned to the *Thomas* they refused to obey Murphy's orders and announced their intention of joining the patriots, whereupon the captain went aboard the *Macedonian* and asked for help to put down the mutiny. First Lieutenant Maury sent a force of sailors and marines aboard the *Thomas* and the mutineers were brought back to the *Macedonian*, where they were put in irons. It so happened that Spry came aboard the American warship for dinner that same evening with Lieutenant William K. Latimer and in the course of the evening became somewhat inebriated. When he and his host were about to leave the ship the Englishman spied the *Thomas'* crewmen on deck in irons. Forgetting that he was no longer serving in His Britannic Majesty's Navy, he became indignant and demanded to know by what authority Englishmen were confined in irons on an American ship. Hot words between him and Latimer followed; the result might have been a duel had not other officers intervened. Deblois, in reporting the incident, was apparently disappointed that the argument ended there. "Spry is a poor bombasting Englishman, & if he goes on at this rate will get into difficulty," he wrote, "our officers are not to be trifled with, he will get challenged and shot."[48]

Downes's services to the merchantmen did not stop at recovery of deserters and maintenance of discipline. Wherever they were needed, he sent men from his own crew to fill out the depleted crews of American vessels. Within the limits of stores available, cordage and ground tackle were supplied subject to reimbursement of the government for their cost. When the whale ship *Peru* entered Valparaiso, for example, Downes let it have a kedge anchor. The master of the *Peru* became dangerously ill and delayed the sailing of his ship for several weeks while receiving medical care from the *Macedonian*'s surgeons. It was also customary for ships to provide towing service for each other in such evolutions as getting underway and anchoring when the winds were not favorable. The *Macedonian* did her share of this type of duty and in return was helped when she required it. One of the greatest services rendered by men-of-war was lending artificers to help merchantmen make repairs. Whenever their services could be spared, carpenters, blacksmiths, armorers, sailmakers, and other technicians were sent to work on merchant ships, which paid them the prevailing wage for the port. This service was not restricted to United States ships. Thus, *Macedonian* calkers were sent to calk the deck and upper works of the British brig *Rebecca* and received $2.50 a day besides their regular pay. Entries in the *Macedonian*'s log for April indicate that carpenters were employed aboard the American brig *Ellen Maria*, the whaler *Ocean*, and the British brig *Livonia*, among others. On April 15 an unidentified Swedish ship was assisted in getting underway.[49]

Deblois' thirst for blood was satisfied some two weeks later to the sorrow of all hands on board. Dueling was prevalent in the old navy as an honorable method of settling disputes. Hot-blooded midshipmen were especially addicted to this method of asserting their status and proving their manhood.[50] The *Macedonian* was no exception. Among its midshipmen there was much bickering and petty quarreling, which resulted in many challenges. Thus, on March 2 a group of midshipmen went ashore in Valparaiso to settle their differences on the field of honor. Three separate challenges had been given and accepted, but the first two sets to take the field settled their differences by mutual apologies. The third set, midshipmen Alexander G. Gordon, aged eighteen, and John B. Abercrombie, aged twenty-three, could not be reconciled and the duel went off as scheduled. Abercrombie was hit on the first exchange of shots and died almost instantly.[51]

The midshipman was given a modified military funeral on March 3. His grave had to be dug on the beach near one of the forts, as permission could not be obtained to bury him in a Catholic cemetery and there were no others. The spot selected was near the place where the victims of the *Essex-Phoebe* battle had been buried some five years before. It had been reported that many of the bodies of the *Essex* crew had been dug up and robbed of clothing. Since Abercrombie's obsequies attracted a large crowd of disreputable looking riffraff and soldiers, the officers of the *Macedonian* feared the same treatment would be accorded their former shipmate's body. To prevent such desecration of the grave, heavy stones requiring three men to lift them were put on the mound. The following morning a special detail was sent ashore to see if the grave had been disturbed. The ship's company was relieved to hear that it had not been touched.[52]

Downes was very angry over the affair and restricted the midshipmen involved to the ship. He intended to send Gordon and the two seconds back to the United States on the whale ship *Factor*, which, having filled up with sperm oil, was preparing to go home. This plan had to be abandoned since the *Factor* could not accommodate the midshipmen for such a long voyage. Gordon and the seconds were subsequently restored to full duty and no further disciplinary action was taken.[53]

Another duel occurred between Lieutenant Josiah Tattnall and an English officer serving in Cochrane's squadron. In it the Englishman was wounded in the shoulder. Later in the year, Tattnall was present at a party in Valparaiso during which Midshipman Richard Pinkney made some derogatory remarks about Lord Cochrane and was promptly challenged by one of Cochrane's English officers. Each principal selected two seconds, Tattnall being chosen as one of Pinkney's, and the company adjourned to the moonlit beach of the Almendral. At the beach a general argument ensued over the terms of the duel—whether it was to be fought at five or ten paces. Tattnall lost his temper with one of the Englishman's seconds and, calling him "a coward and a scoundrel," challenged him to a duel before the main event. The English second declined Tattnall's challenge and apologized, after which the original duel proceeded at ten paces as the American lieutenant had insisted. Pinkney and his antagonist exhausted their ammunition without doing any harm, and since the militia were threatening interference, a reconciliation was effected. When Tattnall heard later that his actions were criticized by Cochrane's officers he sent word he would be most happy to fight any officer in the Chilean squadron from "cockpit" to "cabin door."[54]

In order to counteract the bad effects on discipline of a long period at anchor and desiring to exercise the crew at sea, Downes made a brief inspection trip to Coquimbo. Hill went along as guest. The short cruise up the coast and back was a most pleasant break from the activity of Valparaiso. In Coquimbo they were met by the American vice-consul, Washington Stewart, and made the acquaintance of a young Scottish physician, Doctor R. C. Wyllie, who afterwards became prime minister of the king of the Sandwich Islands.[55]

After returning to Valparaiso, Downes accompanied Prevost to Santiago, where he again failed in a final attempt to collect the Aguirre bills of exchange. The bills were subsequently returned to Washington for further action.[56] Otherwise the visit to Santiago was something of a personal triumph. Downes was given a banquet by the supreme director and Prevost wrote Adams that during a fortnight's visit the naval officer, by "associating with the members of the government," had "sensibly diminished their jealousies."[57]

April was fairly quiet in Valparaiso. Most of the foreign ladies, including Lady Cochrane, had gone to the country, with the result that there was little social activity. There seemed to be fewer robberies and murders and less disorder. Carpenters and calkers were sent to various ships in the harbor, including the "French" whaler *Archimedes*, obviously a Yankee sailing under French papers to gain the advantage of a 10 per cent premium on sperm oil paid by the French government. To relieve the tedium, Deblois invested in some new clothing but did not dare make the outlay for a complete outfit. Inflation was rampant in Valparaiso. Boots, shoes, and hats were "uncommonly" expensive. Coats which cost $28.00 in the United States were $45.00–$50.00 in Valparaiso; $18.00–$20.00 were asked for $12.00 pantaloons; and $5.00 vests were going at $10.00–$12.00.[58]

All hands were happy to take to the sea again on April 25, when the *Macedonian* left Valparaiso for a cruise of nearly six months along the coasts of Peru and Mexico. The primary object of this voyage was to carry out that portion of Downes's instructions that directed him to "fall in with" United States "Whale Fishery or Merchant Ships in that quarter" in order to ascertain whether "any interruption" had been given to them. It had also been the captain's intention to visit Callao, the seaport for Lima, but at the earnest request of the Chilean minister of state for foreign affairs, Downes agreed to postpone his visit to that port.[59]

At the time of the *Macedonian's* departure for the northern ports, Callao was being blockaded by the patriot squadron. On January 16, 1819, the first division of the new Chilean fleet, composed of the *O'Higgins, San Martín, Lautaro,* and *Chacabuco,* had sailed under Cochrane's command to make a surprise attack on Callao, but a heavy fog delayed the Chilean fleet and spoiled the chances for a surprise. After an ineffectual attack against the forts and royalist ships at Callao, Cochrane's fleet withdrew to seaward and the admiral announced a blockade of the royalist coast from Guayaquil to Atacama. O'Higgins gave the Chilean government's sanction to the blockade by decree dated April 20, 1819.[60] Nothing illustrates the shift of sea power in the Southeast Pacific from royalist to patriot hands so clearly as the failure of the Spanish fleet to leave the security of their anchorage under the guns of Callao to challenge the blockading ships.

United States naval commanders were vitally concerned with the shift in the balance of forces. In the protection of neutral United States commerce with the belligerents in South America, they were guided by the common usages of international law and the so-called "treaty plan of 1776" as modified by specific treaties with particular nations. This plan, adopted by the Continental Congress, covered four important principles governing neutral commerce, which successive United States administrations attempted to incorporate in commercial treaties with foreign powers. These were: (1) nationals of a neutral nation could engage in trade with enemies of a belligerent, not only between neutral ports and enemy ports but also from port to port of the enemy; (2) "free ships" should "give a Freedom of Goods," except contraband—that is, that enemy goods on a neutral vessel were immune to capture; (3) contraband was limited to arms, munitions of war, and horses; (4) neutral goods in enemy ships were liable to confiscation. In the commercial treaty of 1795 between the United States and Spain three of these principles had been recognized: trade from port to port of an enemy;

confirmation of the contraband list; and free ships make free goods. The United States had been unable to reach an agreement with Britain recognizing the principle of free ships make free goods. In fact, the Jay Treaty of 1794 with Britain contained an article permitting the confiscation of enemy goods in neutral vessels.[61]

The principles of the treaty plan of 1776 would have been most advantageous to United States shipping and commerce on the west coast of South America if unequivocal adherence to them could have been achieved. Such, however, was not possible. Spain did not recognize the patriot governments as belligerents but considered them as rebels. She insisted that as colonies of Spain the Laws of the Indies governed neutral commerce with them rather than the provisions of the treaties between the Madrid government and other nations. Moreover, there were no commercial treaties between the United States and the new governments.[62] Thus there was no mechanism for regulation of neutral commerce with either of the belligerents that was binding on the opposite party except the accepted principles of international law. In Chile, Lord Cochrane and his officers, the majority of whom were English, applied British principles to neutral commerce. In the British concept there was no provision for "free ships, free goods" or for any other traffic with an enemy except on British terms. Even contraband was subject to redefinition in British maritime warfare. It was inevitable that Cochrane's ideas of maritime trade should produce misunderstanding with United States merchantmen and their protectors, the United States Navy.

No question generated more friction between United States naval commanders in the Pacific and the belligerents, both royalists and patriots, than seizure and condemnation of American merchantmen for alleged violation of blockades. It was, and is, an accepted principle of international law that any ship attempting to break a blockade may be subject to capture, provided the blockade is valid. It was on this point—the definition of what constituted a legal blockade—that disputes arose. The United States has always held that to be valid and binding, the power declaring a blockade must maintain a force off the place under blockade sufficient to make communication with such a place hazardous.[63] This has been the usual position of all maritime nations, including Britain. But during the Napoleonic wars Britain and France departed from this concept and each declared the entire coastal areas of the other under blockade without any real effort to station ships to enforce their edicts. Thus their announced blockades became legal nets by which the warring parties could seize neutral vessels trading with the enemy wherever found and hail them before the prize courts for violation of blockade. British naval forces had been active in seizing neutrals in this manner although it should be noted that judges in British prize courts continued to hold that a blockade to be legal must be effective.[64]

The position of the United States on paper blockades was consistent. Successive administrations vigorously protested the practice. In 1801 Secretary of State Madison made it clear that the United States would not recognize such blockades. Writing to the United States minister to Spain, Madison said: "Mere liability by neutral vessels to capture by belligerent cruisers hovering around a coast, cannot constitute a blockade of a port on such coast."[65] In 1804 he denounced the fictitious blockades of Britain as being "one of the greatest abuses ever committed on the high seas."[66] As president, Madison termed "mock blockades" one of the causes of the War of 1812.[67] In 1816 Monroe, as secretary of state, protested the announced blockade of the Colombian and Mosquito coasts by the Spanish General Morillo as being a "paper" blockade and in a protest to Onís clearly stated United States opposition to it.[68]

On the west coast of South America both royalists and patriots declared sweeping blockades of the other's coast line. In respect to these blockades, United States naval commanders following Biddle became more apprehensive of the growing Chilean war fleet than of the Spanish ships as it increased in strength and efficiency under the energetic Lord Cochrane. Prevost noted the shift in control of the seas when he reported to Adams: "The Changes brought about in one short twelve months are almost incredible. . . . At this period all is confidence, the patriot Flag waves triumphantly on the ocean and upwards of forty large vessels [merchantmen] at Valparaiso proclaim its success. . . ."[69] He also reported that Cochrane was capturing many American vessels as prizes and bringing them to Valparaiso for adjudication.

Prevost and Downes differed in their attitude toward the capture of American ships. Prevost believed the best procedure was to allow the patriots to make their captures and trust to the fairness of the Chilean tribunals to see that justice was done. When Downes proposed to go to Lima to help any American merchantmen caught in Peruvian ports by Cochrane's blockade, he was dissuaded by Prevost, who advised patience in allowing the cases of ships seized for carrying enemy property or for violation of the blockade to come before the courts as a "right" of the belligerents. In advising Downes against going to Lima, Prevost said: "It was never intended by your presence to invalidate the right to arrest and send a disputed ship into some port for judicial investigation, . . . your interference on such occasions can extend only to promote a decision, and whether just or unjust the agency there ends and it becomes a subject of discussion between the Governments."[70]

Prevost was much concerned with the unfavorable impression any signs of disagreement with, or opposition to, the patriots might have on the image of the United States as a champion of democracy. In a report to Adams concerning the cases of the *Montezuma*, captured entering Lima with a cargo of arms and munitions, and the confiscation by Cochrane's forces of some $140,000 belonging to the merchant brig *Macedonian*, operated by Captain Eliphalet Smith,[71] Prevost remarked that he was "vexed and mortified" at the occurrences, not merely because of the immediate effect on the interests of his countrymen but because such cases tended to increase "those unfavorable impressions which I have increasingly to contend with since the last imprudent visit of Capt. Biddle." He then went on to explain the reaction of the patriots to American attempts to trade with the royalists: "There exists a peculiar sensibility to every act emanating from the Government [of the U.S.] or done by an individual although strictly neutral. They seem to claim a sympathy from us in their struggle that they look for nowhere else, and cannot bear any circumstances that lead to a contrary feeling."[72]

Downes had a much broader concept of his obligations to American shipping than had Prevost. He conceived it to be his duty to prevent illegal seizure of American merchantmen by either party for whatever cause and proposed to use the limited force at his disposal to do so. To clarify his position he wrote to the supreme director of Chile and the viceroys of Peru and Mexico protesting the unwarranted and illegal seizure of American ships. Respecting the capture of American ships attempting to enter ports along the blockaded Peruvian coast, he informed the supreme director of Chile that the blockade would not be recognized as legal, adding: "The undersigned also informs his Excellency that the object of this Ship in the Pacific is the Protection of American Commerce against unlawful interruptions. ... The undersigned conceives it to be his duty to use the force placed at his disposal, for the protection of the Ships of the United States against all unlawful interruptions."[73] The letters to the viceroys of Peru and Mexico contained almost identical statements.[74]

In spite of his peremptory tone, the *Macedonian*'s captain was uncertain as to how far he was authorized to go in protecting the merchantmen. In a long report to the Navy Department he outlined his position on the blockade and asked for instructions as to the extent of force he could use. There was not the slightest doubt in his mind that Cochrane's blockade of Peru was illegal and merited no consideration whatsoever. The idea that the Chilean commander's force of three frigates, one corvette, and three brigs could maintain a coast of twelve hundred miles in a state of rigorous blockade was termed "ridiculous." "He continues but a few days before any place," he wrote of Cochrane, "under such circumstances I cannot consider any part of the coast of Peru as blockaded." He added, however, that if the blockade were actually confined to one or two ports he "would be inclined to respect it."[75]

In order that there should be no doubt in Washington about his intention in case of seizures of American ships by Cochrane's forces, Downes wrote the secretary of the navy: "Our vessels are suffering on the coast of Peru by the depredations of Lord Cochrane. If I were present I would not allow him to take possession of an American vessel under any circumstances, but if he takes or sends a vessel to Valparaiso during my absence, and it is regularly condemned there I conceive the affair is to be decided between the Governments and that I have nothing to do in such a case."[76]

The last sentence was in conformance with Prevost's instructions. Accordingly, the troubled Downes advised the Navy Department that he had assumed no responsibility in the cases of the *Montezuma* and of Smith's specie. He considered these cases the responsibility of Prevost and Hill since they had been taken before the Chilean tribunal before he knew of them.

The northern cruise was a welcome change for Downes and the crew of the *Macedonian*. En route to San Blas, the northernmost port visited, the ship made brief stops at Arica, Guarmey, Trujillo, Túmbez, and Guayaquil in the expectation of finding in some of them United States merchantmen that might require assistance.

No American ships were encountered before arrival at San Blas, but off Arica between May 5 and 14 the *Macedonian* rendezvoused a number of times with the British brig *Thomas*, which with three other vessels had been engaged in clandestine trade in the Arica area. While in company with the British brig a "considerable" amount of specie was received from her.[77] In agreeing to accept the specie for safekeeping and transportation Downes was following the standard practice of warships for that period and the precedent set by Biddle for United States ships in the Pacific. Moreover, the service to commercial firms was invaluable because it provided a safe means of transmitting cash through the perils of war and piracy. At this stage of the Wars for Independence the service was far more important to merchants trading with the royalists than with the patriots since it was virtually the only way of getting cash out of Spanish-held territory without risk of interception and confiscation by the patriots.[78]

Quite naturally the patriots protested the transportation of specie as an unneutral act and claimed that some carried by neutral warships was actually property of the Spanish government. Prevost, fearing the practice would do damage to United States relations with the patriot government, sought to dissuade Downes from taking specie on board the *Macedonian*. Henry Hill, however, with the merchant's viewpoint, encouraged the naval commander and "expressed the opinion that it was proper for him to be remunerated for the great care and responsibility connected with this important service."[79] The United States government, shortly after receipt of the Chilean complaint against Biddle, indirectly condoned the practice, even for belligerents, when it excepted specie from a confidential instruction designed to prohibit the transportation of property of belligerent nationals. The instruction read: "You will therefore decline taking on board for either party, either Men, Money, provisions or Supplies to be carried from such party to any other Port or Country whatsoever except Specie which you have permission to bring to the U.S. . . ."[80] In practice, Downes extended the authorization to carrying specie for Spanish merchants, as well as for neutrals, between ports on the South American coast while he was in the Pacific. Altogether, he took on board close to $2,000,000 during the two-year cruise.[81]

One of the objects of the visit to San Blas was to ascertain the fate of the schooner *Traveller* and her crew. The *Traveller* had been captured by the Spanish in the Gulf of California in 1818, and the crew imprisoned. The marine officer of the *Macedonian*, Lieutenant Samuel B. Johnston, was sent sixty miles inland to Tepic to ascertain the facts of the case. On his return, Johnston reported that the crew had been freed and the owner, one Wilcox, had decided to remain in the country, become a Roman Catholic, and marry a Spanish woman. There was little for Downes to do except protest the capture to the viceroy. While in San Blas, Downes learned that the American brig *Cossack* had also been captured in the Gulf of California, but the particulars were not available.[82] At the end of the northern summer the ship left San Blas for Valparaiso and arrived there on October 10, making only one stop on the way—at Acapulco—to send a protest to the viceroy on the captures of the *Traveller* and *Cossack*.[83]

The first eight months of the *Macedonian*'s cruise in the Pacific had been relatively quiet. Although Downes had maintained cordial relations with the patriot leaders the effects of the blockade of Peru on American shipping continued to weigh on his mind. As yet there had been no direct contact with the blockading squadron off Callao or with the viceroy of Peru. As the blockade assumed increasing importance it became imperative that he go to Callao to observe conditions there as well as to pay his respects to the viceroy.

Chapter VI

*Peru, 1820 — Downes,
Cochrane, Pezuela, and San Martín*

The *Macedonian* remained in Valparaiso three weeks preparing for her long-delayed visit to Callao and performing various services for the United States merchant ships present. Altogether there were about fifty ships of all flags in the harbor.¹ One of them was the *Andromache*, which sent over two deserters from American ships whom she had been keeping in accordance with the two commanders' agreement.² If there was any extensive social activity it was not recorded.³

Only one event occurred to mar the amicable relations between the Americans and Chileans during this visit to Valparaiso. The ship's purser desired to purchase some shoes and spirits from a merchantman in the harbor and requested that the sale be made duty free as a courtesy to a United States man-of-war. When informed by the collector of customs that he was authorized to allow duty-free sales to British but not to United States warships, Downes wrote a protest to the supreme director designed to get action but hardly calculated to win friends. Some of the naval commander's growing impatience at the inconsistency and pettiness of Chilean officials revealed itself in his letter, which read in part: "I have the honor to address your Excellency upon a subject which I little anticipated; however experience proves to me how little this government is disposed to reciprocate civilities. It also further proves that the British Ships of War in this Port are treated with more liberality than ships of War belonging to the United States of North America."[4]

In his answer to Downes, which apparently was never received by the naval commander, Echeverría maintained that in the absence of commercial or other treaties, the question of collection of customs from warships of different nations was a question solely within the discretion of his government. However, he extended to the *Macedonian* the same privileges enjoyed by the British. A few days later he forwarded a copy of his action to Prevost together with a complaint against the tone of Downes's letter. Without consultation with the naval officer, Prevost forwarded the Chilean's complaint to Adams. Some eight months later the concession regarding customs-exempt sales to United States men-of-war was confirmed by directorial decree.[5]

Downes's irritation at the Chileans was no doubt intensified by rumors current in Valparaiso that Cochrane had boasted he would not allow the *Macedonian* to enter Callao harbor through his blockade. According to Henry Hill, the volcanic Downes could hardly restrain himself on hearing these reports and immediately made plans to fight his way into Callao if necessary. His plan, as confided to Hill, was simply to concentrate his fire on Cochrane's flagship, hoping to sink her at once, and then, if that was successful, to deal with the two smaller vessels reported to be in the blockading force.[6]

When the *Macedonian* left Valparaiso for Callao on November 1, all hands on board expected a showdown with the Chilean fleet off Callao. En route every precaution was taken to make ready for the expected fight. Gun crews were exercised at quarters daily and extra round shot was routed up from the magazines. On approaching Callao at daybreak on November 9, the

Macedonian beat to quarters and prepared for action. Decks were sanded, guns run out, and "matches lighted" by the gunners. True enough, two sail were sighted off San Lorenzo Island at the harbor entrance. These proved to be the Chilean frigate *O'Higgins*, Cochrane's flagship, and the corvette *Independencia*, both of which bore down on the *Macedonian* and took station on either quarter in menacing positions, thereby strengthening the conviction of the crew that Cochrane intended to deny the American warship entry to the harbor. A boarding officer from the *O'Higgins* came alongside, enquired as to their destination, and returned to the flagship. The *Macedonian* resumed her course to the anchorage still prepared to do battle if necessary. No effort was made to stop her, however, and soon thereafter Cochrane sent a signal wishing her a pleasant passage to her anchorage.[7]

The junior officers of the *Macedonian* considered that their show of readiness to fight before the *O'Higgins*' boarding officer had influenced Cochrane's decision not to oppose them. It is doubtful, however, if this incident was the dramatic showdown the young, impressionable officers of the *Macedonian* imagined it to be. Cochrane was aware of the implications of the use of force against a public vessel of a foreign power and had no desire to complicate his problems by a battle with a United States man-of-war, no matter what he may have said prior to that warship's appearance off the port. In his final report Downes did not attach much importance to the incident, merely stating that he spoke to Lord Cochrane's flagship on the way into Callao and his lordship was "very polite."[8]

Whether or not the confrontation off Callao was a "showdown," more was at stake than either Downes or Cochrane realized, for it had repercussions in far-off places. Partially as a result of this incident, England determined to strengthen her naval forces in the Southeast Pacific by sending out two ships of the line under the command of Sir Thomas Hardy. In London, Irisarri, now Chilean representative to the European courts, believed this action was taken "because of the reports which have reached here that Lord Cochrane tried to search the frigate *An-*

dromaca [sic] and the *Ontario*, and had threatened to open fire on the *Macedonian* in case it did not respect the blockade of Callao."⁹

Another, rather plaintive, passage in Irisarri's report to his government indicates Chilean resentment toward what they considered as disregard for their rights as a sovereign nation by the great naval powers. Respecting the British attitude toward Chile, he wrote: "they will scoff at us as abject men who are inclined to take all sorts of insults. This opinion is due to the contempt with which this nation as well as the United States have viewed us; they send their merchant ships to our ports as they would send them to an uninhabited coast, threatening us with their warships as they would the negroes of Senegal."¹⁰

Relations with the viceroy followed much the same pattern as had those of Biddle with the Spanish official. Downes received a vigorous but dignified reply to his bellicose letter of the previous May announcing his intention to use force to protect American shipping against mistreatment by royalist naval ships. Pezuela pointed to concessions granted Biddle as proof of his desire to remain on good terms with the United States in spite of the extensive aid that its citizens and ships were giving to the patriots. The viceroy asked for specific cases in which American ships had been wronged and assured the *Macedonian*'s commander that satisfaction would be given under the Spanish law in such cases. Ending by decrying the resort to force to settle differences, he adroitly contrasted the conciliatory tenor of his reply to the belligerent tone of Downes's letter as evidence before their respective governments that if any altercation should take place the responsibility would rest on the North American. Downes, in his turn, denied any intent to use threats and came as close as his nature would permit to apologizing for the strong language of his first letter, which he assured the viceroy had been misinterpreted. The case of the *Eliza Barker*, which had not yet been settled, was cited as his example of mistreatment of United States ships by Spanish men-of-war. Without attempting to explain the intricacies of the United States neutrality acts, which actually did not prohibit sales of arms to belligerents outside the limits of the states, Downes declared that the sale of articles of war did not meet the approval of his government and that he was personally opposed to it.[11]

Desiring to retain the friendship of Downes, Pezuela consented to the release of five of fifteen prisoners from the *Maipú*—two at Callao and three at Guayaquil—with the understanding that they would be kept on board the *Macedonian* until she left the area. Downes believed he would be able to secure release of the remainder on his next trip to Callao.[12] Among the prisoners released was Thomas Bradshaw, whom Pezuela gave up because he had been a shipmate of Downes on the *Essex*.

Another motive of Pezuela's was to insure protection for the sizeable fleet of United States merchantmen that had been, in effect, enlisted in the royalist service in return for the privilege of trading along the coast of the Peruvian viceroyalty. With the advent of the patriot blockade Pezuela had been forced to further relax the regal ban against foreign trade, and by the end of 1819 Lima was largely dependent on neutral ships for its supplies. Thus, the *Beaver* was given permission to trade with Spanish ports in order to provide a means of transporting food from the northern provinces to the capital. Another reason for granting special permits to the *Beaver* as well as the *Canton*, according to Pezuela, was to compensate them for losses sustained in Talcahuano during their illegal detention. Other American merchantmen favored by the viceroy were the merchant brigs *Macedonian*, *Pallas*, *Ellen Marie*, and the schooner *Amanda*. For the most part these ships simply carried produce and non-contraband merchandise from port to port, but they also performed invaluable and unneutral service for the royalists in keeping lines of communication open with Panama and Chiloé. Thus, the *Canton* was sent to warn a convoy en route from Panama to Callao of the patriot blockade, after which she was sent southward to Valdivia with important messages. The *Pallas* and *Amanda* both brought cargoes of arms and munitions to Callao and remained to trade. The supercargo of the *Amanda*, George Bier, undertook a special trip to Valparaiso to obtain information for the viceroy.[13] These services were especially valuable to the royalists in view of the erratic nature of the patriot blockade.

Bier was a passenger on the *Macedonian* from Valparaiso to

Callao, although there is no reason to suppose that Downes had any knowledge of his mission for the royalists.[14] Other passengers from Valparaiso were a Mr. Gerauld and a Baron Kavanaugh. These gentlemen remained on board for passage to Panama when the ship left Callao to spend the South American summer in the Gulf of California.[15] The *Macedonian* narrowly missed having another very important passenger from Callao to Panama. José de la Serna, former commander of the Army of Upper Peru, who had resigned his command because of ill-health and disagreements with Pezuela, arranged with Downes for transportation to Panama and actually had his baggage on board when Pezuela recalled him to the command in Upper Peru with promotion to the rank of lieutenant general. This action was forced on Pezuela by leading members of the government because of the threat of Bolívar's armies in the north.[16]

The *Macedonian*—with her namesake, the merchant brig *Macedonian*, and the brig *Ellen Marie* of Boston in company—got underway for Panama on December 5. Before she sailed the viceroy entertained her captain at his country house in Magdalena and earnestly solicited him not to take on board any undeclared specie as most foreign warships were in the habit of doing when they left Callao. Downes gave his word of honor not to do so but asked if it would be satisfactory to carry specie for the Spanish merchants of Lima if properly registered. The viceroy gave a qualified answer to the effect that the request should be made by the merchants to the government. Apparently a satisfactory arrangement was made, because the ship took on board $480,000 at Lima, part of which was carried for the merchant brig *Macedonian* and part destined for Panama and the United States.[17]

The Christmas season was celebrated at Panama. The warship continued to aid United States merchant vessels wherever she found them in need. At Panama her beneficence extended to two oceans. Crew members were sent fifty-one miles across the Isthmus to the schooners *Sea Serpent* of New York and *Nymph* of Philadelphia, when it was learned that those vessels were immobilized at Chagres because most of their crews had died of fever.[18]

From February 23 to May 10, 1820, the *Macedonian* remained at San Blas, a popular rendezvous point for United States ships, then headed south for Valparaiso, once more stopping en route at Panama. While at Panama, Downes gave asylum to several English and Irish prisoners who had eluded their Spanish captors with the help of the ship's officers. One, a surgeon, was loaned a uniform by one of the *Macedonian*'s lieutenants to pass the Spanish sentries.[19] Downes's account follows: "I have preserved a good understanding with those in power and all the inhabitants at every place we have been except Panama, where the Governor General was much insenc'd in consequence of five prisoners having made their escape from the shore, and he supposed they had taken shelter on board my ship (which is the fact) altho' he could not have known it. They were two Irish and three Englishmen, taken at Portobello when Genl. McGregor was driven out, if I had have given them up, they would have been immediately shot. I trust the Government will not disapprove my having done so."[20]

When the governor protested the flight of his prisoners a Spanish officer was allowed to make a search of the ship accompanied by one of the ship's officers. Fortunately the stowaways were not found. The Spanish official was not fooled, however, and in retaliation refused passports to a number of American officers and men who had intended to cross the Isthmus to take passage for the United States. The disappointed travelers were obliged to return to Valparaiso aboard the *Macedonian*.[21]

When the *Macedonian* arrived at Valparaiso on June 13, 1820, the Chilean fleet was at anchor, preparing for the impending invasion of Peru. Downes sent Maury to the flagship with an offer to salute Cochrane's flag, provided it was returned gun for gun. When the first lieutenant returned with a message from the admiral that he would answer gun for gun if the American commander would give him assurance that an even exchange was always required by United States ships regardless of the relative ranks of the commanders, the hot-tempered Downes became disgusted. Believing that Cochrane was attempting to belittle him and the United States he told Henry Hill, who was visiting aboard the warship, that he would give no such assurance, fire no salute, and do nothing further about it. Hill, to prevent a repetition of the Biddle-Cochrane contretemps, persuaded his friend to give Cochrane the desired assurances, which were in accord with navy regulations. A salute of seventeen guns was fired and was returned gun for gun.[22]

The outstanding event of 1820 on the Pacific coast was the Chilean expedition led by San Martín against the royalist stronghold of Peru. The patriot general's plans were well known and preparations were watched with great interest by Downes and his officers. San Martín planned to land his small force of about five thousand Argentine and Chilean troops on the coast of Peru with the expectation that the inhabitants would rally to the rebel cause. The Chilean treasury was exhausted and it was rumored that San Martín had promised to repay the cost of outfitting the expedition from the booty of the first places taken.[23]

After a year and a half in South American waters the enthusiasm of the North Americans for the invasion was somewhat less than it might have been on their first visit to Valparaiso. Many of them were becoming disenchanted with the South American brand of democracy. Deblois had expressed the sentiments of many of his shipmates when he wrote: "I was ere we arrd. here from N. America, very much in favor of the Patriot Cause, but I have seen & heard so much of their villaneous [sic] Conduct that I am done with them."[24] After a visit to the capital, Gauntt wrote: "During my stay in 'Santiago' I learned that the people of Chili experienced from the reigning power more oppression and more tyranny is exercised over them than when the old Spaniards ruled."[25] Part of Gauntt's dislike of the Chilean government was caused by the harsh treatment of O'Higgins' political enemies. The American lieutenant witnessed the banishment from Valparaiso of one member of the Carrera family, who "were oppressed beyond measure."

Downes, in his official reports to Washington, avoided party politics and confined his criticism of the patriot government to Cochrane, the blockade, and the treatment of United States ships. In his communications with the Chilean officials he exercised diplomatic restraint unless a point of national prestige was at stake, as when he had written O'Higgins demanding the same privileges for the *Macedonian* as those granted British warships.²⁶ The commander's main arguments were reserved for the blockade, which he considered illegal and as being operated by Cochrane for his own aggrandizement and to the advantage of British ships.²⁷ There is some basis for his belief that the blockade was not enforced impartially. Irisarri found it necessary to caution O'Higgins to watch the administration of naval matters so that Britain was not granted favors to the exclusion of other nations, and especially the United States. He cited an article in the London *Morning Chronicle*, which he attributed to Álvarez Condarco, indicating that Britain had been granted special privileges. The article read: "Lord Cochrane has shown great partiality to British interests in the South Sea; and at his advise, the government of Chile has permitted all British ships to enter and leave the blockaded ports of the Pacific, while the ships of all other nations are not permitted any commerce with such ports."²⁸

Irisarri professed not to believe in the authenticity of the article but noted that whether true or not the reported mistreatment of United States ships was alienating a portion of the North American public. He deplored the tendency to give Britain advantages without securing comparable favors in return and suggested a careful examination of his government's policy. Castlereagh, the British foreign secretary, apparently believed that his countrymen were faring satisfactorily in regard to the blockade. After telling Irisarri in August, 1819, that his government considered the blockade illegal, he reversed himself in January, 1820, and informed the Chilean representative that Britain would recognize whatever blockade the patriots should "legally" make. Irisarri took this as acceptance of the blockade although he himself believed it was illegal under international law.²⁹

Downes became uneasy at the prospect of American ships being caught in Callao after arrival of the patriot forces. The lack of fresh arrivals in Valparaiso from the Peruvian port convinced him that the royalists had declared an embargo on ship departures. He reasoned that if the Americans at Callao could not get out under existing circumstances their plight would be worse when the patriots arrived and established a new blockade. Therefore, he decided it was necessary for him to go to their aid. Informing the Navy Department of his intentions to go to Callao he wrote of the merchantmen: "Their chance to escape will be very slender unless I go to their assistance."[30] The American commander informed the supreme director of Chile of his intentions and with delicacy indicated that he would delay his arrival until after the patriot forces had arrived on the coast of Peru, "provided no objections would then be made to my entering the Port of Callao."[31] José Ignacio Zenteno, minister of marine, advised that "by Order of the Supreme Director" there would be no difficulty in the *Macedonian*'s entry into the port of Callao.

San Martín's expedition sailed from Valparaiso on August 20, 1820. The same day O'Higgins issued a decree declaring that from August 25 all the Pacific coast from Iquique to Guayaquil was once more to be considered in a rigorous state of blockade. One of the specific provisions of the decree was that any neutral vessel taking on board "property or effects belonging to the subjects of the King of Spain" was to be captured and sent to Valparaiso for adjudication.[32] Downes did not consider this new blockade any more legal than the old.

The *Macedonian* remained quietly at anchor until the twenty-third in order to give the slow-moving expeditionary force a head start. En route to Coquimbo, the ship rescued a derelict launch from the San Martín expedition loaded with guns, carriages, and pack saddles. The launch was taken into port and turned over to the governor of Coquimbo.[33] This was the only recorded act of direct assistance to the patriots by the *Macedonian*. The ship *Two Catherines* and the brigs *Warrior* and *Chesapeake* were at anchor at Coquimbo. The former was about to sail for the United States and, being short of men, was furnished with six seamen from the man-of-war. Cochrane had been in the port a few days before and taken twelve men from the *Chesapeake*. The captain of the *Warrior*, Lieutenant Zachariah W. Nixon, on leave from the U.S. Navy, went on board the *Macedonian* to Lima in order to wind up his business there. Shortly after the American warship left the harbor, the governor of Coquimbo seized the *Warrior* by order of the Chilean government and removed her sails, rigging, guns, spars, and rudder on the charge that she had been employed by the Peruvians to carry arms and munitions to Chiloé.[34]

From Coquimbo the *Macedonian* proceeded to Callao, arriving there on September 10. There was no problem about entering the royalist port since the Chilean expedition had not yet arrived; it had stopped at Pisco, where Cochrane's forces took the American brig *Canton*, in ballast, and the British brig *Rebecca*, loaded with *aguardiente*, as prizes. There were six United States vessels at Callao—the ships *Panther* of Boston and *Zephyr* of Providence, the brigs *Savage* of Baltimore, *Dick* of Baltimore, and *Pallas* of Boston, and the schooner *Rampart* of Baltimore.[35] The months of September and October passed peaceably. Downes re-established his friendly relations with Viceroy Pezuela and was granted permission to visit the Spanish prisons for the purpose of securing the release of such men as he requested. Fifteen persons claiming United States citizenship were released to him.[36]

On October 29 the Chilean expedition of twenty-three sails appeared and anchored off Callao. A battle appeared imminent, but the following day the transports continued to Ancon while the naval squadron remained to invest Callao.[37] On the night of October 30, the patriots shot a few rockets into the shipping in Callao harbor. No damage resulted, but the following day Downes, expecting a full-scale attack on the harbor, moved the *Macedonian* and the American merchantmen further up the harbor to clear the anticipated line of fire. During the movement the *Zephyr* lagged behind the other ships and the *O'Higgins* approached as if she intended to cut the merchantman out. The *Macedonian* got underway and stood toward the *Zephyr* whereupon the *O'Higgins* hauled off. A few days later at the request of the commandant of the port, the *Macedonian* and her merchantmen again shifted berths to a supposedly safe location quite near the Spanish ships and one of their protectors, the warship *Esmeralda*. The British frigate *Hyperion* was also assigned a berth near the *Esmeralda*.[38]

Then occurred a series of events which disrupted the amicable relations between the Americans and Spanish and threatened to lead to open hostilities. During the night of November 5-6, the Chileans under the personal command of Lord Cochrane boarded the *Esmeralda* and after a bloody hand-to-hand fight captured her. During the battle the Spanish ship, which had been cast loose from her moorings, drifted so close to the *Macedonian* that the cries of her wounded could be clearly heard and pistol shot landed on the American warship's decks. When the Spanish on shore realized what was happening, they opened fire on the *Esmeralda* from the forts. But the *Macedonian* and the *Hyperion* were so close to the Spanish ship they were caught in the line of fire. Acting on a previous agreement with the royalist commandant, the American and Englishman hoisted recognition lights to identify their neutral character. The Chileans, now in secure possession of the *Esmeralda*, were quick to copy the lights of the two neutrals. The fire from the forts continued and both *Macedonian* and *Hyperion* suffered hits but no casualties to personnel. Eventually, the *Macedonian* managed to slip her anchor cable and make sail. Followed by several merchantmen she succeeded in anchoring clear of the fire of the forts. The *Esmeralda*, in possession of Cochrane, made good her escape and joined the Chilean squadron off Callao.[39]

Whether or not the presence of the *Macedonian* and the use of her neutral recognition lights had any bearing on the outcome of the battle is a matter for conjecture. Neither she nor any of her personnel gave any direct aid to the patriots during the attack. Lord Cochrane, thirty-nine years later, spoke with warmth of the well-wishes of the *Macedonian's* officers as his boats approached the *Esmeralda*, whereas the *Hyperion's* sentry challenged his boats so loudly that it might well have given alarm to the Spanish.[40] However, the commander of the Chilean squadron did not let his appreciation for a few kind words prevent him from sending boats at night among the American merchantmen in an attempt to entice their seamen to desert to his ships. The nocturnal visits were stopped when Downes ordered a boat to "row guard" around the American ships each night.[41]

The garrison and civilians of Callao were enraged at the loss of the *Esmeralda*. Rumors spread that the Americans and English had participated in the battle on the side of the patriots. Early the following morning an angry mob of soldiers and civilians attacked the *Buckskin*, the *Macedonian*'s tender, which had gone in to the landing on its regular marketing trip. Two sailors were killed and six others wounded before responsible Spanish officers stopped the mob and removed the wounded crewmen to a hospital. The tender was ransacked before it was rescued by the *Hyperion*'s boat and delivered alongside the *Macedonian* later in the day. American and English ships in the harbor were boarded by mobs and looted. Meanwhile, anti-foreign sentiment spread to Lima and several foreigners in that city were murdered.[42] Although the viceroy had very little sympathy for the victims, he wished to avoid international complications and passed the word along to the ninety-one foreigners then in Lima, most of whom were merchants, masters, and supercargoes of ships lying at Callao, that they should stay off the streets and return to their ships by way of Chorillos, a small port about twelve miles south of Lima. Among the foreigners in Lima at the time of the riots was the commander of the *Macedonian*, who took refuge in the viceregal palace. Concerned for the safety of his ship, he organized a party of masters and supercargoes of American and British ships and led them to Chorillos, where they were picked up by the *Macedonian*'s boats and taken to their ships in Callao harbor.[43] Downes was infuriated at the loss of his men and the attack on the *Buckskin*. He demanded from the viceroy punishment of the assassins and, in the name of the United States, redress "as to the insult offered to the flag."[44]

The same day that Downes returned on board the *Macedonian* from Lima—November 8—the schooner *Rampart*, flying the United States ensign, was fired on by the Spanish ships as she approached her anchorage under the guns of the forts to unload cargo. Either in a spirit of animosity or in a genuine belief that the Chileans were making an attack under cover of the American flag, the shore batteries joined in the fire, which became so heavy that the merchant captain and his crew were forced to abandon ship. The *Rampart* suffered extensive damage and inevitably she was plundered of all valuables. Downes immediately demanded an explanation of this new attack on the United States flag, which he said "could only have been that of a declared enemy." There followed a rapid exchange of letters between the naval officer and the viceroy. During the exchange Downes somewhat irrelevantly brought up the question of payment of $11,000 owed to Francis Coffin of the *Canton* for services rendered the Peruvian government.[45]

For political reasons and somewhat against his personal inclinations, Pezuela was conciliatory. He promised a full investigation of the attacks on the *Buckskin* and the *Rampart* and punishment of those found guilty according to Spanish law. The *Rampart* was returned to her captain and the debt to Coffin was acknowledged with a statement that it would be paid. Pezuela stoutly denied the complicity of his government in either of the attacks, attributing them to mob action.[46]

Downes admitted that the attack on the *Macedonian*'s boat might be considered the act of a mob but vehemently maintained that the attack on the *Rampart* came from batteries manned by royal troops under command of Spanish officers and, therefore, was an official act of the government. His anger was somewhat mollified by the return of the *Rampart* to her captain, but he continued to press for payment of damages amounting to $8,008 as evidence of the viceroy's disavowal of the acts of his subordinates. The question was never fully settled. Downes remained far more calm than his statements to Pezuela indicated. He was no more anxious than the Spanish official for an open break and just before leaving Callao wrote the viceroy that he would submit an account of the affairs to Washington for decision between the respective governments. Pezuela indicated full assent to this procedure.[47]

Not entirely happy with the outcome of his quarrel with the viceroy, Downes left Callao on November 21 to check on American shipping in the northern ports. When he left the harbor he escorted a sizeable fleet of United States and English merchantmen through the patriot blockade. With the exception of the *Rampart*, which chose to remain behind to take on a cargo for trade on the coast, all the American vessels in the harbor—the *Zephyr, Panther, Dick, Savage,* and *Pallas*—took advantage of the opportunity to make good their escape from the blockaded port. The English ships accompanying them were the *Egham, Matilda,* and *Royal Sovereign.* The convoy passed the blockading squadron on the way to sea; but Cochrane made no effort to stop them, nor was there any communication between the two groups. As the *Macedonian* got underway she exchanged a thirteen-gun salute with His Britannic Majesty's frigate *Hyperion*.[48] This display of Anglo-American solidarity served as a subtle warning to Lord Cochrane not to interfere with ships under the protection of United States and British naval power.

Once clear of the blockading force only the *Zephyr* and *Panther* remained with the *Macedonian* during visits to Samanco and Paita. Off Paita a small royalist battery fired a few rounds at the man-of-war that fortunately missed their mark. The fire was not returned and Downes was content to send word to the commanding officer ashore that nothing but his friendly disposition towards the Spaniards prevented him from chastising them for such hostile conduct. At Paita the whale ship *Columbus*, four months out of Nantucket, gave the welcome news that she had encountered the U.S.S. *Constellation* in the Atlantic en route to Valparaiso as relief for the *Macedonian*.[49] During the visit Downes secured the release of Jabez Gillespie, former mate of the American whale ship *Golconda*, who had left that ship at Túmbez only to be imprisoned by the Spaniards as a suspected spy. There were other American seamen, deserters from the *Golconda*, whom the Spanish governor was willing to release but they were not at the port and Downes could not wait for them to be brought from the interior. The *Macedonian* with the *Zephyr* and *Panther* left Paita on December 11. Off the port the two merchantmen parted company and headed for Gibraltar while the warship headed for Huacho to take on water.[50]

On Christmas Day, 1820, the *Macedonian* anchored at Huacho, where she found the Chilean transports, protected by the warships *Lautaro* and *Galvarino*. San Martín's headquarters were located at Huara, four miles from the port. In the harbor were four merchant vessels that had been captured by Cochrane's fleet and were being held for adjudication before the admiralty courts at Valparaiso. Among them was the United States ship *Louisa*, which had been captured nearly a month before while attempting to enter Callao.

Captain Hicks, commander of the *Louisa*, complained to

Downes that he was being held without any apparent effort to settle his case one way or the other. In the meantime his crew were being put aboard the patriot ships; those who agreed to join the patriot forces were given preferential treatment over the remainder. Although not certain in his own mind as to the guilt or innocence of the *Louisa,* the naval commander was very much concerned that she was being held without any attempt to bring her to trial while her crew deserted and her cargo deteriorated. On the day after Christmas, he personally proceeded to Huara and urged San Martín either to release the merchantman or order her to Valparaiso for regular admiralty proceedings.[51]

San Martín attempted to evade any responsibility for the *Louisa,* claiming that naval affairs came under Cochrane. At Downes's insistence, however, he agreed either to send the vessel to Valparaiso within eight days for admiralty proceedings or to order her release and consented that this agreement be confirmed in writing. Downes returned to the *Macedonian* satisfied. The next day the promised letter from San Martín arrived but contained reservations to the effect that the *Louisa* would be sent to Valparaiso within eight days or released "provided that from the examination of her papers nothing should appear which might make the condemnation probable." This reservation, as interpreted by Downes, made the agreement pointless and negated his principal contention that a neutral vessel seized as a prize had a right to a speedy hearing in order to determine guilt or innocence. He refused to accept the reservation and wrote San Martín that he could not leave the *Louisa* under such circumstances and that unless his demands were met he would take the ship to sea with him when he left Huacho, implying the use of force. This letter was sent to San Martín's headquarters by Lieutenant Gauntt. Unfortunately, San Martín was not present to clarify the reservation when the messenger arrived, having taken to the field with his troops. In the absence of any definite assurances that the merchant ship would receive a speedy trial Downes determined to take the responsibility of releasing her himself. Thus, when the *Macedonian* put to sea on December 28, she was accompanied by the *Louisa.* The *Lautaro* made motions as if to stop the *Louisa* but took no direct action to prevent her escape.⁵²

Downes correctly anticipated that his arbitrary action would create a furor. In order to defend the release of the *Louisa* he wrote letters of explanation to the supreme director of Chile, Prevost, and the secretary of the navy. Since the affair caused intense resentment among the Chilean officials, extracts from his explanation are quoted at some length. To O'Higgins he wrote:

> Whether her [the *Louisa's*] detention in the first Instance was legal or illegal, I do not pretend to say. But your Excellency will readily perceive the enormity of the outrage in detaining a neutral vessel upwards of a month without sending her in for adjudication.
>
> . . . I was therefore under the painful necessity of releasing the Louisa that she might proceed on her voyage.
>
> Your Excellency will readily perceive the pernicious tendency his Lordships [Cochrane's] Conduct will have. The partiality that he extends to His Countrymen and His extreme Hostility to the Citizens of the United States are too glaring not to be perceived by every one.
>
> It appears to me that His Lordship, is determined if possible to destroy the American Commerce on this Coast and to effect his purpose he after capturing a vessel, detains her until the Cargo is damaged, then if she be cleared, the property is [lost] to the owners and His Lordship's ends are accomplished.⁵³

To Prevost, Downes wrote:

> I flattered myself that I should escape from this Country, without getting into difficulty with the Chilean Government, and I still have hopes that the case of the Ship Louisa, will be received in its proper light by these People. . . .
>
> It is perhaps a fortunate circumstance for [me] that I am about to leave the Coast, for I feel satisfied that I should get into some difficulty with His Lordship, if I were to remain on it.⁵⁴

There was much resentment among the patriot high command. San Martín indignantly reported the affair to O'Higgins, who, answering through the minister of marine, Zenteno, wisely counseled patience. Zenteno termed Downes's action as "hasty and inconsiderate" but resignedly remarked that such "outrages" had to be borne with a certain amount of tolerance until Chile's independence was secured. Bernardo Monteagudo made the practical suggestion of establishing prize courts in ports occupied by the patriots to eliminate the long, expensive process of sending prizes to Valparaiso for adjudication, but no action was taken to implement his plan.[55]

Prevost discussed the affair with O'Higgins, who "appeared chagrined and mortified at the conduct of this officer [Downes], ... in forcibly releasing the ship Louisa after having obtained from the General the pledge he asked for on the subject." The agent halfheartedly defended Downes's actions to the supreme director, assuring him that no disrespect was meant to the Chilean government.[56] The Chileans did not make an official issue of the subject, perhaps because they were preoccupied with the Peruvian campaign, which was entering a crucial stage.

From Huacho the *Macedonian* proceeded to Valparaiso, stopping at Mollendo and Coquimbo en route. At Mollendo, the center of the guano trade and a favorite resort of smugglers, a considerable amount of specie was taken aboard—$500,000 from the shore and $100,000 from the British ship *Thais*.[57] At Coquimbo it was learned from Washington Stewart, the American vice-consul, that the *Constellation* had arrived at Valparaiso. The *Chesapeake* and *Warrior* had not been able to escape Coquimbo. The latter was still under detention by the Chilean government and immobilized by the removal of her rigging. Downes considered her detention illegal but in view of her condition could not repeat his performance with the *Louisa*, even had he so desired. He decided to continue to Valparaiso, where he could turn the *Warrior*'s case over to the *Constellation* for further action.[58]

The *Macedonian* arrived in Valparaiso on March 4, and Downes began to turn over his information on the Pacific duty to Captain Charles G. Ridgely, commander of the *Constellation*. The officers and men of the *Macedonian* were saddened to hear of the death of their beloved chaplain, Azariah Wilson, who had been left in Valparaiso on their last visit because he was too weak and sick to stand the life on ship. They were comforted to learn that the chaplain had been given a decent burial by the ship's company of H.M.S. *Conway*. Although the burial had to take place in unconsecrated ground, the governor had provided a plot inside the walls of the arsenal where the grave would be free from molestation.⁵⁹

During the greater part of the *Macedonian*'s cruise in the Pacific, there had been little contact with Prevost, who had been in Buenos Aires from November, 1819, to November, 1820, returning to Valparaiso via the Horn in January, 1821. Downes practically invited the agent to a duel when an unidentified merchant informed him that Prevost had termed his conduct "disgraceful" and had said that the "business of carrying money was ungentlemanly and low on the part of an officer" and that "Captain Downes had distinguished himself in it." The naval officer wrote the agent a stinging letter asking for an explanation, adding: "To admit that you have expressed yourself in the manner stated would prove you to be a character unworthy the respect of any gentleman." Prevost denied having made accusations against Downes personally but reiterated his stand against the transportation of specie on warships.⁶⁰

In justice to Prevost it must be stated that in spite of his differences with the naval commanders in the Pacific he tried to keep the quarrels within the family. On his return to Chile in 1821 he delivered to Chilean Foreign Minister Echeverría, Adams' answer to the protest of March 16, 1819, against Biddle's actions, as well as a copy of the secretary of the navy's instructions prohibiting naval officers from carrying goods, money, or personnel for either of the belligerents in the war. The Chilean was also informed that the viceroy's gift to Biddle—the sword— had been deposited with the United States government and that the president was satisfied there was no ulterior motive in Biddle's acceptance of it. Echeverría professed satisfaction with these explanations. Prevost himself was not so easily pleased and privately complained to Adams that the instructions for naval commanders still gave them too much latitude in determining the neutral nature of goods or money.⁶¹

Just before the *Macedonian*'s departure for home Ridgely asked that Downes stop at Arauco to try to effect the release of the captain and several crew members of the whale ship *Hero*, who had been captured by the royalist guerrilla leader, Vicente Benavides. Prevost added a request that the *Macedonian* stop by the adjacent island of Santa María to check on any whale ships that might be endangered by the guerrilla activities. Downes declined to divert the *Macedonian* from its homeward route for either of these tasks, stating that the ship was already overdue and too much time would be wasted with no assurance of success. He suggested that Ridgely take upon himself the humanitarian project of releasing the personnel of the *Hero*. To Prevost he wrote: "If I remained here until my services could be dispensed with, without having one ship exposed in some quarter of this coast, I apprehend there would be no end to my cruise."[62]

On March 18, 1821, the *Macedonian* began the long voyage home. Off Juan Fernández, Robinson Crusoe's island, four American whale ships were sighted and boarded. Finding that they were in need of no assistance, the *Macedonian* continued her voyage, stopping only at Rio de Janeiro, where one million dollars from various west coast ports was landed. On June 19, 1821, the *Macedonian* anchored off Charlestown Navy Yard, having logged 58,878 miles since her departure from there two years and nine months before.[63]

Chapter VII

Ridgely, 1821

Like his predecessor on the Pacific Station, Charles Goodwin Ridgely entered the navy as a midshipman during the undeclared naval war with France in 1799. Born Charles Goodwin in Baltimore, he changed his name to Ridgely as one of the conditions for receiving a legacy from an uncle, Charles Ridgely.[1] During the Tripolitan War he distinguished himself on *Gunboat No. 1* in the assaults on Tripoli under the direct command of Lieutenant Richard Somers.[2] As one of "Preble's Boys," his rise in the service was steady if not spectacular. In 1820 he was in command of the Baltimore Station and was extremely anxious to get a command at sea.

Ridgely's outstanding characteristic was forthrightness. He believed in coming directly to the point, whether in the field of action or of words. While an acting lieutenant in the Sicilian port of Messina, he had—after an evening of libations—impulsively gone to the assistance of an English-speaking stranger who was menaced by a gang of waterfront toughs. The following day the man whom he had helped, the mate of an English merchant ship, was found stabbed to death and Ridgely was accused of the murder. To avoid international complications, the young lieutenant voluntarily surrendered himself for trial. He was tried before a military court in Sicily and after nearly a year was acquitted of the crime.[3]

Typical of his direct approach to a question was the manner in which he came to command of the Baltimore Naval Station. When his brother-in-law died suddenly in the Maryland city, leaving his sister and four children without means of support, Ridgely demanded duty there in order to be near them. With little regard for the convenience of the incumbent in command he stated his reasons bluntly: "The Captain Spence who is and has been for many years stationed there is *junior* to myself, is not a native of Maryland and is *rich*, all that is dear to me is in Baltimore and I am poor." Ridgely usually got what he went after, and he took command of the Baltimore Naval Station on July 8, 1819.[4]

His reports to the Navy Department were crisp and to the point. Those from South America have the ring of sincerity, with no attempt on Ridgely's part to conceal or to exaggerate his own actions in that troubled area. He was outspoken in his criticism of both Downes and Prevost for what he considered failures to subordinate their personal desires to the business of protecting United States commerce—Downes for refusing to delay return of the *Macedonian* to the United States in order to go to the assistance of United States seamen reported imprisoned at Arauco, and Prevost for leaving Chile to go to Lima while the cases of several American ships requiring his attention were pending in Chile.[5]

Early in May, 1820, having heard that the frigate *Constellation* was fitting out in Norfolk for a cruise to the South Seas, Ridgely submitted a request to the Navy Department for her command. His request reached Washington at an opportune time. Commodore Sinclair, who had been offered the command, was forced to withdraw because of ill-health while Ridgely's letter was still before the secretary. Orders for the Baltimorean to report as commanding officer of the *Constellation* were issued on May 13.[6]

The *Constellation* was ready for sea on July 10, and on July 25, 1820, she left New York for the Pacific with instructions to stop at Rio de Janeiro and Buenos Aires en route. Ridgely's instructions did not differ in essential details from those given to Downes two years previously. The purpose of the cruise was stated in the first paragraph, which read: "You have been appointed to the command of the United States Frigate Constellation destined upon a Cruise in the Pacific Ocean, for the purpose of affording protection and relief to the Commerce and Whale fishery of the United States in that quarter." He was ordered "to receive on board, as passenger, John M. Forbes, Esq., as an Agent appointed on the part of the United States to the Governments of South America, and whose final destination will be determined after his arrival at Buenos Ayres."[7]

Two new admonitions were added to Ridgely's instructions. En route to the equator he was ordered to be on the alert for, and to apprehend, "any Slave Vessels or those of a piratical character," as defined in the new laws relative to the suppression of the slave trade and piracy. A concluding paragraph, incorporating the instructions issued to Downes in August, 1819, prohibited taking on board for either of the embattled parties in Chile and Peru "men, money, provisions or supplies, . . . except Specie," which he was permitted to bring to the United States on his return.[8]

Forbes had been appointed agent for commerce and seamen for "either" Buenos Aires or Chile. The reasons for his appointment were twofold: to provide an agent on both sides of the Andes in southern South America and to give a balance to Prevost's pronounced preference for the patriots. In deference to Monroe's protégé, Adams had written Forbes's instructions so that Prevost could choose either Buenos Aires or Chile for his post, leaving the other to the newcomer. However, Adams gave Forbes exclusive responsibility for carrying on negotiations with the Chilean government on behalf of the owners of the merchant brig *Macedonian* for recovery of the specie taken by Cochrane from her master, Eliphalet Smith, in 1819; and Prevost was specifically warned not to interfere in those negotiations because of his suspected preference for the patriots.[9]

The well-worn bills of exchange drawn by Aguirre on the governments of Buenos Aires and Chile were turned over to Forbes by the Navy Department with a request that he attempt to collect them from the governments concerned. It was pointed out that the bills remained valid although for two years attempts to collect them had been unsuccessful. When the money was collected, the agent was to turn it over to the commander of the *Constellation* for the purchase of supplies in South America.[10]

Ridgely was pleased with his new command. When the *Constellation* fell in with the homeward-bound *John Adams*, seventeen days out of New York, he sent back a report to the secretary of the navy that he considered his officers and crew as fine a body of men "as ever went afloat." He took great pride in maintaining his crew in peak condition, a challenging task considering the extended periods at sea between ports and the lack of fresh provisions on board ship. On arrival at Valparaiso after seven months away from home, he could report that he had lost not one man from sickness or accident. His formula for maintaining the health of the crew was to avoid "all hands" evolutions at night, to provide plenty of pickles and raisins, "sour crout," and lemon acid in the diet, to require the crew to change "frocks and pantaloons" four times weekly, and to issue the grog rations at meals rather than "at the barrel."[11]

The loss of officers from disciplinary action was less praiseworthy. During a layover in Rio de Janeiro, where a damaged mainmast was being replaced, Ridgely encountered much trouble with the quarrelsome midshipmen because of dueling. Four were sent back to the United States because they refused to give a pledge not to take part in duels on shore leave. Another officer, Lieutenant John H. Bell, was returned under arrest because of threatening and contemptuous language to the first lieutenant, John H. Clack. The latter had suspended Bell from duty for leaving the quarter-deck in charge of a midshipman during the official visit of Portuguese General Carlos Frederico Lecor at Montevideo.[12]

The *Constellation* departed from Rio de Janeiro on December 21, 1820, and arrived at Valparaiso on February 6, 1821, where she anchored to await the arrival of the *Macedonian*. The harbor was crowded with merchant ships, six of them flying the flag of the United States. The month's wait was not wasted. The time was spent in getting acquainted with the Chileans and foreigners of the city. On February 12 the ship fired a salute in honor of the third anniversary of the battle of Chacabuco, and Ridgely, accompanied by some of his officers, visited Santiago from February 10 to 21.[13]

One other disciplinary action occurred before Ridgely could consider the *Constellation* purged of troublemakers. An American businessman, Daniel S. Griswold, had been granted passage from New York to Valparaiso. En route he had become very friendly with some of the young officers. On arrival in Valparaiso, Ridgely learned that Griswold had a poor reputation among the respectable English and American merchants there. On the visit to Santiago he found that Griswold had defrauded another American of $2,500. Concluding that his former passenger was not a fit person for his officers to be associated with, Ridgely sent back word from Santiago that Griswold was not to be allowed on board the *Constellation*. This action created a schism among the ship's officers, a small clique adhering to Griswold and deliberately seeking his company on shore to show their disapproval of the commander's orders. When he returned to Valparaiso, Ridgely learned of the dissension among his officers and hearing that four duels were pending over the question called a conference in his cabin to explain the reasons for the ban on Griswold. During the conference three officers— Lieutenants John P. Cambreleng and Robert B. Randolph of the navy and Marine Lieutenant Joseph C. Hall—evidently acting in concert, defied Ridgely to forbid their associating with Griswold. In the interest of discipline, the commander had no recourse but to arrest the three lieutenants and to return them on the *Macedonian* to the United States to stand trial for "seditious, mutinous, and contemptuous language."[14] After this action, there were no more problems with personnel and the *Constellation*'s crew gave their commander loyal support.

Early in March the British whaler *Indian* brought the mate and two surviving crewmen from the whale ship *Essex* of Nantucket into Valparaiso. The *Essex* had foundered far to the westward in November of the previous year as the result of being rammed head on by a maddened whale. The survivors of the *Essex* told a harrowing tale of having been eighty-nine days in an open boat and being "compelled to subsist on the body of one of the crew who died." The mate reported that the captain and part of the crew had made for the "Island of Esther [Easter]" and that three other men were on Ducie Island. Believing it his duty to take care of American seamen in distress wherever they might be, Ridgely gave Captain Thomas Raines of the English ship *Surrey*, bound for the Far East, $500 to call on the islands to effect the rescue of these men. The trip to Easter Island proved unnecessary, however, since word was received via the whaler *Hero* that Captain Pollard and one boy of the *Essex* had been picked up at sea by the *Diana* of New York. It was reported that they too had been forced to eat the flesh of their dead companions. Some seven months later Ridgely received a letter from Raines stating that he had arrived at Ducie Island just in time to rescue the three stranded men from almost certain death by starvation and madness.[15]

The *Hero*, which brought the news of Captain Pollard's rescue, had herself gone through a most distressing experience. Captured at Santa María by Benavides, the royalist guerrilla leader, she was taken to Arauco, where she was plundered of provisions. The guerrillas had cut her adrift, thinking that she would run aground, but the mate and part of the crew had managed to make sail and bring her to Valparaiso. The captain and nine crewmen remained in the hands of Benavides.[16]

After a thorough briefing by Downes, Ridgely assumed responsibility for the protection of American commerce and shipping on the coasts of Chile and Peru. He decided to proceed as soon as practicable to Coquimbo to assist the *Chesapeake* and *Warrior*, which were reported in a precarious situation. From Coquimbo it was Ridgely's intention to work the *Constellation* up the coast of Peru as far as Lima, which was still under blockade, checking on United States ships along the way. Accordingly, the *Constellation* sailed for Coquimbo, arriving there on March 12.[17]

Between them, Downes and Henry Hill had given Ridgely a most unfavorable impression of the Chilean government. This opinion was reflected in his subsequent reports to the Navy Department, which included comments on political questions as well as on military affairs. In reporting San Martín's campaign in the north, he wrote from Coquimbo: "There is no doubt the whole of Chili & Peru will be called Republicks [*sic*], each government will be independent of the other but neither will embrace any of the liberal institutions which form our happy republic. At present those in power here (Chili) are perfectly despotic. . . ."[18]

In his first report from Chile the newcomer echoed Downes's opinion of Lord Cochrane. The Chilean naval commander, he said, took American ships on the coast wherever he found them, removed their crews, and detained them so long before sending them to Valparaiso for adjudication that their voyages were "ruined" financially. Another unfavorable comment on the patriots concerned their efforts to enlist English and American sailors. During Ridgely's cruise the whalers were the chief victims of this particular abuse. The *Constellation*'s commander reported that "there was hardly an instance" of a whaler anchoring in a patriot port without the greater part of the crew deserting, leaving her helpless. The patriots offered a $30.00 bonus besides high monthly wages, and the authorities took no interest in returning deserters. Ridgely seemed to have a sense of social justice, for he blamed part of the difficulties of the whalers on the avariciousness of their New England owners, who bought up all of the shares, or interests of the crewmen, in the profits of the cruise before the ship ever left the United States. According to the navy man, the poor sailor had nothing to look forward to at the end of the cruise; hence he was an easy mark for the blandishments of the patriot recruiters. He recommended that the owners forego this source of profit in order to secure the co-operation of the seamen in a mutually profitable venture.[19]

Ridgely entered into arrangements with the British commodore on the station to afford mutual protection to the ships of their respective nations "against the excessive outrages committed daily by the Chilean crews" and "from the impossibility of the masters of the merchantmen receiving protection from the Chili authorities in the ports of Chili." He was convinced that he had made an excellent deal because the United States had more commercial ships and fewer men-of-war in the area than the British. He was frankly envious of British naval power, noting that they had four warships on the station. Ridgely strongly urged additional United States warships to provide simultaneous coverage off Chile and Peru.[20]

It is interesting to note that the British attitude toward Chile's paper blockade was the same as that of the United States, despite the fact that during the Napoleonic Wars England had adopted the tactics that Cochrane was now using. Commodore Sir Thomas Hardy, who relieved Bowles as senior British naval officer on the South American Station, protested to O'Higgins against the blockade of Peru, declaring that it was illegal under international law.[21] In instructions to Captain Thomas Searle, commanding officer of the *Hyperion*, Hardy stated: "The law of nations or of blockade . . . require that the force must be fully equal to the places said to be blockaded, but if, for instance, three or more places are said to be under blockade, and one or two only decidedly so, that is by having a sufficient force off these two places only and none off the others, the whole of the blockade is null and void, for this has been the doctrine held by his Majesty's government and by the Admiralty courts. . . ."[22] In the same set of instructions, Searle was enjoined to insist at all times that His Majesty's warships enter and leave freely all blockaded ports.

In Coquimbo, Ridgely found the *Chesapeake* and *Warrior* in poor repair and in great need of men. The *Chesapeake* had been severely damaged from overloading with copper, and some $9,000 in unwrought gold she was carrying had been removed by the patriots. Because the gold had been declared contraband, Ridgely feared the ship and its entire cargo would be confiscated although she was still technically free. The *Warrior* remained under detention by order of the authorities. The governor finally agreed to liberate both ships, but the American officer was unsuccessful in his attempts to have the *Chesapeake*'s gold returned. Repairmen from the *Constellation* were sent aboard the two ships to get them ready for sea and a crew was provided the *Chesapeake* from the *Constellation*.[23]

Upon receipt of an appeal from Prevost for protection from Benavides' guerrillas for American ships in the vicinity of Santa María and Downes's announcement that he would not go to the rescue of the *Hero*'s crew at Arauco, Ridgely decided to undertake those tasks himself. Leaving carpenters to continue the work on the *Chesapeake*, the *Constellation* proceeded to Santa María. An American whaler fishing off the island reported no indications of trouble there and later attempts to contact Benavides at Arauco were fruitless. Evidence of royalist guerrilla activity at Arauco was seen in the presence of a wrecked and stripped hulk offshore, which proved to be the English ship *Perseverance*. One of the *Constellation*'s boats investigating the hulk was fired on from the beach, but the fire was not returned because it was feared fire directed at the shore might be claimed as an unneutral act against Spanish territory.[24]

The disappointed Ridgely reluctantly concluded that the one ship at his command would be more effectively employed in the protection of American lives and property at the center of military action than in the chase of elusive guerrillas off southern Chile. Accordingly, he issued a circular letter warning American ships to keep clear of the Santa María-Arauco area until the region was pacified, and returned to his original plan to visit Peru, stopping at Valparaiso and Coquimbo en route. At Coquimbo extra effort was exerted to make the *Chesapeake* seaworthy before the departure of the *Constellation* since Ridgely was convinced the patriots would take possession of her once his protection was removed.[25]

By May, 1821, it appeared that San Martín's conquest of Peru would soon be successfully terminated. Viceroy Pezuela had been deposed by a junta of royalist military leaders on January 29, and La Serna had been chosen to succeed him. The patriot blockade of Peru was rigorously enforced at Callao if not at other points, and Lima began to feel its effects as guerrillas blocked supplies by land. Decisive action was prevented by a series of epidemics that swept San Martín's army as well as Lima and Callao. Not until the end of April was San Martín able to move his army from Huara and tighten the siege of Lima.[26] In the meantime, negotiations were being carried on between the royalists and patriots to end the war—the royalists urging acceptance of the Spanish Constitution of 1812, and San Martín, on behalf of the patriots, proposing the independence of Peru as a constitutional monarchy with a Bourbon prince as king. Although the two parties were unable to agree on terms for a cease fire, an armistice was arranged for twenty days beginning May 19, with the provision that San Martín and La Serna should meet to discuss a lasting peace. The meeting, held June 2 at Punchauca, produced no results, but on June 11 the armistice was extended for an additional twelve days before hostilities were resumed. During this period San Martín permitted relaxation of the blockade to allow the entrance of enough food to meet the daily needs of the people of Lima.[27]

The first phase of the armistice was in effect when the *Constellation* sailed into Callao harbor on June 4. In consideration of the fact that Callao was a Spanish port, Ridgely would permit no communication with the patriot blockading squadron until he had paid the Spanish the courtesy of obtaining their consent, and his first act was to go to Lima to pay his respects to the new viceroy, La Serna. The latter readily gave his assent to intercourse between the patriot squadron and the American warship. After returning to Callao on June 7, Ridgely sent his first lieutenant to the Chilean flagship, the *Independencia*, to arrange an exchange of visits with Captain Robert Forster, current commander of the blockading force.

While these courtesies were being exchanged, events were developing that brought the disfavor of the patriot high command down on the head of the *Constellation*'s commander. On his return from Lima, Ridgely had directed the United States merchant ship *General Brown* to shift from a berth under the guns of Callao's forts to an anchorage near the *Constellation*. All money aboard the merchantman was transferred to the warship for safekeeping. This maneuver was watched with interest by the patriots, for they wanted the *General Brown* not only for violating the blockade of Callao but also because she had on board a number of Spanish passengers trying to get away from Lima. Most of these were noncombatants, but among them was the former viceroy, Pezuela, his son-in-law, Colonel Rafael de Cevallos, and several of his loyal staff officers.[28]

Following his deposition, Pezuela, accompanied by his family and some close supporters, had gone to his country house in Magdalena, where he remained for nearly four months under virtual arrest. In April, his wife and the nonmilitary members of the family, with the consent of Cochrane, were granted passage to Europe on the British frigate *Andromache*. But Captain Shirreff had refused passage to Pezuela and other officers because of their military status.[29] Pezuela then secretly secured passage for himself and his son-in-law on the *General Brown*, which planned to slip out of Callao under cover of night and elude the blockade by her superior sailing qualities. Pezuela and his son-in-law went aboard on the afternoon of May 26, the prearranged date, expecting that the merchantman would attempt to run the blockade before moonrise. The departure was postponed, however, and the presence of the former viceroy on board the *General Brown* quickly became known to the patriots, who augmented their blockade to prevent the escape of so important a figure.[30]

This was the situation when Ridgely returned from Lima and ordered the *General Brown* to anchor under the protection of the *Constellation*.[31] The naval officer had more than routine interest in the merchantman. Her master was the bearer of a letter from the secretary of the navy to Ridgely directing that the ship, which belonged to Henry Eckford of New York, be given special attention and rendered every lawful aid and protection during her voyage in the Pacific.[32]

The patriots were keeping a strict watch on the *General Brown*, and when she moved from the shelter of the forts to the protection of the *Constellation*, Forster sent a note to the American commander demanding to know his intentions in regard to the merchantman. The blockade commander pointedly forwarded a copy of Cochrane's instructions regarding merchantmen entering or leaving a blockaded port under the protection of a neutral warship. These were, simply, to capture or seize such a ship in the same manner as any other vessel attempting to run the blockade unless the commander of the neutral warship would state in writing his intention to use force; if he would not so state, the blockading ship was then to proceed with the capture of the merchantman—unless and until the escort actually used force to prevent it. Either procedure, of course, placed the onus on the neutral man-of-war. The matter would then become a question for argument between the Chilean government and the government of the neutral commander.[33]

In the voluminous correspondence that followed, Ridgely pressed for the free passage of the *General Brown*. He denied that she had knowingly broken the blockade, since she had left the United States the same month the blockade was declared and had entered Callao without being challenged or warned by any blockading ship. He declared that she had no cargo on board, but did admit to the outward-bound passengers. Ridgely disavowed any desire to protect vessels engaged in "illicit trade," but wrote: "At the same time I will afford protection to every vessel of the U. States engaged in a lawful commerce." Forster in reply admitted that the *General Brown* might have entered Callao without being challenged, but he contended that if she went to sea with the "intent of convoying the late Vice King" it would be a breach of blockade, and added: "I am compelled from an imperious sense of duty to the Govt. which I have the honor to serve, to detain that ship, should she put to sea so laden, unless protected by the ship under your command." To this the American replied that he had no intention of taking Pezuela and the other passengers out of the harbor without consent. "I shall not attempt to give them protection," he wrote, but continued, "I regret that you should feel yourself compelled from an imperious sense of your duty . . . to detain the *General Brown*, should she put to sea without those passengers, because my imperative duty will justify me in giving protection to this American ship, as far as my slender means can be used. I did state the *General Brown* had no cargo; and I now assert she has not a cargo, but only a few articles belonging to the supercargo."[34]

In the meantime, Pezuela sought asylum in the *Constellation*, where he was treated with respect and kindness. He addressed a dignified letter to Ridgely asking protection for himself and his son-in-law. In his reply the American informed the Spaniard his instructions would not permit him to provide protection to persons from either side in the conflict. However, he did offer the ex-viceroy his cabin, promising that no "violence" would be done him while he was under the United States flag and that he would do all that was possible to get permission for the fugitive to depart in peace.[35] Pezuela remained on board the frigate for several weeks.

San Martín arived in Callao on June 7 following the meeting with La Serna at Punchauca. There he and La Serna had reached a tentative agreement to establish an independent Peru under a regency, pending approval of the Spanish government for a separate monarchy under a Bourbon prince. Although the armistice was extended, the tentative agreement for a regency fell through. In the meantime, La Serna asked Ridgely whether he could, in the name of the United States government, guarantee compliance with the treaty that was expected to result from the conferences. Ridgely declined on the grounds that he had no diplomatic powers but offered to serve in a personal capacity in any way possible to further the peace.[36]

One evening San Martín was invited aboard the *Constellation* to see a theatrical performance put on by the sailors of the ship. There ensued a meeting between him and Pezuela, and in spite of the latter's initial embarrassment, the two got along very well. They discussed the deposition of the viceroy, who took the occasion to ask permission for the *General Brown*, with him on board, to proceed to sea. The patriot general was emphatic in his refusal but did tell Pezuela that he expected Lima to fall in a few days and that after that event the Spanish official would be free to go wherever he wished.[37]

Ridgely also tried to persuade San Martín to let the *General Brown* leave Callao with her passengers. San Martín was adamant in his refusal to let Pezuela and the military officers go but agreed to allow the *General Brown* and the civilian passengers to proceed without them. With this understanding, Ridgely arranged to take the merchantman to sea without the military personnel, and Pezuela and four Spanish officers were put ashore on June 28. The same day, the *Constellation* and the *General Brown* passed through the blockading fleet after an inspection of the latter by the commander of the insurgent ship *Valdivia*.[38]

Before the Spanish officers were sent ashore the master and supercargo of the *General Brown* and Pezuela made a private agreement between themselves that the merchant ship would return to the coast near Chiras to re-embark the banned officers. Ridgely was not made an official party to this scheme because the conspirators feared the naval officer would prohibit it.[39] Unofficially, the commander of the warship could hardly have failed to realize that some such plan was afoot, if he were not actually a party to it, since the Marquesa of Casares, wife of one of the officers sent ashore with Pezuela, accompanied by the sister of the Inquisitor of Lima, went aboard the warship to make the passage to sea rather than remain on the *General Brown*. The reason assigned in Pezuela's *Memoria* for this procedure was that it was feared the patriot inspecting party might spot the Marquesa among the passengers on the merchantman and suspect the plan to rescue her husband and the former viceroy. Once safely at sea the ladies, together with some equipment of the *General Brown*'s passengers, were to have been returned at the same time the money taken aboard the warship in Callao for safekeeping was returned.[40]

The second night out of Callao the *General Brown* slipped away from the *Constellation* and returned to the coast where she picked up Pezuela's party at considerable risk to both the Spanish officers and the ship. She then hurried back to sea expecting to rendezvous with the *Constellation*, to effect the transfer of passengers and money, and to proceed on her way. The *Constellation*, on missing the merchantman, spent several days in the vicinity searching for her without success, then proceeded to Huacho for provisions. The two ships never made contact. Not daring to remain too long in Peruvian waters, the master of the *General Brown* with the concurrence of his passengers gave up the search after ten days and headed to Huacho to leave the supercargo, John Heffernan, with instructions to contact the *Constellation* and look out for their "interests and equipment." Narrowly missing the *Constellation* at Huacho, the *General Brown* dropped Heffernan and set course on July 11 for Cape Horn and Rio de Janeiro. The Spanish refugees were not reunited with their belongings and their ladies until some months later in Rio de Janeiro, where they were brought by the supercargo aboard His British Majesty's Ship *Owen Glendower*, which had received them from the *Constellation* via the British corvette *Rosa*.[41]

No sooner had the search for the *General Brown* been abandoned than the misfortunes of another United States merchantman demanded the attention of the *Constellation* and her commander. This was the *Galen* of Boston. When the *Constellation* first arrived at Callao, the master of the *Galen* had reported to Ridgely that his ship had been detained for fifty days on charges of having Spanish property on board. No attempt had been made to bring her case to a hearing and her crew had been put aboard the Chilean man-of-war *Valdivia*, formerly the royalist ship *Esmeralda*. Ridgely argued her case with San Martín and Forster and obtained her release. Forster further agreed to put a Chilean navy crew aboard her to take her to Salinas Bay with an order to pick up her own crew from the *Valdivia*. On arrival in Huacho, Captain Henry Cobbett of the *Valdivia* not only refused to release the *Galen*'s regular crew but took the temporary Chilean crew away, leaving her immobilized. Ridgely found her in this state when he reached Huacho on July 8.[42]

The navy commander put a crew from the *Constellation* on board the *Galen* with instructions to work her back to Callao, where it was understood the *Valdivia* had gone. The two ships started to Callao in company, but the *Galen* stopped at Chancay for provisions while the warship continued straight to the blockaded port, arriving there on the night of July 12. Drastic changes had occurred during the two weeks' absence of the *Constellation*. The entire Chilean naval force under Lord Cochrane had returned to Callao Bay. On July 11 San Martín had entered Lima unopposed and proceeded to establish an independent government for Peru. The *cabildo* of Lima proclaimed the independence of Peru on July 28, and on August 3 a provisional government was formed with San Martín at its head with the title of Protector.[43] In the meantime, Callao remained in the hands of the royalists, and the patriots issued an order declaring the port city under a new and strict blockade from July 11. All intercourse of any kind with the "port, town, or forts of Callao" was prohibited.[44]

Ridgely began correspondence with Cochrane at once to secure release of the *Galen*'s crew. Official visits were exchanged and the *Constellation* rendered a salute of seventeen guns to the patriot admiral when he came aboard on July 14. On the morning of Cochrane's visit, however, the *Constellation*'s boat, en route to the port, was brought to by a shot from the *San Martin* and ordered back to the ship. Ridgely protested officially that this was an insult to the American flag. Cochrane replied that he recognized no neutral flags at such times, but attempted to be conciliatory. He insisted that he desired to maintain friendly relations with the United States and pointed out that the port of Callao was in rigorous blockade and, reasonably enough, that his forces had no way of knowing the true nationality or mission of boats making for the port regardless of the flag displayed. Ridgely considered the reply unsatisfactory but there were so many other issues at stake and he was so badly outnumbered that he considered it prudent to take the Chilean admiral's reply "for an apology."[45]

Cochrane sailed for Chorillos on the seventeenth without answering Ridgely's representations regarding the *Galen*. When it was learned that the English brig *Walsingham*, which had been detained under circumstances similar to those of the United States merchantman, had been taken a second time, Ridgely became alarmed that the *Galen*, which had arrived in Callao on July 18, would also be repossessed. His suspicions were correct. A Captain Simpson from the Chilean squadron attempted to board the *Galen*. Not being allowed to board by the United States naval crew then in possession of the ship, he proceeded to the *Constellation* and announced that he had orders to put a prize crew on board the merchant ship. Ridgely refused to surrender the *Galen*:

> I certainly could not submit. . . . I regretted his Adml. should have imposed on me the necessity of assuming a defensive attitude against such vile aggressions on the rights of our neutrality, that I felt assured my conduct would be approved by resisting with force any attempt on the Galen even if it were to the sinking of my ship which I was determined they should do and I begged he would state so to his Admiral, he asked if I would give it him in writing. I declined having any further official communication with his Adml. until my letter of the 13th [concerning the *Galen* and American deserters] had been satisfactorily answered.[46]

One reason no communication had been heard from the admiral was that the Chilean flagship, the *San Martin*, had run aground at Chorillos with the loss of the ship and an estimated $900,000 in goods that had been taken from various English ships along the coast.[47]

Cochrane had indeed begun to bear down on his countrymen to the annoyance of Hardy, who made vigorous protests on the legality of Cochrane's actions. At the British commodore's insistence, the Chilean government on June 22, 1821, modified the blockade of August 20, 1820, restricting it to the area between Ancon and Pisco.[48] Other practices of Cochrane that aroused the ire of the British were the levying of a duty of 18 per cent on cargoes bound for the newly-liberated ports, which the admiral himself collected, and the application to the coasts of Peru of Britain's own "rule of 1756" governing neutral trade. Cochrane claimed that the question of the adequacy of the blockading force off the royalist ports was immaterial since the neutrals were restricted to the trade they enjoyed before the war and could not, because of the war, open up trade with ports that had been closed to them in peace. In his letter to Hardy on the latter point Cochrane pointedly wrote: "I am most willing to hope that this [British] government has not adopted one law for war, and another for convenience in peace; that they have not established one rule for the strong and another for the weak. . . ."[49]

On July 19 the *Constellation*, with the *Galen* in company, weighed anchor for Ancon, the port through which neutrals were allowed to trade with Lima. While at Ancon, Ridgely visited Lima and had a very uncomfortable conference with San Martín at the palace. San Martín was "much displeased" at the escape of Pezuela and upbraided the American naval officer for his part in the affair. He said he would make representations to the United States government requiring the punishment of the master of the *General Brown* and satisfaction for the conduct of Downes in releasing the *Louisa* the previous year. San Martín threatened to "close *his* ports to the American commerce until *he* obtained satisfaction." In a more mellow mood, the general assured the American of his personal regard and stated that he had directed a search for the *General Brown*. He proposed entering into an official correspondence on the subject with Ridgely "in a few days," which the latter took to be a ruse to keep him in Lima, since news had been received that the supercargo of the *General Brown* was at Ancon.[50] Ridgely hurried back to meet the latter.

John Heffernan, the *General Brown*'s supercargo, confessed to the plot to spirit Pezuela and his officers from Peru, for which he and the master were to collect a "large amount" of passage money. He made a statement covering the facts and absolving Ridgely from complicity. In turn, the effects belonging to the *General Brown* and her passengers were turned over to the supercargo.[51]

Having received a letter from Eliphalet Smith "that he had been robbed by Lord Cochrane of upwards of $70,000" near Arequipa, Ridgely decided to go to Mollendo to do what he could to assist Smith, then to proceed to Valparaiso to lay the case of the *Galen* before the supreme director. The supercargo of the *General Brown* went as passenger to Mollendo in order "that he might be near his funds."[52]

The *Constellation* anchored in Mollendo Roads on August 15. Ridgely contacted Smith at Arequipa and learned the details of his latest loss, which were strikingly similar to those of the seizure of the brig *Macedonian*'s specie by Cochrane's forces on the road between Lima and Ancon in April, 1819. In the latest incident, which occurred on May 7, 1821, a raiding party under orders of Cochrane's marine officer, Colonel William Miller, had seized $70,000 in coined money and bar silver from a mule train in the valley of Sitana, between Tacna and Arequipa. Smith had engaged the mule train to transport the money and merchandise from his vessel, the same *Macedonian*, from Arica and Tacna to Arequipa, where he hoped to sell the merchandise. He claimed the money was the property of United States citizens, being the lawful proceeds from the sale of part of the cargo of the brig. The patriots claimed, as they had in 1819, that the money was Spanish property and distributed it among the crews of the Chilean ships without the formality of judicial condemnation. In addition, Smith charged that Miller had forcibly requisitioned the *Macedonian* to transport troops from Arica to northern ports.[53]

Since nothing could be done in the royalist-dominated Intermedios ports to help Smith recover his money, Ridgely continued on to Valparaiso intending to enlist Prevost's aid in presenting Smith's case to the patriot government along with requests for release of the *Galen*'s crew and return of various United States seamen known to have deserted to the patriot service. When the *Constellation* arrived at Valparaiso on August 31, Prevost was on the point of sailing for Lima. Much to the disgust of the naval officer the special agent refused to delay his departure to make the necessary representations to the Chilean government and suggested that the matters be turned over to the new commercial agent at Valparaiso, Michael Hogan, for action.[54]

Ridgely himself proceeded to Santiago and laid his complaints before the O'Higgins government. He was moderately successful, the supreme director and his ministers being as usual more inclined to give favorable consideration to the representations of foreigners than were their subordinates. The government agreed to return the crew of the *Galen* and the deserting seamen and promised to give Smith's complaints a hearing before a prize court according to the "proofs and justice of the case."[55]

While the *Constellation* was lying at Valparaiso, Captain James P. Sheffield of the American brig *Hersilia* and William S.

Lane, mate of the brig *Ocean*, with six men of their crews, made their way into the harbor in an open whale boat. They had escaped from Arauco, where the two brigs had been captured, sacked, and wrecked by Benavides. The merchant officers reported that twenty-three Americans from their ships and the *Hero* were still held by Benavides and forced to serve with his guerrillas. They also reported that two British vessels had been similarly mistreated.[56]

Commodore Hardy being then in Valparaiso, Ridgely immediately conferred with him on action to be taken to protect their respective countrymen from the royalist irregulars. Hardy agreed to send the frigate *Conway*, under the command of Captain Basil Hall, to Arauco to treat for the release of the crewmen of both countries. Hall's efforts to contact Benavides were futile, since that leader had been driven inland by patriot forces under Colonel Joaquín Prieto and had taken with him the captive Americans and Englishmen.[57] Both Hall and Ridgely were fearful that even if their countrymen should escape from Benavides they would be summarily dispatched by the patriot forces without investigation or trial, or would fall into the hands of the untamed Arauco Indians. The best Ridgely could do was to address letters to both Benavides and the patriot officials invoking protection for the men as citizens of the United States, a neutral nation at peace with both belligerents. He offered to pay the patriots any expenses incurred in the rescue of the men, including payment of ransom to the Indians, should the sailors fall into the hands of the Araucanians.[58]

Ridgely had been unable to take the *Constellation* to Arauco because inspection of his main and mizzenmasts revealed rot at the step end. It was necessary to lift the mainmast and cut off three feet from the base. Two carpenters and a sailing master from the British warships *Creole* and *Owen Glendower* were members of the survey board that recommended this action to the American commander—another example of Anglo-American naval cooperation in the Pacific.[59]

When an official dispatch was received in Valparaiso announcing the fall of Callao to San Martín's forces on September 21, the American naval commander considered the independence of

Lower Peru inevitable. A cheering aspect of the news was that it would end the blockade because most of the coastal area would be in possession of the patriots. A notable exception was the Intermedios, the ports serving Upper Peru, which had been reoccupied by the royalists. Ridgely conjectured that the patriot blockade would be restricted to those ports "from Pisco as far south as Chile."[60] Not so cheering was news of a serious rift between San Martín and Cochrane, which culminated in Cochrane's seizure of a reported $600,000 in funds belonging to the Peruvian government from one of the transports at Ancon. It was reported that there was a serious schism in the fleet and that most of the European officers and seamen had left the Chilean squadron to join the Peruvian forces. It was said that Cochrane himself dared not leave his ship because San Martín had threatened to arrest and imprison him if he were caught ashore.[61]

Cochrane had indeed confiscated the Peruvian government's funds, variously estimated from 205,000 pesos, a sum admitted by the admiral, to $600,000, the amount reported by Ridgely. The money was used to pay back wages of the officers and men of the Chilean squadron, who were near mutiny because of arrears in pay and scant rations.[62] This bold action was characteristic of Cochrane and is reminiscent of San Martín's own refusal in 1814 to relinquish $36,000 in his possession on demand of the Buenos Aires government because the money was needed to keep his Army of the North together.[63] One result of the quarrel between the patriot leaders was the creation of a Peruvian squadron under Captain George Martin Guise, to which many of the officers and men of the Chilean squadron defected. The break between the admiral and the general was complete. When Cochrane entered into independent negotiations with the royalists for the surrender of the Callao forts, he was peremptorily ordered to leave Peruvian waters.[64] The breakup of the powerful land-sea combination of San Martín and Cochrane marked the beginning of the decline of both men in Spanish American affairs.

There was little sympathy for Cochrane among the neutral naval officers but much anxiety lest he turn to freebooting. Ridgely's report to the Navy Department read: "The Government have sent Adml. Blanco . . . it is said, to take the fleet from

Cochrane, it is very doubtful he will resign the command; if he should, he will be troublesome no longer; if he should not, he must be watched very sharp, this Govmt., I have no doubt, will outlaw him and he will then buccaneer on a large scale."[65]

On November 2 it was reported that Cochrane had sailed with the fleet, supposedly to Mexico. In view of the uncertain naval situation in the north and a fear of what Cochrane would do if deprived of his command, Ridgely decided to follow the Chilean squadron in order to keep a "very sharp" watch on Cochrane to see that he did "no injury to our Commerce with impunity."

This decision to shadow Cochrane was announced to the Navy Department in a lengthy report from Valparaiso. As usual, Ridgely included an account of the health of his crew in this report. Not one man had been lost from sickness but three had met violent deaths. A carpenter had been robbed and murdered in Valparaiso; a marine had been stabbed to death by the drummer on board ship; and the cooper "was killed by an oxcart passing over his body while on shore on liberty."[66]

One other matter demanded the attention of Ridgely before he could return to Peru. In October the New Bedford whaler *Persia* came into Valparaiso with the news that the inmates of the prison island of Juan Fernández, mostly exiled royalists and adherents to the Carrera party, had succeeded in gaining control of the island and had deposed the governor. The mutineers had captured a boat of the *Persia* with the mate and six men, who were held as hostages to force the *Persia* to carry the exiles to the mainland. The master, Latham Cross, refused to bargain for release of the men and made directly for Valparaiso to secure assistance. When Ridgely heard Cross's story he immediately applied to the supreme director for the rescue of his countrymen. Since the Chileans had no ship available for this task the naval officer volunteered to take a detachment of patriot troops to Juan Fernández to restore order.

In the meantime, a boatload of exiles from the prison colony boarded and captured the American frigate *Washington* near Más Afuera Island. With them were four of the *Persia*'s captive crewmen. The captain and crew of the *Washington* regained control of their ship after a sharp fight on deck in which two of the

Spaniards were killed, and set course for Valparaiso, arriving there on October 20. As three of the *Persia*'s crew were still held on Juan Fernández, Ridgely carried out the original plan. The Chilean troops were transported to the island and the authority of the patriot governor was restored.[67]

From Juan Fernández the *Constellation* proceeded to Callao by way of Coquimbo and Mollendo. On December 18, 1821, she left Callao with Prevost on board to go to Guayaquil to investigate the detention of the United States merchant ship *Tea Plant* by the revolutionary junta of that place. The trip was made at the request of Prevost, who once more consented to board a naval vessel, not only to free the *Tea Plant* but also to ascertain the political situation in the Quito presidency. It was the agent's intention to seek out Bolívar in order to obtain his views on the revolution, since it had been reported that the Liberator was on his way to Guayaquil with a large force.[68]

The *Tea Plant* had already been freed and had sailed for Gibraltar by the time the *Constellation* arrived at the entrance to the Bay of Guayaquil and the visit accomplished little except for conversations with local revolutionary leaders, who were divided on the question of whether to join Peru or Colombia, or to remain independent. Prevost's plans to visit Bolívar were frustrated by the loss of his baggage when the boat in which it had been placed was upset in the turbulent Guayaquil River. Not wishing to face the Liberator in dirty linen, he decided not to remain in Guayaquil until Bolívar arrived.[69]

On their return to Callao, Ridgely did not tarry long but got the *Constellation* underway on February 2, 1822, to proceed to Valparaiso, via the royalist-held ports of the Intermedios. Prevost had intended to return to Chile in the *Constellation* but gave up the idea when he learned that Ridgely was determined to visit the blockaded royalist ports, The agent believed that taking the ship through the blockade would create "unfriendly feelings" among the patriots.[70]

One reason for returning to Chile by way of the Intermedios was a request from Eliphalet Smith that the *Constellation* stop at Mollendo to take out specie belonging to American citizens. On arrival at Mollendo in March, 1822, Ridgely wrote to Smith at

Arequipa advising him to liquidate all his holdings, because the fall of the southern city to the patriots then appeared likely. Smith took the advice but was forced to accept chinchilla skins in lieu of cash from some of his debtors because of the short notice. These skins were carried aboard the *Constellation* together with approximately $320,000 in specie. Ridgely had expected the specie but not the chinchilla skins, which were put aboard without his knowledge. He was so annoyed at Smith for placing him in the position of breaking the naval regulation prohibiting carrying merchandise for private individuals that he refused to unload the skins at Valparaiso and took them to New York, where he reported them to the collector of customs. Of the specie, $120,000 was transferred for Smith to the U.S.S. *Franklin* in Valparaiso and the remainder consigned to Boston mercantile firms.[71]

The *Constellation* arrived in Valparaiso on March 28 and found that her relief, the U.S.S. *Franklin*, had been waiting there two months. In compliance with his orders, Ridgely turned over all information and correspondence to Commodore Charles Stewart and prepared his ship for the passage around the Horn.

One new instruction issued after Ridgely reached the Pacific was undoubtedly discussed by the two officers. This instruction concerned the patriot blockade of Peru, which had been proclaimed in August, 1820, but was not known in Washington until March, 1821. Secretary of the Navy Smith Thompson, with the reports of Biddle and Downes before him, apparently feared that the vigorous efforts of his commanders in the Pacific in support of American commerce would lead to an open clash with the patriot navy. To forestall such an event he had dispatched supplemental instructions on the new blockade reiterating the administration's policy of "benevolent neutrality" toward the patriot governments.

Thompson had written that the United States did not recognize the legality of the blockade, but in view of their "struggle for liberty and independence," the United States did "not desire a collision with the patriots governments"—the policy remained, "as always, to observe strict neutrality." Ridgely was cautioned to avoid collision with the Chilean squadron under Cochrane, allowing "nothing but protection of the American Flag" to lead him to "open conflict with any vessel under Cochrane's command." For the present, action was to be confined to the defensive, and if any violations of United States rights occurred the naval officer was to make representations through the public agents to the government of Chile.[72] In effect these instructions directed the naval commander to protect American commerce against an admittedly illegal blockade but in the interest of democratic solidarity to stop short of open conflict with the patriots. Balancing the requirements of amicable relations with the patriots and the protection of American shipping required considerable restraint on the part of the American naval commanders throughout the next three years.

On May 6, 1822, the *Constellation* left Valparaiso homeward bound. From Rio de Janeiro, Ridgely summed up the situation in Chile and Peru for the benefit of the secretary of the navy. As of April, Upper Peru was quiescent under the control of the royalists, but San Martín had raised an army of six thousand men and was expected to take the field against La Serna's mountain strongholds. The entire coastal area, except for a section between Pisco and the northern frontier of Chile and the Archipelago of Chiloé, was in the hands of the patriots. The former was under blockade and a small expeditionary force had been sent against Chiloé. The last two Spanish frigates in the Pacific, the *Prueba* and *Venganza*, had surrendered to San Martín's forces but Cochrane had forcibly taken possession of the *Venganza* at Guayaquil, claiming her for the Chilean Navy. Regarding the rupture between San Martín and Cochrane, Ridgely reported that the Chilean government supported their commander's actions publicly, but it was his belief that there was a secret agreement between O'Higgins and San Martín. "Lord Cochrane must & will be *sacrificed*, whenever he shall have returned to Chile with *his fleet*," he wrote, "the whole object is to get their fleet back—in fact the Director told me so."[73]

Ridgely arrived off Sandy Hook on July 30, 1822, eighty-four days out of Valparaiso. He faced no such inquisition at the hands of the press and Congress as had Biddle, probably because the pro-patriot faction in the United States had won the battle for recognition of the South American republics. During his fifteen-month tour in the Pacific, Ridgely had continued and refined his predecessors' policies in the protection of American merchantmen and their crews from both belligerents. Unlike them he had been able to maintain reasonably good relations with the patriots and had been successful in obtaining the release of the *Chesapeake* and *Warrior* at Coquimbo and the *Galen* and *General Brown* at Callao. The very presence of the *Constellation* had been beneficial to other Americans. It is true that in his zeal to serve his countrymen Ridgely had allowed the *General Brown*, under his protection, to commit a serious breach of neutrality in the rescue of the deposed viceroy, Pezuela. He did not himself, however, attempt to break patriot blockades and clearly stated that he would not extend the protection of the United States naval forces to the *General Brown* or any other merchantman engaged in illegal activities. Thanks to favorable progress by the patriot forces in the conquest of Peru, the incident of the *General Brown* was soon forgotten, although his part in the freeing of Pezuela led to unofficial accusations of breach of faith with San Martín.[74]

Indeed, when the *Constellation* left the Pacific, threats to American shipping had diminished considerably although there were still troubled areas along the Intermedios and some apprehension among shippers as to Lord Cochrane's intentions after his break with San Martín. Regardless of the improved political situation, United States seamen on the western coast felt more secure because of the presence of warships commanded by energetic officers alert to their problems. Ignacio Manning, master of one of the whale ships, expressed this feeling when he praised the actions of Ridgely to Jeremy Robinson: "The Constellation Frigate is now in the bay of Calou [*sic*], Capt. Ridgely's conduct has been most energetic and decisive, he will do both honor to himself and Country." Manning had less kind words for the United States agents: "I am informed that there is shortly to be sent from the U. States a Consul Genl. & Navy Agent, for Buenos Ayres, Chili, & Peru. If so I am in hopes that we shall have no mor[e] Frothy Mercantile speculators to assume the garb and name of Consul of the U. States of Amer. who are more capable of Bobbing for Eels than that of supporting the rites [*sic*]of their Countrymen, or the Dignity and Honor of the Nation."[75]

Chapter VIII

*Captain Charles Stewart
— The Pacific Squadron, 1822–1824*

In the fall of 1821 United States naval forces in the Pacific were given squadron status when Commodore Charles Stewart was ordered to take the seventy-four-gun ship *Franklin* and the schooner *Dolphin* to relieve the *Constellation*.[1] Stewart held two commands, for he remained commanding officer of the *Franklin* while flying the broad command pennant of a squadron commander from her main-truck. The lesser ship of his squadron was spanking new, fresh off the building ways of the Philadelphia Navy Yard. Her commanding officer, Lieutenant David Conner, was an old hand in the Southeast Pacific, having been first lieutenant of the *Ontario* in 1818.[2]

Stewart was one of the ranking captains of the service in 1821. As a boy in Philadelphia he attended Doctor Abercrombie's Academy with Stephen Decatur, Richard Somers, and Richard Rush, but ran away to sea at the age of thirteen. During the quasi war with France he entered the navy at the age of twenty, with an original commission as lieutenant because of his former merchant-ship experience. His early reputation in the naval service was earned in the Mediterranean, under Preble, as commanding officer of the schooner *Experiment*. He attained a navy-wide reputation, not only as a fighter, but as an excellent organizer and as an authority on constitutional and international law. As commander of "Old Ironsides" during the War of 1812 he gained nationwide fame. After the war he became a confidant of Madison and Monroe and was reported to have declined a cabinet post under the latter.[3]

Notwithstanding his reputation for tact and diplomacy, Stewart was a stern disciplinarian. In 1817 he was assigned command of the Mediterranean squadron to restore lagging discipline. His measures were effective, if Draconian. When he returned to the United States the squadron had been restored to its former efficiency. He wasted little time on the lower ranks but concentrated on the commanding officers, holding them strictly accountable for all happenings in their commands. At one point in 1819 he relieved most of the senior commanding officers of the squadron and replaced them with juniors of his own choosing. Among those relieved was Thomas MacDonough, commander of the *Guerrière* and hero of the battle of Lake Champlain—because of a dispute over the proceedings of a court-martial.[4] He willingly accepted the restraints of discipline himself and obeyed orders implicitly. James Fenimore Cooper relates that Stewart once put to sea in the *Experiment*, towing the mainmast astern, in obedience to a petulant order of Commodore Thomas Truxtun.[5]

As commander of the Mediterranean squadron, Stewart took a keen interest in United States-Spanish relations and gained some insight into the revolutions in South America. He was a firm believer in the use of available force to achieve national objectives. In 1819 he proposed to John Forsyth, minister to Spain, and again in 1820 to the secretary of the navy, that he make a show of force with the fleet off the Spanish coast to frighten Ferdinand into signing the pending Florida Treaty but received no encouragement in his plans.[6]

The *Franklin* was outfitted in New York in the summer of

1821 for the Pacific cruise and most of her crew were recruited there. By mid-September, Stewart reported the ship "in readiness to receive the orders of government for her destination,"[7] and sailing orders were received on October 1. With the season for making a safe passage around the Horn fast approaching, Stewart wasted little time in getting his ships to sea. The *Franklin* and *Dolphin* left New York on October 10, 1821, bound for the Pacific.[8]

The sailing orders were essentially the same as those issued to Downes and Ridgely, with variations dictated by experience and the changing political situation in Chile and Peru. One of these was the enlargement of naval operations from a single-ship basis to a squadron basis. Paper blockades remained a major concern —the special instruction to Ridgely prohibiting use of force to secure neutral rights in the face of an admittedly illegal blockade was incorporated verbatim in Stewart's orders. The annoyance of the secretary of the navy at the paucity of reports from the Pacific was shown by a new paragraph that recommended "frequent communications" to the department relative to all "movements and the events which may take place." The primary mission remained the protection of American lives and property in the Pacific Ocean.[9]

Stewart anticipated a pleasant, relaxed cruise in the Pacific, uncomplicated by the multifarious problems he had faced in the Mediterranean. The offer of a master commandant as flag captain was declined because he believed the command in the Pacific would be very limited and would not require divided attention.[10] Evidence that he expected no trouble is indicated by the fact that Mrs. Stewart and his children accompanied him in the *Franklin* to South America. Mindful of navy regulations, which stated that "No captain shall carry any woman to sea without an order from the Secretary of the Navy or from the commander of the fleet or squadron to which he belongs," Stewart asked and received from Secretary Thompson permission for Mrs. Stewart to accompany him in the warship.[11]

Before returning to the United States he was to be disillusioned about the ease of duty in the Pacific. Problems undreamed of in the Mediterranean were to plague him in South America, and he returned to the United States at the end of the cruise to face a court-martial for alleged misconduct as commander of the Pacific Station.[12]

In late January, 1822, after a "boisterous and tedious trip around the Horn," the *Franklin* and *Dolphin* arrived off Juan Fernández Island where they fell in with the merchantman *Canton*.[13] The latter remained under the protection of the *Franklin* for the next seven months. Owned by LeRoy, Bayard & Company of New York, the *Canton* had left the United States for Chile about the same time as the *Franklin* with a cargo of wine and French, German, and English dry goods. In addition to her regular cargo she carried several cases of firearms. Her master and supercargo was John O'Sullivan and the assistant supercargo was Horatio G. Ward. The rendezvous off Juan Fernández was prearranged. Before leaving New York, Commodore Stewart had advised the masters of three ships lying there —the *America*, *Post Captain*, and *Canton*—that he would provide convoy for them if they would meet at Juan Fernández, but only the *Canton* took advantage of the offer.[14]

The three ships arrived at Valparaiso on February 5, 1822. The *Franklin* did not again get underway until she had relieved the *Constellation*, but in March, Stewart sent the *Dolphin* on a scouting mission off Concepción and Santa María to ascertain how the whaling and sealing ships in that area were faring. Conner returned to Valparaiso in April and reported that American vessels to the southward could operate in complete safety.[15] This became the pattern of future operations. The *Franklin*, because of her deep draft—about twenty-five feet fully loaded—would remain at anchor while the *Dolphin* investigated conditions along the coast and in the small harbors.

On March 19 a serious accident took the lives of six officers and two seamen of the flagship. On a hunting expedition to Quintero Bay, near Lord Cochrane's country estate, one of the *Franklin*'s boats capsized while attempting to land through the heavy surf. One of the victims was Lieutenant James A. Perry, brother of Commodore Perry. Another was Cornelius De Puy, a naturalist, who was carried on the ship's rolls as second sailing master but actually performed duties as Stewart's clerk.[16] Ward, the assistant supercargo of the *Canton*, was named as the commodore's clerk the following August.[17]

The *Constellation* arrived on March 28. Stewart, expecting Prevost to come from Lima on the frigate, had delayed making a visit to Santiago to meet the Chilean leaders because he considered it desirable to have the special agent present him to the supreme director.[18] In the absence of Prevost, Ridgely took the commodore and Mrs. Stewart to Santiago to present them to O'Higgins and at the same time make his own farewell. During the four-day visit Stewart was coolly received and on his part would accept no civilities from the government.[19]

During this period Stewart formed a very unfavorable opinion of the patriots—an opinion that remained unchanged throughout his tour of duty and that undoubtedly adversely affected his relations with the patriot officials. Characteristically, having made up his mind regarding them he was far more outspoken in his criticisms than any of his predecessors. His comments on the Cochrane and San Martín quarrel were searing. Characterizing the two patriots as "two of the greatest rogues ever existing," he believed that the ambition of each to "overreach" the other was actually preventing the liberation of Peru—each of them was engaged in plunder. "Deception is their forte," Stewart wrote, "and when they profess most it is necessary to be most on your guard." When word reached Valparaiso that the brig *Macedonian* had been condemned in Lima as property of the Spanish Philippine Company, Stewart's comment was: "When they want a thing they find no difficulty in making a pretext, as they acknowledge no law but expediency."[20]

At this time Stewart thought the fall of Lima and Callao to the patriots would render the presence of the *Franklin* in the Pacific unnecessary, "unless government should be desirous of enforcing rigidly all their neutral rights," which appeared to him "the only mode of gaining the respect" of the patriots. "Submission is construed into fear," he said; "they cannot be brought to believe that 'respect for them and the cause they are engaged in' would induce any nation to submit, unless they had higher interests to subserve."[21] In anticipation of an early peace, the commodore recommended three smaller ships for the station—

two sloops to be stationed in Lima and Valparaiso, and a schooner to patrol the coast. Such a fleet, he thought, would best serve the needs of the American merchants, principally as a place of deposit for their specie, "where it would not be subject to the seizure of every governor or officer who chose to lay violent hands on it."[22]

The newcomer's opinions were no doubt based on reports by Ridgely and Eliphalet Smith, who had accompanied his specie and chinchilla pelts as a passenger on the *Constellation* from Mollendo to Valparaiso. Smith's primary reason for the journey was to enlist the aid of Stewart in recovery of the money taken by Cochrane's raiding parties in 1819 and 1821, but he also took advantage of the visit to charter the *Canton* and purchase the greater part of her cargo for sale at the Intermedios ports.[23] Since Adams had specifically requested the commodore's assistance in obtaining settlement of the *Macedonian*'s claim of 1819, he gladly undertook to obtain a promise from the supreme director for a speedy decision on both of the pending cases.[24] Besides his obligation to a fellow citizen, Stewart was eager to help Smith because of a long friendship dating back to the years when he had been commander of the Mediterranean Squadron and the merchant had been a trader on the Spanish coast.[25]

Smith was a typical example of early nineteenth-century American merchant navigators, to whom the excitement and adventure of travel and trade were almost as important as the profits they made. Often these merchants would keep to the sea for years—buying, selling, and trading cargoes from one port to another—before returning to their home bases to retire on their gains or to seek new backing to recoup losses. Smith had come to the Pacific in 1818 as captain of the merchant brig *Macedonian*. Unlike many of his compatriots, he did little trading with the insurgents but quickly established business connections with the royalists and carried on a profitable trade with the Spanish merchants of Peru. He co-operated fully with the royalist officials and operated strictly in accordance with Spanish law.[26] But in so doing, he violated many of the patriot proclamations concerning blockades and contraband. Smith and the *Macedonian* became anathemas to the patriots. San Martín is reputed to have said that he did more damage to the cause of liberty than any other man.[27] Twice, large sums of money were taken from him by the patriots, but restitution was made eventually for each seizure on proof that the money was, in fact, private, neutral property.[28]

Smith also took full advantage of his friendship with the commodore to further his private interests and was a frequent visitor to the *Franklin*. He was a passenger on board from July, 1822, to April, 1823, making a complete circuit from Quilca, to Callao, to Valparaiso, and back to Quilca—a trip that took the better part of a year. He originally went aboard for passage to Callao to investigate the condemnation by the patriots of the *Macedonian* and her cargo, valued at $90,000, but on the invitation of the commodore returned with the *Franklin* to Valparaiso, where both men expected to have some fresh instructions from the United States supporting the merchant captain's claims against the Chilean government.[29] While aboard the *Franklin*, Smith continued the direction of his various business affairs. Prevost claimed these included arrangements for the supply and transportation of contraband arms to the royalists—an action detrimental to United States relations with the patriots. When the agent complained that Smith had shipped arms for the royalists from Arica to Chiloé in a schooner that he had chartered while enjoying the hospitality of the *Franklin*, Stewart hotly defended his friend, stating that he had been received on board the warship "as any other unfortunate citizen would have been," and that he had "been many years intimate with him" and had "always believed his integrity unimpeachable."[30]

At various times the *Franklin* carried large amounts of money for Smith and throughout June and July, 1822, remained in the Intermedios ports for the protection of the *Canton*, then under charter to Smith. In August, 1822, the commodore made strong, but futile protests to the patriots over the confiscation of Smith's vessel, the *Macedonian*.[31] These facts, coupled with the prolonged sojourn of the merchant on the *Franklin* and the appointment of Ward as secretary to the commodore, gave rise to unpleasant gossip among the pro-patriot American merchants at Lima and Callao that Stewart had a financial interest in Smith's enterprises and was using the *Franklin* to further their private affairs to the neglect of the welfare of other United States citizens in the area. Spokesman for the critics of the naval officer appears to have been Platt H. Crosby, a young American living in Lima. His ardent sympathy for the patriots is attested by the fact that he was the translator of Vincente Pazos' *Letters on the United Provinces of South America*, which was addressed to Henry Clay.[32] In May, 1823, Crosby composed a twenty-page phillipic attacking Stewart as a pawn of Smith and accusing him of neglecting other Americans in Peru to serve Smith's interests. In it Crosby referred to Smith as the "supercargo of the *Franklin*."[33] This vitriolic document eventually reached Washington and became the basis for most of the charges against Stewart at his court-martial in 1825.

The accusations against Stewart were thoroughly aired during his trial in 1825 and no legal basis was found to sustain them. Nevertheless, it appears that in the name of friendship he committed an error in judgment in permitting a person with known sympathies for, and extensive business connections with, the royalists to reside so long on a public vessel of the United States. There can be little doubt that Smith exerted an influence in favor of the royalists—not a difficult task in view of the antipathy for the patriots the commodore had already acquired from his predecessors on the Pacific Station.

When Smith first went to Valparaiso to contact Stewart he brought with him a letter inspired by himself but signed by General Juan Ramírez, commander of the royalist forces in the southern provinces of Peru. In the letter Ramírez offered to negotiate a commercial treaty with Stewart that would "secure to his Countrymen the right to land their goods and merchandise from their vessels on this coast, and from which great and mutual advantages are to be derived by both the parties contracting." Stewart's reply was cautious. He told Ramírez that it was the "invariable policy" of the United States to maintain a strict neutrality between warring parties while keeping commerce freely open to both "under the laws of nations." Such a policy would preclude granting the authorities of Peru an "equivalent" for any relaxation they might make of Spain's rigid colonial policy.[34]

Stewart's letter to Ramírez was entrusted to Smith for delivery since Smith was desirous of returning to Peru and would be able to interpret it for the Spanish general. The *Dolphin*, which was bound for Callao, was ordered to take Smith as a passenger, touching at Arica or Mollendo to put him ashore.[35]

One of the three or four trunks that Smith took aboard the *Dolphin* contained samples of ginghams and silks from the recently purchased cargo of the *Canton*. In Arica, Conner imprudently permitted display of the samples to visiting Spanish merchants in the captain's cabin. Ordinarily this would have caused no comment but it so happened that a Lieutenant Horace B. Sawyer, himself under arrest for disobedience to orders, saw the display and reported his captain to Stewart for violation of navy regulations. Stewart considered the charge trivial and took no action against Conner.

Nonetheless, Sawyer's accusations reached the States, and Stewart was charged with neglect of duty for not disciplining the *Dolphin*'s commander. Conner himself was tried by court-martial in 1824 in New York. He was charged with disobedience to orders for violating naval regulations against receiving "goods and merchandise not for sole use of his vessel" and with unofficer-like conduct for permitting public display of dry goods for commercial purposes, "thereby tending to the subversion of discipline, and prostituting the said vessel of the United States to purposes of private trade and traffic." Another specification in the charge was that he received smuggled plate and bullion in Callao in June, 1822. Conner was acquitted of all charges except permitting "a public display of dry goods," for which he received a reprimand.[36]

Another item Stewart's critics used against him was the construction, out of his personal funds, of a small schooner to facilitate communications between his ships and Washington. Communications of previous commanders with Washington had been most unsatisfactory. A letter took from three to six months, sometimes longer, to go from Valparaiso to the United States. There were three possible routes: (1) around the Horn; (2) across the Andes to Buenos Aires, thence by ship; (3) to Panama, thence across the Isthmus, and by ship from the Caribbean side. Use of the Panama route was preferable to the others; but merchant sailings were irregular, and sending one of the two regular ships of the squadron would mean her absence from the trouble spots in Chile and Peru for several months because of the adverse head winds on the return trip south.

Stewart gave a great deal of thought to the problem and in an early report recommended to the Navy Department that a small dispatch or pilot boat be sent out to facilitate communications with Panama, the route suggested in his basic instructions.[37] There was little hope of receiving favorable action in less than a year. In the meantime, the arrival in Valparaiso of the brig *Pearl* of Boston provided a practical, if unauthorized solution. In the *Pearl*'s hold were the frames and material for building three small schooners intended for sale in the Sandwich Islands. When Stewart learned of this he tried to buy one of the knockdown vessels on his own account for use of the squadron, but the master of the *Pearl*, Samuel Chandler, was unwilling to bargain for only one. An agreement was made by which the commodore undertook to build all three of the small craft with the understanding that he retain one of them on payment of $500 in cash. On completion, the other two were to be delivered to the master of the *Pearl* in the port of Oahu in the Sandwich Islands.

In accordance with this agreement, the *Water Witch* was built at Arica in June, 1822, the *Peruviano* at Quilca in July, 1822, and the *Robinson Crusoe* at Juan Fernández in January, 1823, by crewmen of the *Franklin*. The artificers who did the work were paid additional money to their regular pay and the carpenter's mate was promised a bonus of $100 by the commodore to get the vessels launched quickly. Material from the *Franklin* used in their construction was replaced by Hogan at Valparaiso from the commodore's private account. The *Water Witch*, the first to be finished, was pressed into service immediately under command of Lieutenant Henry Henry with a crew from the *Franklin*. She and the *Robinson Crusoe* were eventually delivered to Chandler or his agents on the coast of South America, and the *Peruviano* was retained for use of the squadron with Henry in command.[38]

The fast, sturdy schooners provided invaluable services to the squadron; they carried messages between the commodore, the *Dolphin*, and officials in various ports of the coast, delivered provisions, transported passengers, and performed similar functions that they could do more quickly and efficiently than the larger ships. The *Peruviano*, before she was fully completed and manned by a naval crew and while she was under tow by the *Franklin*, was utilized for storage of silks from the *Canton*. After she was operating on her own with a naval crew, she performed the more heroic task of recapturing the schooner *Adonis* of Baltimore from a prize crew of the royalist privateer *Quintanilla*.[39]

The status of these vessels was anomalous. While in service of the squadron they were manned by naval personnel and were considered public vessels by authorities of the ports they visited, yet they were privately owned. Stewart never asked nor received any compensation for use of the *Peruviano* but did recommend approval of Henry's request for additional pay as her commanding officer, which was granted by the secretary of the navy.[40] The use of these craft formed one of the key charges against Stewart in the investigation of his conduct while in command in the Pacific in 1825—one specification alleging that he caused the craft to be built with public funds and used them for private speculations. Henry testified at Stewart's trial that the schooners were "employed in carrying dispatches and other public services connected with the squadron, and upon no other duties whatever."[41] He considered carrying specie and passengers as a public duty, as his later testimony showed.

When Stewart returned to the United States, he sold the *Peruviano* to Mr. Nixon of the firm Nixon & McCall of Lima for $4,000 or $4,500.[42] This was the same Lieutenant Nixon of the U. S. Navy who had been captain of the *Warrior* in 1820 and was still, in 1824, on furlough from the naval service. Stewart undoubtedly made a profit on the *Peruviano*—but for two years she filled a vital gap in the squadron's organization without cost to the government.

The affairs of Smith's ships—the chartered *Canton* and the brig *Macedonian*—took up much of the commodore's time during his first year on the Pacific Station. When the merchant purchased part of the *Canton*'s cargo at Valparaiso he also chartered the ship for $3,500 a month.[43] Under terms of the sale O'Sullivan contracted to deliver the merchandise at Arica or Quilca and was to receive part of the proceeds of the sale. Smith was to have the privilege of filling, freight free, any vacant cargo space on the *Canton* with his own merchandise purchased in Valparaiso. He agreed to deposit the proceeds of the sale of the cargo on board the *Franklin* within two months after its delivery in the Intermedios ports. At Stewart's trial Smith testified that he sold the cargo for approximately $300,000 under special license from the viceroy of Peru and that the proceeds were put aboard the *Franklin* in specie and bullion with the knowledge and approval of the viceroy and the collector of customs of Arequipa.

Part of the cargo of the *Canton* was sold in Valparaiso, including a large quantity of canvas and wine purchased by the *Franklin*. The wine was intended for issue to the midshipmen as a substitute for ardent spirits. Two or three casks spoiled, but an eventual saving to the government resulted since they were converted into vinegar, a commodity that cost a dollar a gallon on shore whereas wine cost only fifty cents a gallon.[44]

The arms the *Canton* carried became a source of embarrassment to both Stewart and the Chilean government. The special envoys of Peru then at Santiago—Juan García del Río and Diego Paroissien—informing the Chilean government that they had information that the *Canton* had left the United States with armament for the royalists and had made an agreement to meet the *Franklin* at Juan Fernández, requested that the *Canton* be prevented from sailing to royalist-held ports with the arms on board.[45] The Chileans, unwilling to go so far as to prohibit the sailing, assured the Peruvians that the *Canton* would not sail without adequate bonds and safeguards that the arms would not be turned over to the royalists. The Peruvians politely acquiesced in any action the Chileans proposed. Stewart, learning of the arms, declined to extend the protection of convoy to the *Canton* as long as she had contraband on board. To satisfy all parties, the arms carried as cargo were landed and placed in the customs house at Valparaiso, only those registered with the United States for defense of the ship remaining on board.[46]

After the merchantman had landed her contraband arms, the

commodore assumed full responsibility for her protection on the war-torn coast, and the *Franklin* and *Canton* left Valparaiso for Arica on May 22. At the same time he refused to take the *Pearl* under convoy as it was known she had on board a quantity of arms destined for trade with the Indians on the northwest coast of North America. Nonetheless, the *Pearl* and a British brig, the *Sarah*, made sail about the same time as the *Franklin* and *Canton* and remained in sight during most of the voyage along the coast. They thus became an unofficial part of the convoy although Stewart told the officers of the deck that they were not under his protection and no attention should be given to them. It is interesting to speculate what action Stewart would have taken if a warship of either of the belligerents had attempted to molest the *Pearl* or even the British *Sarah*. No such event occurred and all four vessels reached Arica without incident on June 5. Indeed, no warships of either of the belligerents were seen until after the group arrived at Arica.[47]

When Stewart left Valparaiso he was under the impression that the blockade of the coast of Peru was no longer effective; therefore the presence of contraband on board ships under his protection was of more concern to him than the prospect of encountering a blockade.[48] As Ridgely had predicted, the shortened blockade of the coast from Ancon to Pisco, declared by the supreme director of Chile on June 22, 1821, was rendered unnecessary by the fall of Callao; but on October 15, 1821, San Martín, as protector of Peru, had declared eight hundred miles of royalist-held coast from 15° S. Lat. to 22° 30′ S. Lat. (approximately from Puerto Caballas to Punta Cobija) under blockade.[49] Apparently, San Martín's decree was confusing and not widely disseminated. Even Prevost, in commenting on its use as a reference for a new blockade in 1823, had this to say concerning it: "As that Decree gives effect to the Blockade only upon the arrival of vessels of War at the Station destined to render it efficient, it appeared to me imprudent to cavil at the loose manner in which it is announced and unnecessary to ask explanations as to the Force employed, when its competency must be a Subject of enquiry should any case occur claiming my Interference."[50]

In Arica the *Canton* sold and landed part of her cargo. The day after their arrival the Peruvian naval schooner *Sacramento* came into Arica and spent several days bombarding royalist positions on shore, departing on June 9. She made no attempt to interfere with any of the activities of the American ships. Whether she made protests regarding violation of blockade is not clear. Stewart later said that she was not "wearing" the same flag as other Peruvian warships and that her conduct was so irregular and equivocal that he was later "led to believe she was piratical." The ships remained three to four weeks in Arica, after which the *Franklin* and the *Canton* went on to Quilca, while the *Pearl* set sail for the Northwest Coast.[51]

Before the *Franklin* left Arica, Henry, who had been supervising the building of the *Water Witch* on shore, reported to Stewart that someone had asked him if guns had been landed from either the *Canton* or the *Pearl*. The commodore immediately sent the first lieutenant and Lieutenant Thomas S. Hammersley to the *Pearl* to ascertain if any of the guns known to be on board had been landed. Those officers boarded the *Pearl* as she stood out to sea and after a thorough search reported to the commodore that the guns carried on board the merchantman tallied with her invoice.[52]

At Quilca the remainder of the *Canton*'s cargo was sold. In port also was the French ship *Telegraph*, unloading cargo for Arequipa. Some time after the arrival of the American ships, the Peruvian schooner *Cruz* entered the harbor and took possession of the Frenchman for trading in violation of the blockade, but made no attempt to interfere with the *Canton*. On July 8 the Peruvian brig of war *Belgrano* entered the harbor and her commander, Captain William Prunier, inquired of Stewart what ships were present. On Stewart's reply that they were the American ship *Canton* and the French ship *Telegraph*, Prunier further asked if the *Canton* was a public or private vessel, to which Stewart replied that she was a private, armed merchant ship, belonging to citizens of the United States. On July 10 Prunier informed Stewart by letter that he "had sufficient motives to detain the ship *Canton* and to send her to the disposal of the government" and that he proposed to do so the next day. The same day he wrote another letter, which seemed to ask the commodore's concurrence in the seizure of the *Canton*. It stated that he would be happy to have Stewart's "determination [i.e., his views on the proposed seizure], in order if it were possible to conciliate them" with the performance of his, Prunier's, duties.[53] Stewart's own duty demanded defense of the American merchantman and as Prunier had thus far given no concrete reasons for taking the *Canton* he refused to surrender her: "I have to inform you that I am sent into this sea with the naval forces of the United States under my command, to protect the citizens (and their property) of the United States in all their lawful pursuits. As the ship Canton has done no act contrary to the laws of nations, you can have no legal pretext for interfering with her. She is entitled to protection, and will be defended as property of citizens of the United States."[54]

Stewart's statement that he would defend the *Canton* elicited from Prunier the charge that the *Canton* had been trading in the ports of Arica, Mollendo, and Quilca under the protection of the *Franklin* in violation of a formally declared, rigorous blockade from 15° S. Lat. to 22° S. Lat. and since he, a commissioned commander of the Peruvian Navy, had found her trading in Quilca, he had ordered her to proceed to Callao to determine her guilt or innocence "of an infraction of the law of blockade." This was too much for Stewart, who informed Prunier that the blockade of seven degrees of coast without sufficient force was illegal "by any international law." Furthermore, the Peruvian government had failed to station a competent force off the ports claimed by Prunier as being specially blockaded, to prevent the entrance of neutrals or to warn them away. The commodore wrote to Prunier: "On the entrance of the Ship *Canton* to Arica and this port, no such force appeared, and although I have been six weeks on this coast, which you assert to be blockaded, your vessel and the schooner in company are the only vessels we have seen in all that time, carrying the flag you wear." He continued: "Thus, sir, you will perceive that the ship *Canton* has violated no law which the flag of our nation is bound to respect, or gives you a right to lay your injunction on her commander, or your government judicial authority over her."[55]

It was one thing to capture an undefended merchantman and

another to take her from under the guns of a formidable warship. Prunier left without the *Canton*. In his report to Tomás Guido, minister of war and marine of the patriot government at Lima, the frustrated Prunier claimed that the *Canton* was masquerading as a United States warship. Since none of the French warships in the Pacific were present at Quilca to prevent it, the unfortunate *Telegraph* was sent to Callao for adjudication.[56]

Under the existing circumstances Stewart was not only justified in preventing seizure of the *Canton* but required to do so. As his counsel pointed out at his trial in 1825, to have acquiesced in the seizure of the *Canton* after Prunier had sought his concurrence would have been tantamount to acknowledging the legality of the blockade. Stewart also had to consider the probability of a fair hearing under international law for the *Canton*. His counsel alluded to the "known profligacy of public and private citizens of both belligerents" and the "yet green and inexperienced" prize courts of the revolutionary governments, which "could not be expected to deny, by their sentence, the legality of a blockade ordered by their government."[57]

Stewart made no secret of his distrust of patriot tribunals even in official correspondence with their officials, as he demonstrated in his correspondence with Francisco Valdivieso, Peruvian foreign minister, over the condemnation at Callao of Smith's *Macedonian*.

A few weeks after Prunier's rebuff, the *Franklin*, with the partially completed forty-ton *Peruviano* in tow, left Quilca for Callao, where she arrived on August 2. The *Canton* sailed in company as far as San Lorenzo Island, off the port, but, understandably, did not choose to expose herself to the patriots of Callao and continued on to Guayaquil to load a cargo of cacao.

At Callao, numerous complaints of the imprisonment of United States citizens and seizure of their property by the government of Lima were investigated.[58] One of these was the case of the *Macedonian*, which had been condemned and converted to a patriot naval vessel after the removal and sale of her cargo by the government. This action had been taken on the grounds that half of the ship had been sold by Philip Mercier of Baltimore to José Arismendi, a Spanish refugee whose property had been confiscated by the patriot government and who, with Smith, had paid the royalist government $100,000 for the privilege of bringing goods from Canton, China, to Callao before the latter port had fallen to the patriots. Stewart claimed that the property belonged wholly to Americans since Arismendi had never completed the terms of the sale. He further claimed that the *Macedonian* had been "condemned by some secret tribunal or inquisition," a charge that the minister of state, Francisco Valdivieso, denied with considerable asperity, contending that the owners of the *Macedonian* were amply represented at hearings by the presence of the supercargo and ship's officers. He refused to concede that the case was one for discussion between governments and maintained that it was purely a matter of personal interests and that the claimants had the privilege of appealing to higher tribunals of the Peruvian government if dissatisfied with the ruling of the lower court.[59]

The commodore was shocked to learn that four seamen of the *Macedonian* had been imprisoned by the patriots in order to obtain testimony from them. Such practice was "obnoxious" to the government of the United States, he said, and destroyed the validity of any testimony the prisoners might give. "Those who have suffered personal injury and insult, and stand in personal fear," he wrote Valdivieso, "are not the tools by which justice works her ends."[60] Valdivieso's reply in defense of the incarceration of the seamen did little to increase the naval officer's respect for judicial procedures of the patriot government. The minister's explanation stated: "The detention of a small part of the crew has been magnified into oppression. This is far from being true, and the detention was only intended for the procurement of the truth, which cannot always be elicited when witnesses are at liberty to make depositions. The crew of the Macedonia[n] that was detained suffered no violence." He added that the crewmen were liberated "as soon as the truth was discovered."[61]

Stewart was unsuccessful in his representations for release of the *Macedonian*, and that vessel remained part of Peru's navy. His opinion of South American justice was expressed in a note to the minister, in which he said: "The claimants, having been excluded from a hearing in defence of their property before the first tribunal, as also from making their protests and reservations before the proper authority, have little to expect from the justice of any other tribunal before which they could bring it." He continued: "I can assure your excellency that if so unjust and nefarious a transaction has not been resisted by force of arms, you owe it exclusively to the respect the Government of the United States desires to feel for the patriot cause of South America."[62]

In approaching the patriot officials directly on such matters, Stewart was exceeding the authority of his instructions, which directed that any such appeals were to be made through the special agent. He justified his failure to do so by the absence of Prevost from Peru, the extreme urgency of the complaints, and the fact that he believed there would soon be a drastic change in the government. The former minister of war and marine, Bernardo Monteagudo, had been sent into exile and the commodore was convinced that San Martín would soon follow. It seemed to him desirable to make the protests a matter of record before the government that had authorized the protested acts was overthrown, in order "to keep alive any just claim we might have on the future government of that place, as well as to exhibit to them that we are not indifferent to injuries, and that they would not be passed unnoticed."[63] His evaluation was correct; San Martín resigned as protector in September to leave Peru forever. The government was reorganized and entrusted to a three-man junta ruling in the name of the Congress.

The complaints were not all one-sided. Valdivieso asked for an explanation of the alleged landing of two thousand muskets from the *Canton* at Arica under the protection of the *Franklin*'s guns. He forwarded correspondence from Del Río and Paroissien at Santiago and from Prunier at Quilca purporting to prove that the muskets were on the *Canton* and had been landed at Arica because the *Franklin* prevented interference by the Peruvian blockading squadron. Stewart flatly denied the allegation, forwarding an affidavit of Ward, assistant supercargo of the *Canton*, wherein the latter stated under oath that all arms not carried for the defense of the *Canton* were landed at the customs house in Valparaiso and that none were landed in Arica. There were some Americans who believed Valdivieso's accusations, among them Prevost and Crosby.[64]

In September the commodore received news that a piratical schooner was cruising off the coast of Guayaquil and that the former Chilean brig of war *Araucano*, now turned pirate, was also operating in those waters. Having in mind the *Canton*, which was loading cacao at Guayaquil, Stewart ordered Conner in the *Dolphin* to proceed to Guayaquil in order to provide convoy for any United States vessels ready to sail to southern ports and to capture the pirates if they should be found. The *Dolphin* performed another service on her mission to Guayaquil. In response to a request from O'Sullivan, $50,000 of the specie carried on the *Franklin* for LeRoy, Bayard and Company was delivered to him via the schooner. Another $100,000 was delivered to an Englishman named Lang then in Guayaquil.[65]

As with their predecessors in the Pacific, the handling of specie and bullion for merchants and shippers became big business for the ships of Stewart's squadron, to the mutual advantage of the shippers and the commanding officers. The precious metals were received for deposit as well as for transportation. Lieutenant Henry of the *Peruviano* testified that the fee for deposit was 1 per cent, and for transportation $2\frac{1}{2}$ per cent. The *Peruviano* did a brisk business carrying specie, which her young commander considered "absolutely indispensable" since "there was no security for it on the shore, under either of the governments." Unlike his counterpart in the Caribbean, Commodore David Porter, Stewart did not demand a percentage of the fees collected by his subordinate commanders. When Henry asked what proportion of the fees should be turned over to him as squadron commander, the commodore told him: "You have taken all the responsibility, and are consequently entitled to all the emolument."[66]

In essence, the naval vessels became floating banks in addition to their normal functions. The squadron was ideally situated to perform this service. The *Franklin*, in effect, became the central bank and clearing house while the *Dolphin* and *Peruviano* were highly mobile branches. During Stewart's court-martial, his counsel, General Robert D. Taylor, explained the service in these words: "When money or bullion were taken on deposit or for transportation, receipts or bills of lading were given for them, signed by the commander of the ship, which passed in those seas in the purchase of produce or goods as so much cash, it being the most convenient and safe mode of carrying funds from place to place, and being known the money would always be paid on presenting them to the ship."[67]

The system was loosely managed and subject to many abuses. Stewart did refuse, however, to accept specie or bullion from either of the belligerents or any that was not brought on board openly, and issued orders to his subordinate commanders to receive none but neutral property.[68]

Money was frequently taken on account for neutrals of other nationality. On one occasion Stewart agreed to transport $70,000 from Arica to Lima for an English merchant but in deference to his instructions would not grant the Englishman himself passage. At another time he agreed to transship some money for Baron Mackau of the French warship *Clorinde* on the assurance of the Frenchman that it was neutral property.[69]

Money to be shipped back to the United States or overseas was put on board other men-of-war or merchant ships leaving the coast. Transfer to men-of-war was safely made at any time but transfer to merchantmen was usually made just before the vessel sailed in order to lessen the time it was subject to confiscation by one or the other of the belligerents. Thus, when the American brig *Cora* was about to sail from Callao, the *Franklin* sent over $50,000 or $60,000 to be shipped out in her that evening, but the master refused to accept it on board until after the vessel was underway and insisted that the transfer be made in the warship's boat. It so happened that while the transfer was taking place an armed patriot boat came out to investigate the ship, was warned off by the captain of the *Cora* with the concurrence of the *Franklin*'s boat officer, and returned to shore after the warship's boat alongside was identified. A few days later the commodore received a complaint from the patriot government that his boat had interfered with one of their revenue boats.[70]

Crosby claimed the money transferred from the *Franklin* to the *Cora* was smuggled. His version of the affair revealed that the true cause of the patriot's anger was the presence of an absconding treasury officer on board the brig. Quite independently of the *Franklin*, the director of the mint, an Italian, had boarded the *Cora* the afternoon of her departure with some $80,000 to $100,000 of government funds. The revenue boat was attempting to apprehend this official when it overtook the *Cora* and had been frustrated in its mission by the presence of the *Franklin*'s boat alongside.[71] This gentleman had previously attempted to deposit his loot on the *Franklin* but had been refused by Stewart because "he was a Spaniard and one of the belligerents."[72]

There is no indication whether the money put aboard the *Cora* from the *Franklin* was cleared through the patriot customs or, indeed, whether it was subject to revenue regulations. According to the officers of the *Franklin* the money came from the *Dolphin* and merchant ships in the harbor, the masters of which presumably were responsible for its legal status whether it was taken aboard in China or Peru. The fact was that warships accepting money had no convenient way of checking its ownership or customs status beyond the statements of the depositors. As a result, it is very likely that much specie and bullion found its way aboard the warships without the payment of export duties. It is equally likely that much money actually belonging to Spanish royalists was spirited out of patriot territory under the guise of neutral property. Yet, although the warships did not keep open registers of specie received on board, as was required of merchantmen, they did not attempt to evade customs. Conner, for example, was careful to obtain permission of the minister of war before receiving deposits for safekeeping on board the *Dolphin* at Callao.[73]

In the fall, the prospect of renewed military activity at the Intermedios made it necessary for the *Franklin* to return to that area. The governing junta had decided to carry out San Martín's plan to dislodge the royalists from Upper Peru by simultaneous attacks from the center and the Intermedios. The Army of the South, designated to make the assault through the Intermedios, boarded transports in Callao expecting to depart in late September. The expedition was delayed until October because of difficulties with the transports, which departed, one or two at a time, between the first and fifteenth of October in a poorly coordinated movement.[74]

The *Franklin* arrived at Quilca on October 23, in advance of the patriot expedition.[75] Unknown to Stewart, the *Franklin* carried an unauthorized passenger from Callao to Quilca. This combination of circumstances gave rise to accusations by the patriots that the *Franklin* carried advance news of the expedition to the royalists by means of a Spanish spy secreted aboard.

As the warship was getting underway from Callao a poorly dressed, harrassed-looking Spaniard—one Madrid—came on board and, asking for Mrs. Stewart, begged her protection and help in getting passage away from Lima. He professed to be in danger of imprisonment, perhaps of being shot as a deserter, if he remained there, since he had no passport. He presented a note to Mrs. Stewart from a friend of hers, the Countess of Vallehermosa, asking her help in obtaining a passage for him. Perplexed and not wanting to take the responsibility on herself, Mrs. Stewart consulted Eliphalet Smith, who was returning to Quilca on the *Franklin*. Smith wisely advised her to inform the commodore, but she, knowing her husband would not allow the Spaniard on board and believing that he was in danger of being shot if returned to Callao, disregarded the advice and turned Madrid over to Peter Birch, the commodore's steward, with instructions to care for and feed him without letting her husband know he was aboard. Birch kept him fed and gave him some decent clothes in return for which he was required to do odd jobs such as dishwashing and shining silver. The cabin pantry proved to be the best possible place for Madrid to remain without being seen by the commodore. Nearly everyone else, including the first lieutenant, knew of his presence on the ship. The first lieutenant assumed that it was with the commodore's permission since he was subsisting in the cabin pantry.[76]

A year later in Valparaiso, Stewart learned from Henry of the unauthorized guest. There is no record of what he said to Mrs. Stewart but he had the "painful task" of informing the secretary of the navy of his passenger. "This circumstance," he wrote, "is doubly afflicting to me, as it deeply involves a wife, whose conduct and confidence towards me ought to have been different, and who should have preferred my duty to any act of grace she could possibly confer on another."⁷⁷ Stewart further informed the secretary that this event might "also involve a complaint on the part of the government of Lima"—a surmise that proved accurate. Two years later, after the royalists had retaken Lima, Madrid paid a visit to the *Franklin* in Callao, wearing the uniform of a royalist officer; he was recognized by a number of the officers but neither the commodore nor Mrs. Stewart would speak to him. One of the charges of Stewart's court-martial was that he received on board the *Franklin* "spies and officers in the royalist army" and protected "said persons from seizure and punishment, contrary to the express instructions given. . . ." From evidence given at the trial by the ship's officers, some of whom had no reason to favor Stewart, it appears that he actually knew nothing of the affair until long after it was over.⁷⁸

There was little for the *Franklin* to do in Quilca. Lieutenant Thomas S. Hammersley's journal for November expresses perfectly the reason for being there and some of the boredom of the task: "From the First of November 1822/Lying at anchor at Quilca protecting a number of Merchant Ship[s] from the Blockading Squadron of Peru/until the 2 December—During which time nothing material occurred."⁷⁹ On the latter date the *Franklin* left Quilca for Valparaiso with four American vessels under her protection. She was to spend the months of January, February, and March at Valparaiso and Juan Fernández before returning to Peru. When the *Franklin* arrived in Valparaiso on December 29, that city was in ruins as the result of an earthquake, and the country was in revolt against the O'Higgins regime. Neither of these circumstances seems to have affected the *Franklin* or American shipping to Chile in any great degree. Stewart reported to his superiors in Washington that the revolt would terminate in favor of General Ramón Freire, whose movement was popular throughout the country.⁸⁰

Stewart took advantage of Prevost's presence in Santiago to contact the special agent as required by his basic instructions. Stewart's letter, dated January 2, 1823, was the first contact between two men who should have been working in close unison during the past year. Each had expected the other to make the first move. After receipt of Stewart's letter, Prevost forwarded it and his reply to Adams with the sarcastic complaint: "After having passed eleven months on this coast within reach of me, Capt. Stewart was pleased to make the enclosed comment...."[81] Prevost's mental anguish was heightened by the fact that he had a son serving under Stewart's command. In his letter to Prevost, Stewart expressed "disappointment" at not having found the agent in Peru, "particularly as that was the only quarter in which the conduct of the government of Lima appeared to require our exertions." The commodore explained to Prevost, as he had to the secretary of the navy, his reasons for making protests against seizures of American property to the Lima government without going through him, as agent. The commodore gave as his reasons the "urgency of our fellow citizens" and "the changes, which it was not difficult to foresee were about to take place in that government...."[82] This, of course, was a not too subtle criticism of Prevost for failure to look after United States interests in Peru and for not foreseeing the fall of San Martín's government.

The basic difference in attitudes and reactions toward the South American revolutions and the patriots, which had been apparent between Prevost and Stewart's predecessors on the Pacific Station, was laid bare in the acrimonious correspondence that followed between the two. Stewart was an exponent of the use of the force under his command to prevent "depredations on our commerce" and to procure "respect for our interests and flag." He was confident that he had "a force adequate to the object."[83] Conversely, Prevost believed, now that the United States had recognized the independence of South American countries, that the first task was to "cultivate American feelings, to cherish a national character, and to foster sentiments of good will." Obviously he considered these aims more important than protection of the neutral rights of commerce. Turning to seizures of American property in Peru, he advocated a passive attitude and bluntly told Stewart: "I do not hesitate to advise a total silence on your part, and to leave the redress to the agency of the minister contemplated from the United States, who may, by treaty obtain full reparation."[84]

The blockade of the Intermedios and the protection of American ships in respect to it became one of the major points of dispute between the two Americans. Prevost was in complete disagreement with Stewart on the blockade's legality: "I should have offered my ideas of the blockade of Arica, or of any other of the intermediate ports before which a vessel-of-war was lying, and have shown that a force in station at any one place competent as to the enemy, was equally so to the neutral." He then unjustly criticized Stewart for affording protection to the *Pearl* and other merchantmen and thus defeating the "liberal and noble policy of the government of the United States."[85]

To Stewart, adherence to Prevost's ideas meant abrogation of long-cherished United States rights to the lawless whims of vacillating, unstable governments. Regarding the blockade of the Intermedios and Prevost's opinion as to its legality he wrote: "The ideas . . . you now entertain, are not in unison with those of the Government of the United States, and you ought to know they have expended too much blood and treasure in contending with Great Britain for just principles to yield it now inconsistently, however desirable it may be to you."[86] Stewart denied that he had afforded protection to the *Pearl* but emphasized that the inadequacy of the Peruvian force at Arica had rendered any protection unnecessary.

Stewart declared that the acknowledgement of the independence of the South American countries had produced no change in his responsibilities; he had received no new instructions and would continue to act in accordance with the instruction given him on departure from the United States. Respecting his duty to uphold the interests of the United States and his obligations toward the new governments he wrote:

> If the obedience I owe to the government [of the U.S.], and the duties I am bound to perform in consequence, should not comport with the erroneous ideas of these governments [the patriots] as respects justice to ourselves, they must blame none but themselves and not attribute it to improper sentiments of the Government of the United States or myself toward them. There was no disposition on the part of our government to incur so much expense, in sending a naval force to this sea which could be so advantageously employed in suppressing *pirates* nearer home, had these governments and the officers under their authority not exhibited so much avidity in depredating our commerce, imprisoning our citizens, in fine, by exercising every unfriendly act toward those who were alone their best friends;

and the fact of a necessity existing of keeping up a naval force in the Pacific is a strong proof that the Government of the United States are not willing to abandon either their rights or their commerce in this sea, and argues strongly the sense they entertain of the good will and justice these governments have for us.[87]

The argument between Prevost and Stewart was interrupted for a few months when the *Franklin* left Valparaiso for a month's visit to Juan Fernández. In the meantime, Prevost returned to Lima, and it was not until May that the *Franklin* returned to Callao by way of Iquique and Quilca.[88]

Before the *Franklin* returned to the north several significant changes occurred in Chile. In January, Lord Cochrane left Chile to take command of the naval forces of Emperor Pedro I of Brazil, leaving behind him a Chilean fleet that was in a state of disintegration.[89] On January 28, O'Higgins surrendered his executive authority to a provisional government, without bloodshed, before an open *cabildo* in Santiago, thus demonstrating the growing political maturity of the Chilean nation.[90] In March the *Franklin* left one of its carpenters in Valparaiso to construct a storehouse for the squadron—an indication of the permanence of the United States naval squadron in the Pacific.[91]

The debate between Prevost and Stewart was briefly resumed in early May when the *Franklin* arrived in Callao, but was confined to discussion of the activities of the *Pearl*, *Canton*, and *Macedonian*. No new light was shed on their affairs. Prevost continued to maintain that their activities had been illegal, and Stewart that these ships had done nothing illegal in Peru.[92]

Several new claims were made against the Lima government. With these Stewart had nothing to do since Prevost was now present to handle them.[93] Nonetheless, he continued to keep a weather eye cocked for any political or military changes affecting United States interests. Insofar as possible he kept the *Franklin* and *Dolphin* in different areas along the coast, utilizing the *Peruviano* as a communications link. Thanks to the extra ships and his careful organization of the small squadron he was in far better condition to respond quickly to appeals for help from United States ships on any part of the coast than had been any of his predecessors.

Chapter IX

Justification by Court-Martial

In 1823 a rapidly changing political and military situation in Peru complicated the tasks of both Stewart and Prevost. In February, José de la Riva Agüero became the first president of the Republic of Peru. In May a new patriot attack, led by General Andrés Santa Cruz, was launched against Upper Peru through the Intermedios. Meanwhile, Riva Agüero obtained Bolívar's promise of military assistance, and a detachment of Colombian troops under General Antonio José de Sucre was sent to Peru. The Colombians arrived at Lima in time to face the assault of nine thousand royalist troops from the valley of Jauja under General José Canterac. Hopelessly outnumbered, the Peruvians and Colombians abandoned the capital and withdrew to Callao, naming Sucre general-in-chief of the combined forces. The royalist army entered Lima on June 17 but, denied control of the port of Callao and the seaways, was unable to maintain provisions and withdrew to the mountains in July. In the face of military reverses the Peruvians disagreed among them-

Justification by Court-Martial

selves, and the dominant faction of Congress invited Bolívar to assume complete authority over the conduct of the war. Bolívar entered Lima on September 1, was granted dictatorial powers with the title of Liberator, and began at once to revitalize the civil and military organizations of the faltering republic. He entrusted civil affairs to the Marquis of Torre Tagle, who was named president to replace Riva Agüero. The latter made a feeble attempt to keep alive the constitutional government at Trujillo but was forced into exile by the Bolívar-Torre Tagle faction.[1]

The reverses of the patriots on land and the coming of Bolívar had little effect on the naval war since the patriots retained control of the seaways, the royalists being unable to do more than commission a few privateers, which operated from bases in Chiloé. Although the privateers posed a definite threat to neutral shipping, by far the gravest problem for the United States naval forces in 1823 continued to be the disputed patriot blockade of the Peruvian coast. Stewart's resolute defense of neutral rights was not entirely without results. In March, shortly after Riva Agüero became president, the blockade was redefined and restricted to the coast between Pisco and a point opposite Cerro Colupo, to the south of Iquique. That same month the American whale ship *O'Cain*, lying at Quilca, was boarded by the patriots with no worse results than having her register endorsed: "you are hereby warned off this coast of Peru from between the Latitude of 14° 00' & 22° 20' South."[2] The gentle treatment accorded the *O'Cain* may have been in deference to her new master, former midshipman Charles Wilkes of the *Franklin*, the future Antarctic and Pacific explorer. In keeping with the well-established policy of naval commanders in the Pacific to provide officers and men for United States merchantmen in emergencies, Wilkes had been sent aboard the merchant ship at Valparaiso as replacement for her master, who had died at sea.[3]

When the royalists entered Lima they took possession of the coast from Chancay to Pisco except for the port of Callao. In June the patriots declared this section of coast blockaded "under the same principles and conditions" as those of the former blockade from Iquique to Pisco.[4] Stewart immediately protested to

Sucre, declaring that he would not respect the blockade. "The United States expressly disavow their legitimacy," he wrote of the blockades, old as well as new. "Whenever it shall please the authorities in Peru to declare a port or ports in a state of blockade, and permanently station before such port or ports a competent naval force to carry it into effect, then such blockade will be respected...."[5]

Sucre claimed the blockade was in accordance with international usage and pointed to the fact that the British had recognized the old blockade and were respecting the new. He contended that the naval force of Peru was adequate to enforce the blockade, "as the Spaniards have not even a barge at command, in all the Pacific."[6] Stewart refused to take British acquiescence in the blockade as cause for accepting it, asserting to Sucre that "the tacit conduct in regard to the blockade of the British naval commanders on this station are not applicable to the United States.... Whatever infraction of her rights she may deem proper to tacitly acquiesce in now, does not and cannot constitute a reason that the Government of the United States should also yield theirs."[7] He asserted that the blockade had often been entrusted for months at a time to a single schooner.

The enforcement of the blockade was the duty of Guise, who had been promoted to vice-admiral and who remained the commander of the Peruvian naval force through the bewildering changes of government and military command on shore. Throughout 1823 something akin to an undeclared war existed between Guise and Stewart as a result of the latter's refusal at Quilca to surrender the *Canton* to the *Belgrano*. One of the casualties of this hostility was the schooner *Robinson Crusoe*, last of the vessels put together under the agreement between Stewart and Captain Chandler of the *Pearl*. In mid-April, after delivery of the schooner to agents of the owners, she was loaded with soap at Valparaiso for delivery at the Intermedios. She carried no papers other than a certificate of nationality signed by Stewart.[8] En route, while still well off the coast, she was stopped by the *Protector*, Guise's flagship, and made a prize. Without the formality of a legal condemnation Guise converted her into a tender for his ships. At the prodding of the owners, Prevost made representations to Valdivieso, who agreed to order the *Robinson Crusoe* to Callao for a legal hearing. At the same time, in a complaint to Adams, Prevost used this case as an example of the loose manner in which ships were given papers by naval commanders permitting them to operate under the American flag in the Pacific. The *Crusoe* never reached Callao because shortly after her capture by the *Protector* she was "retaken" by the American merchant ship *Chauncey*, taken into Quilca, and turned over to the Spanish authorities, who later burned her to prevent her from falling into the hands of the patriots a second time.[9]

Despite Guise's animosity and the extended blockade there was little naval activity along the Peruvian coast from July to October. The retreat of Canterac in July ended the need of a blockade from Chancay to Pisco, and the Intermedios ports were under control of the patriot expedition commanded by Santa Cruz. However, a series of defeats in the fall forced the patriots to abandon the Intermedios and, as the royalists returned to the evacuated ports, the blockade of that area once more came into effect.[10]

In November the American schooner *Adonis* of Baltimore was boarded by an armed party of Peruvian seamen in the harbor of Arica and taken to sea, where she was met by the *Protector*. Captain Leonard Sistare and the crew of the schooner were kept aboard the flagship while a crew of Peruvians returned her to the anchorage at Arica and leisurely routed out the entire cargo in search of contraband and money. Being unable to find anything justifying seizure, the patriot officer in charge permitted the regular crew to return on board. They found part of the badly damaged cargo still exposed on deck and much of the ship's equipment missing. The crowning insult was a demand by the patriots, who still held Arica, that the *Adonis* pay four times the normal harbor charges. This tribute was not paid, for the royalists were approaching Arica and the patriot vessels fled the harbor before it could be collected. The patriots gave Sistare to understand that his detention was "on account of Commodore Stewart assisting their enemies and that a vessel of theirs was taken by an American ship."[11]

In April, Stewart had hurried from Quilca to Callao when he heard that the royalists were moving on Lima. He anticipated the necessity of protecting American property from both belligerents. However, there proved to be little for him to do except protest the extension of the patriot blockade, since Canterac exercised strict discipline over his troops and there was no plundering of neutral property.[12]

In spite of the presence of the Spanish outside Callao and the crowding of the forts by refugees and merchants, the patriot high command was not dismayed and passed the time agreeably. Generals Guido and Miller were frequent visitors to the *Franklin*, where they enjoyed having tea with Mrs. Stewart. They were charmed by the commodore's wife, who was described as talented and beautiful and greatly admired by all. They were not so enthusiastic about her husband, "who was believed to be a partisan of the royalists." The commodore was rarely seen on shore and kept closely to his ship.[13]

Canterac's retreat having ended the blockade from Pisco to Chancay, and there being no reason to remain in Callao, the *Franklin* proceeded to Valparaiso to replenish stores, stopping at Mollendo on the way. All was quiet in Valparaiso when she arrived on September 27.[14] There the commodore learned of the satisfactory outcome of a case involving the ship *Arab*, which had been taken by the royalists at Pisco and sent to Chiloé for admiralty proceedings. The sole charge against her was that her cargo of brandy belonged to a patriot contractor of Lima. While at Callao, Stewart had obtained an order from General Canterac for the release of the *Arab*. Her master, S. Williams, personally took the order to Chiloé, where he was treated most cordially by the governor, Antonio de Quintanilla. The *Arab* and all property except the brandy were returned in perfect condition. When the ship was turned over to Williams, Quintanilla ordered his men to salute the American colors and shout "viva la constitución, viva los Americanos."[15]

The master of the *Arab* reported to Stewart that while he was at Chiloé the royalist privateer *Jeneral Valdez* was fitting out to join the *Quintanilla*, which was already in operation. These two ships, especially the latter, caused the neutral naval commanders on the west coast considerable anxiety. During her active period the *Quintanilla* captured as prize the American brig *Frederick* and looted the brig *Winifred* and the schooner *Amanda* at the royalist port of Quilca.[16] Another vessel, the schooner *Adonis*, was made a prize but was rescued by the *Peruviano*. Early in December, while the *Franklin* was lying in Valparaiso, Stewart learned that the *Quintanilla* was operating off the Peruvian coast and immediately sailed for the Intermedios to put a stop to her depredations.[17]

When the *Franklin* arrived at Quilca, the *Quintanilla* had sailed, but the *Winifred* was still there with much of her equipage missing. On the way back to his flagship from a courtesy call on the commandant of Quilca, the commodore's barge apprehended and took in tow a boat belonging to the privateer. The boat was later returned to the commandant, but the seven crewmen were kept as prisoners on the *Franklin*. From Quilca, Stewart organized an intensive hunt for the privateer. One of her victims, the *Amanda*, was chartered, armed, and manned with a navy crew under Lieutenant Hammersley with orders to patrol the coast. A flotilla of boats was equipped and manned to search the bays and inlets inshore.[18]

All these efforts failed to net the *Quintanilla* and threatened to rupture the hitherto friendly relations Stewart had maintained with the royalist high command. Some of the commodore's measures were highly arbitrary and took place in the territorial waters of the Spanish viceroyalty. On one occasion he summarily suspended all boating at Quilca, and even the commandant's boat, with that official embarked, was ordered back to shore to prevent possible intercourse with the pirate. These measures brought immediate reactions. General Geronimo Valdez, commander of royalist forces in southern Peru, claimed that Stewart's measures were unneutral and constituted acts of war against Spain. Valdez and the viceroy asserted that the *Quintanilla* was lawfully commissioned by an officer of His Catholic Majesty, the governor of Chiloé, and any damage claimed as a result of her actions should be submitted to the

Spanish government, which would willingly make full investigation of the complaints, punish any illegal acts, and make reparations for any damages done contrary to law.

Legally, Stewart was in a shaky position vis-à-vis the royalist government, but he doggedly maintained that it was his duty to protect United States shipping from piratical attacks in the absence of Spanish action to do so. With his usual legal acumen, he seized on the fact that the *Quintanilla* was despoiling neutrals at ports supposedly under the protection of the government that had issued her commission as proof that she was more pirate than privateer. It was a novel experience for the commodore to hear the royalist's accusations that United States naval forces and merchantmen were partial to the cause of the patriots. From La Serna came a protest: "The notoriety of certain acts justifies me in suggesting to you that the dissidents of these countries have been treated with a consideration, both by the officers of the United States naval forces and by those of other nations, neutral toward Spain, which is not consistent with strict neutrality." Colonel Rafael Pero, sent by Valdez to investigate Stewart's campaign against the *Quintanilla*, "demanded" an explanation: "I demand of you, definitively, an explanation of your conduct . . . and reparation for the insult thereby offered to the Spanish nation. . . ." He alleged that the insult to the Spanish people was compounded by denying to them the same consideration paid the "gangs of dissidents," whose "illegal and unrecognized flags" were respected. When Stewart received this belligerent note from Pero he replied by abruptly breaking off any further discussion: "I have no further explanation to give you on that subject, and must now refer you to the Government of the United States, through the Spanish minister resident at the city of Washington."[19] Disregarding Spanish protests he continued to hunt the privateer.

Stewart's vigorous action produced some results. While his hunt was going on, the *Quintanilla* was forced away from the Intermedios ports. Some months later at Callao, he was gratified to hear through his friend Smith that La Serna had issued orders to the governor of Chiloé to restore all American ships and property with idemnification for any damage they may have sustained. The officers and crews accused of piratical acts were to be tried and punished if found guilty.[20] As for the *Quintanilla*, a few months later she was captured by a French sloop of war at Quilca and her captain sent to France for trial as a pirate.[21]

In obedience to orders from the Navy Department, Stewart returned to Valparaiso in February to await the arrival of his relief, Commodore Isaac Hull in the frigate *United States*.[22] The *Franklin* arrived in Valparaiso on February 25, 1824, and the remainder of his ships were ordered to assemble there by April 1.[23]

Once more plans were shattered by one of the frequent changes in the fortunes of war in Peru. The *Franklin* had been in Valparaiso less than three weeks when news was received that the patriot garrison of Callao had mutinied on February 4 and defected to the royalists.[24] Knowing that American shipping and property would be in a precarious position and that the *Dolphin* was no longer at Callao, Stewart hurried back to Peru, leaving orders in Valparaiso for the *Amanda* and *Dolphin* to join him. The *Peruviano* was left in the Chilean port with dispatches for the *United States* explaining the new state of affairs.[25]

When Stewart arrived at Callao he found the royalists in possession of the port city, Lima, and the central coastal area. Royalist General José Ramón Rodil was governor and commander in chief at Callao, and under his direction the Spanish were assembling ships to challenge the patriots' command of the sea. Torre Tagle had followed the example of the troops of Callao and joined the royalists. In the absence of an executive, the remnants of the patriot congress had invested Bolívar with dictatorial powers and moved the government to Trujillo.[26]

On February 15, Admiral Guise had arrived off the port with the *Protector* and four smaller vessels. Guise made the inevitable declaration of blockade—this time the entire coast from Callao to Cobija. The American ships caught in the harbor were, indeed, now in need of protection, both from the royalist garrisons ashore and the patriot ships at sea. When the garrison of the Callao forts mutinied, the merchantmen at anchor had been forbidden to move.[27] A period of anarchy followed in which some of the ships were plundered. In the absence of a United States man-of-war, the American masters appealed for protection to the commander of the British sloop *Fly* only to receive the reply that he dared not interfere because he had been warned that the many Englishmen ashore would be killed if he did so. The American merchantmen organized their own defenses as best they could and established guard boats to repel raiders from the shore. Some, such as the *Sabine*, took advantage of the disorganization among the mutineers to make good their escape, but six Americans remained, trapped under the guns of the Callao forts.[28]

Realizing that he could not hold Lima, Bolívar had ordered the destruction of all property that might be useful to the royalists. The general commanding at Lima, Henríquez Martínez, was instructed to issue orders to Guise in these or "similar" terms: "Vice Admiral Guise must enter Callao with the Squadron, *seize upon and take out all vessels without Exception, and those which he cannot remove he must sink or set on fire*. And all those vessels which he shall succeed in removing, *shall be considered as enemies property, to be condemned as good prizes and that he shall have his share of such prizes agreeably to the laws on the subject*." The General himself was advised: "Your Excellency must imagine that the country being lost, *all the ties of Society are broken, that there is no authority, nothing to be regarded, that you must deprive the enemy of the immense resources of which he is about to take possession*."[29]

Thus, vessels which had been trading with the patriots before the mutiny now became fair "prizes" although there was no legal basis for the metamorphosis. On the night of February 20 during the midwatch, two boatloads of sailors from Guise's ships attempted to take the brig *Herald* out from under the guns of the forts. Since the Peruvians refused to answer hails from the brig and tried to reach her decks by way of the forechains, they were assumed to be looters and were repulsed by the *Herald*'s crew. One of the Peruvians who managed to reach the deck was run through with a pike and pitched overboard. The ship *Providence*, anchored nearby, heard the alarm from the *Herald* and fired into the boats, forcing their withdrawal.[30]

A few nights later, Guise's men succeeded in setting fire to the

Justification by Court-Martial

old Spanish frigate *Venganza,* which was lying near the Americans. To escape the fire the Americans were forced to slip their cables. As they moved they were fired on by Guise's ships, but only the *China* suffered hits. When the master of the *Providence,* Captain P. Bowers, went aboard the *Protector* to protest the firing, Guise's reply was that he "would sink every damned American, that was there at anchor. . . ." During the confusion, Peruvian boats took charge of the *Providence* and *Herald* and towed them to an anchorage near the *Protector.* The remainder of the ships were allowed to anchor in the neutral grounds. Guise threatened to send the *Providence* and *Herald* to Trujillo for hearings before a newly established admiralty court on charges of resisting orders of the naval commander and killing a Peruvian crewman. When Bowers asked what the alternatives were, Guise coolly informed him that if the *Herald* would pay $2,000 to the officers and crew of the boats that had attempted to board her the brig would be released. The *Providence,* being newer and more valuable, was asked to pay $3,000 to escape detention. Under protest, the masters paid the requested amounts rather than face the loss of time and the uncertain outcome of a hearing before the court at Trujillo.[31]

When Stewart arrived in Callao the six American ships left in the harbor placed themselves under his protection with formal complaints against Guise's aggressive actions. Shortly before the *Franklin* left Callao, another incident involving Guise's blockade occurred—an incident that indicated the low state of the Peruvian Navy at that time. In late April the ship *America,* whose master was Henry L. De Koven, arrived off Callao, where she was stopped by the Peruvian brig *Macedonian,* informed of the blockade, and warned off, as required by international law. The commander of the *Macedonian,* one Captain Freeman, told De Koven, however, that if he had no arms or ammunition on board he might enter the port on payment of 25 per cent of the value of the cargo. When De Koven told him there was not that much cash on board, Freeman offered to escort the *America* down to Huacho and take out one-fourth of her cargo in lieu of cash. On De Koven's refusal, Freeman then offered to take the merchant captain into port the next morning to arrange for security until the cargo could be sold. In the meantime, De Koven's chief officer had dispatched a boat into the harbor with a note to Stewart. During the night the *America* managed to slip away from the *Macedonian* and the next morning headed into the harbor. As she entered she met the *Franklin* and *Dolphin* coming out to look for her and was assured of their protection. In his letter of appreciation for this service De Koven wrote: "Captain Freeman informed me there was no Peruvian Government except afloat."[32]

Incredulous at the bizarre demands of the patriot blockading ship, Stewart sent Hammersley out to check De Koven's story with the *Macedonian*'s commander. The lieutenant reported back that Freeman was under orders from Guise to blockade the port but "that the Admiral would not be very hard, and he would allow vessels to go in, that had not contraband of war on board, upon paying only twenty-five percent upon her cargo." Stewart turned this information over to Hull with the comment that it comprised "new principles of blockade and contribution," which "Admiral Guise has determined to enforce for the purpose of plundering neutral commerce."[33]

Stewart established cordial relations with Rodil and urged the latter to accept the recently arrived William Tudor as consul at Lima. His interest was more than casual since Tudor was Mrs. Stewart's brother. Tudor's position was awkward because his commission as consul at Lima and for the ports of Peru was obviously intended to accredit him to the now-defunct republican government. Rodil was willing to accept the commodore's brother-in-law but La Serna was less enthusiastic, and Tudor continued to function in an unofficial capacity. During this period Prevost faithfully continued to represent the United States with Bolívar's government at Trujillo and was critical of Tudor for not joining him there.[34]

A few days after Stewart reached Callao, Commodore Hull, in the *United States*, arrived at Valparaiso, where he received Stewart's dispatches. After provisioning ship, Hull ordered the *United States*, accompanied by the *Peruviano*, on to Callao, where they arrived on April 11.[35]

Stewart and Hull spent two weeks exchanging information

and discussing the problems of the Pacific Station. The two agreed that the *Dolphin* should remain under Hull's command in view of the uncertain military situation, the threats of Spanish privateers, and the patriot blockade. Her commander, Conner, was returned to the United States aboard the *Franklin* to answer the two-year-old charges preferred by Lieutenant Sawyer for permitting the display of Smith's silks in the cabin of the *Dolphin* at Arica. Lieutenant John Percival—he whose horse had been bayoneted from under him at Valparaiso five years previously—was appointed by Hull to command the *Dolphin*. On April 27, Stewart formally advised Hull that his own duties in the Pacific were completed, and directed the latter to assume "direction and command of the Naval Force to remain in the Pacific Ocean."[36] A week later he was homeward bound in the *Franklin*.

Stewart was well aware of the enmity he had incurred from Prevost and other pro-patriots in Peru and Chile. He also knew that his actions were being critically discussed in the home press, a fact that Hull was able to confirm. In his last account from the Pacific to the Navy Department, the homeward-bound commodore mentioned the "false and malicious reports" that he understood were being circulated in the United States to the effect that he had neglected public duties to further his own private interests, especially in the handling of specie. He seemed to believe the latter point comprised the principal complaints against him, and in his report defended the carrying of specie as a necessary and legal service. It is apparent from his remarks that he was as yet unaware of the variety and magnitude of the charges accumulating against him in Washington.[37]

The complaints against Stewart's actions in the Pacific began to reach the State Department in the latter part of 1823. They came from too many sources to be ignored. The most serious, from the viewpoint of inter-American relations, were the official representations of the patriot government of Peru.

In March and May, Valdivieso, the minister of state of Peru, forwarded his complaints through three separate channels: (1) directly to the secretary of state in the absence of Peruvian diplomatic representatives at Washington, (2) through the Colombian legation, and (3) by means of a note addressed to Prevost.[38] In each case the major complaints were that the *Franklin* had protected the landing of arms for use of the royalists and had breached the blockade of the Intermedios by preventing the *Belgrano* from taking the *Canton* at Quilca. Valdivieso's note to Prevost contained the additional charge that the commodore had dispatched a schooner (the *Dolphin*) to warn the royalists of a new patriot expedition, which left Callao for the Intermedios in May, 1823. This note referred to Stewart as an enemy of Peru and specifically asked for his recall.

Prevost forwarded the Peruvian minister's note with only one criticism of Stewart: "I confess I do not wonder at their Irritation as independently of Causes of Complaints involving the neutrality of the vessel under his Command he treats them with the utmost disrespect."[39] In subsequent letters Prevost himself made additional accusations against the naval commander and his subordinate officers. Among them were charges that the officers and men of the *Franklin* engaged in illicit trade with the financial backing of Smith and O'Sullivan; that Smith and Ward used the *Franklin* as a business office; and that a Spanish spy was transported from Callao to Quilca. Prevost's indictments against Stewart became more bitter as time went on and reached a climax in June, 1824, when he himself was called to answer charges of neglecting the interests of his countrymen in Peru.[40]

From Buenos Aires came a complaint that had no other apparent reason than the desire of that government to inform the United States of the unneutral actions its naval commander in the Pacific was performing to the detriment of the "American System." Bernardo Rivadavia, foreign minister of the United Provinces, forwarded a note to Caesar A. Rodney, first United States minister to Buenos Aires, asserting that Stewart was openly protecting and rendering services to the royalist army for no other reason than personal gain. He was alleged to have offered to help La Serna purchase warships in the United States. Rivadavia confessed that the only supporting evidence he had was a note from the "Commissioner of Buenos Ayres near the Authorities of his Catholic Majesty in Peru," but he "presumed" the governments of Peru and Chile would have taken care to inform the United States of events of such importance to American interests.[41]

The accusations in Crosby's article on the *Franklin*, forwarded by Prevost "for the perusal of the President," ranged from charges that Stewart engaged in private speculations with Smith, utilizing schooners built with public funds, to assertions that he transported horses and spies on the *Franklin* in the service of the royalists.[42] Crosby sharply contrasted the difference in treatment accorded the Spanish officers and the patriots by the commodore and officers of the *Franklin* in the realm of social affairs. At the Intermedios, "extravagant civilities were exchanged"; there was feasting and dancing ashore and afloat, plus gambling on shore. The *Franklin* gave a grand supper and ball for one hundred guests, "which was kept up until 'the flambeaux flashed against the morning skies.'" One lieutenant was reported to have won $15,000 gambling, only to lose it again. "The Spaniards staked their money like noble hearted fellows," according to Crosby. By way of contrast, patriot officers and sympathizers were alleged to have been prohibited from visiting the *Franklin* during her first visit to Callao. No salutes were fired and the commodore failed to visit the patriot dignitaries at Lima. An invitation to a reception given by San Martín was ignored by the naval officer.[43]

Another source of criticism of Stewart was Jeremy Robinson. Still hopeful for an appointment as agent or consul in Chile or Peru, Robinson bombarded the Department of State with voluminous reports impartially critical both of the United States naval officers and of the special and commercial agents in the Pacific area. He anticipated some of the gossip of Crosby but went beyond the mere recital of alleged misdeeds to examine the impact of Stewart's disdain for the patriots. Of all the commodore's critics Robinson grasped most fully the bitter resentment of the patriots when their "expectations" were frustrated by Stewart's indifference to their needs and demands.[44] During Stewart's first visit to Valparaiso, Robinson had commented on a diminishing friendliness toward North Americans in Chile and Peru and attributed it to the disappointment of the patriots at not receiving more aid and sympathy from the United States.

"They had expected great friendship from the U. S. and as they have not met with a more active exercise of it towards them compared with European Governments are disappointed and irritated," he wrote to Adams. "This irritation has been [under]-scored by the corruption of the merchants and commerce and the callous prostitution of national interest, primar[ily] by the commanders of neutral vessels of war on th[is] station in prosecution of their own individual private interests, to which they have with few exceptions sacrificed every other . . . consideration." The would-be diplomat continued: "This coolness has been augmented by the apathy of Commodore Stewart who has not met in a spirit of conscious reciprocity the amicable advances of the Government of Chile toward him."[45] One gets the impression that Robinson considered Stewart's "apathy" toward the patriots a greater blow to inter-American friendship than the many other misdeeds attributed to the naval officer.

Once more the administration gave public backing to its naval commander in the Pacific. In reply to Valdivieso, Adams stated "that no muskets, arms or ammunitions were introduced or landed at Arica by, or from, the ship *Canton*, the vessel which at that place, received the protection of Captain Stewart."[46] Adams' letter also served as an indirect repudiation and rebuke to Prevost since it was transmitted through him to the Peruvian minister.[47] After the statement that no arms were landed from the *Canton*, Adams wrote: "This fact is so fully established and so well known to Mr. Prevost, that had the correspondence enclosed in your letter of the 29th March, been communicated to him, it is not doubted that he would have satisfied your Excellency that the charge against Captain Stewart in relation to the Ship Canton is altogether without foundation."[48]

Adams did not deny that protection had been given the *Canton* and specifically asserted the obligation of the naval commander to provide such protection against an illegal blockade. "The only ground alledged of the intention of Captain Prunier to take the Ship Canton, then under the Protection of Captain Stewart, was the *suspicion* that the Canton had broken a blockade, declared by the Government of Peru from the 15th to 22nd degree of South latitude—which the Government of the United states cannot, consistently with the principles which it has invariably maintained, acknowledge as a lawful blockade—and no part of which the naval officers of the United States were, conformably to the Laws of Nations, bound to observe."[49]

In the covering letter to Prevost, Adams bared his teeth. First he told the agent: "I am directed by the President of the United States, to express to you the regret and concern, with which he has been informed of the differences which have occurred between you and the Naval Commanders of the forces of the United States in the Pacific, in regard to the execution of public duties." Then he castigated Prevost for not informing Stewart of the charges against him by Valdivieso and for not making "exertions" to convince the Peruvian government that "the charges against Captain Stewart were founded on erroneous impressions." Adams completely exonerated Stewart to Prevost and stated that the latter's own letters regarding the naval officer were written "without reference to any evidence." To make Prevost's humiliation complete, Adams informed him that the president "directs me to express to you his reliance that you will distinctly inform the Peruvian Government, that no muskets were landed at Arica, from the Ship Canton, the vessel which received the protection from the Franklin, and that no protection was given by Captain Stewart to the Pearl."[50]

In his letter to Prevost, Adams repeated the argument to Valdivieso that the blockade of the Intermedios was not recognized by the United States, and he defended the commodore's actions: "Captain Stewart could not have submitted to see the Canton captured under the very guns of his ships, without formally admitting thereby the validity of the blockade in its most licentious extent." For the benefit of the agent, Adams gave a plain statement of the policy of the United States toward paper blockades with instructions to transmit them to the Peruvian government:

> The President considers a blockade by degrees of Latitude, as unlawful not only in its general extent, but for every Port and Spot included within it. Were it otherwise, the mere fact of capture would legalize in any point within the limits of the proclamation, that which would be unlawful upon every other point. The proclamation is the notice to neutrals of the blockade: and the blockade of the

proclamation, must be precisely the same as the blockade in fact; else the whole is unlawful, and neutrals are not bound by it. This principle is too important to be surrendered to any belligerent party, however favorably disposed we may be to his cause; for we cannot concede it to him without yielding it alike to his enemy. You will distinctly declare this to the Peruvian Minister of State, to be the deliberate sense of the Government of the United States.[51]

In the same letter Prevost was informed of complaints against himself for neglecting his obligations to United States citizens in Peru. He was also reminded that he had never made a satisfactory explanation of a letter of September 30, 1819, purporting to come from Tomás Guido, who in 1819 represented the Buenos Aires government to Chile. Guido had written the supreme director of the United Provinces that Prevost was such an ardent partisan of South American independence that he had already performed several unneutral services on behalf of Chile and could be used to advantage by the patriots for other services if properly "managed."[52]

By a neat diplomatic riposte Adams prevented Peru's charges from becoming a matter of possible friction with other South American states. In reply to the Colombian minister's note Adams wrote that before entering into any discussion of the charges he was directed "to enquire whether the Government of Colombia holds itself responsible to the United States and their citizens for complaints they have to prefer against the officers of Peru and for the indemnities and reparations to which they are justly entitled...."[53] In a private conversation the minister, José María Salazar, declared he would do nothing further in regard to the case after Adams told him that a direct reply had been made to the government of Peru.[54]

After the arrival of the *Franklin* at New York on August 29, Stewart began to appreciate the magnitude of the accusations against him. When Lieutenant William K. Latimer, who had returned to the United States as a passenger in the *Franklin*, began to spread rumors in Stewart's home town of Philadelphia that the commodore had engaged in smuggling on the coast of South America and trading in horses between Valparaiso and the royalist ports, Stewart requested either that he be given a court-martial on Latimer's charges or that the matter be laid before the president so that he could take "such notice of this conduct of Lieut. Latimer, as will put a stop to the lawless looseness of his tongue...."[55]

Inquiry revealed that Latimer's stories were based solely on hearsay.[56] In the meantime, however, the administration determined that the gravity of the charges and the publicity involved, as well as the complaints of Peru, required that Stewart be tried by court-martial to stop all rumors and criticisms. On November 16, the secretary of the navy informed Stewart of this decision. "You have been already apprized that the Government of Peru has made complaints against a part of your official conduct," wrote Southard, "and that those complaints have been seconded by public rumor, and confirmed by the Agent of our Government in that Country. I have also to inform that other complaints have been made, though in a less imposing form."[57]

Stewart was formally suspended from duty on November 29, but the trial was delayed for nearly a year because of the difficulty of assembling the key witnesses or obtaining their testimony through interrogatories from South America. Stewart wished to call Hogan to his defense, but the president refused to recall the consul from Valparaiso for that purpose. He consented to recall Prevost for the dual purpose of testifying at Stewart's trial and giving an account of his own actions in Chile and Peru. Prevost's testimony was never obtained because he died in Peru before the trial. The testimony of another key witness—O'Sullivan, master of the *Canton*—was also debarred by death. The commodore exhibited perfect confidence in his spouse by suggesting that she be summoned by the government as a witness; he believed her evidence material but felt a "delicacy" in calling her himself.[58]

The trial got under way in Washington on August 18, 1824, before a court composed of twelve captains, many of whom had just sat on the court-martial that convicted Commodore Porter of violation of Spanish territorial integrity at Puerto Rico in his campaign against Caribbean pirates. Only the president of Stewart's court, Captain James Barron, was senior to the accused; Stewart's standing of fifth in seniority in all the navy precluded the appointment of a court composed of his seniors. An interesting note is the fact that in 1821 Stewart had been president of a court of inquiry which declared that during the War of 1812 Barron had "absented himself from the United States . . . contrary to his duty as an officer in the Navy of the United States."[59]

Stewart pled not guilty to an imposing array of forty specifications, supporting four general charges of unofficer-like conduct, disobedience of orders, neglect of duty, and oppression and cruelty. The most serious charges were unofficer-like conduct and disobedience of orders based on the accusations of Valdivieso, Prevost, and Crosby.[60]

The trial attracted national attention. The hearing of evidence and arguments of counsels took fifteen days. Most of the witnesses for the prosecution were officers of the *Franklin*. Eliphalet Smith appeared for the defense and swore that no arms were landed from the *Canton* and that there were no financial ties between him and the commodore. Three impressive witnesses were Stewart's predecessors in the Pacific—Captains Biddle, Downes, and Ridgely. These officers were unanimous in their testimony that it was invariable practice for English and American warships to carry passengers. Downes said that he was restricted to nonbelligerents while Biddle stated that he considered himself unrestricted by any orders at the time of his cruise. All three captains agreed that their technicians performed repair work for merchantmen on a reimbursible basis and that such service was essential in the absence of regular repair facilities on the west coast. In cases of necessity they supplied rigging and other material to American merchantmen. Downes stated that he "considered it the duty of the commander of an American man-of-war to supply vessels in all seas, and on all occasions, with articles of indispensable necessity which cannot be procured from the shore."[61]

There was equal unanimity on the practice of taking specie and bullion on board for transportation or safekeeping. Ridgely testified that it was an essential service for merchants in the Pacific; Biddle said the practice was universal. In response to a question by a member of the court as to whether it was difficult for a commanding officer "to avoid the suspicion of being partial," Biddle drove straight to the heart of the problem: "I believe it is impossible for any commanding officer to be in the Pacific without giving offence to one side or the other. The royal party, knowing the general feelings of our countrymen, are jealous of them; the patriots, on the other hand, *expecting too much*, are dissatisfied."[62]

On September 3, the court announced its findings. One by one, Stewart was acquitted of the specifications and charges. The court found the facts alleged in some specifications to be proved, but announced that the facts did not constitute violation of regulations. In regard to the specification that charged Stewart with preventing the Peruvian brig *Belgrano* from taking and sending in for adjudication the ship *Canton*, the court was of the opinion that, in so doing, "the said Charles Stewart was acting in strict obedience to his duty, as indicated both in his instructions and by the laws of nations; and that his conduct on this occasion was highly meritorious and praiseworthy." The performance of work for merchant vessels—in this instance, the making of sails for the *Canton*—was adjudged "in conformity with the practice of the service, in fulfillment of one of the duties which public vessels owe to the commercial interests of the nation, and essentially useful and necessary." The court found no occasion to comment on the highly controversial question of the carrying of specie and bullion, merely finding that the specifications alleging Stewart had done so, or permitted others to do so, in violation of the Peruvian revenue laws and in a clandestine manner at night, as "not proved."[63]

In naval court-martial proceedings a court may render a verdict of not guilty in one of several forms. A simple "acquittal" merely means that the charges are not proved to the satisfaction of the court. If the finding is "fully acquits," the court indicates that it finds no degree of culpability in the accused. A finding of "fully and honorably acquits" indicates not merely lack of culpability but the court's approbation of the actions of the accused in regard to the matters charged. In the case of Stewart the final judgment of the court was that "Captain Stewart has been most fully and most honorably acquitted of every, even the slightest impropriety."[64]

Chapter X

The Pacific Squadron Faces West:
Conclusion

While Stewart was making his way up the Atlantic homeward bound, the war in Peru entered its final phase. The main royalist army under Canterac was defeated by Bolívar at Junín on August 6, 1824. After this defeat the royalist forces in the Lima area withdrew to Callao, and the capital was evacuated in September. Bolívar entered Lima with a small body of troops on December 7. Two days later at Ayacucho, Sucre routed the royalist army under the personal command of La Serna. For all practical purposes the victory at Ayacucho ended the Wars of Independence in South America.[1]

It is fortunate that during this period the commander of the Pacific squadron was an officer with the temperament of Commodore Hull. Although by no means willing to abandon United States neutral rights to arbitrary seizures and the hazards of paper blockades, "Uncle Isaac," as he was affectionately known to his officers and men, was genuinely sympathetic to the patriot cause and deliberately tried to establish cordial relations with the new leaders.

Before leaving the United States, Hull was thoroughly briefed on the difficulties of his predecessors in the Pacific. He was given a copy of Stewart's orders as basic instructions, but the complaints against that officer gave rise to a whole battery of special instructions covering Hull's conduct as well as that of his officers and crew on station. He was informed of the charges against Stewart under investigation and directed to avoid such use of his ships. Explicit obedience to the orders prohibiting the carrying of property of either belligerent was enjoined. The authority to receive on board specie and other articles granted by the "act for the better government of the navy" was specifically restricted to property of United States citizens. Under no condition was it to be publicly advertised that specie would be taken on board. As a control measure, reports were to be made from time to time of the specie and other articles carried, with full details as to the amounts, the owners, the port of origin and destination, and the terms and conditions under which it was carried. Hull was warned to maintain friendly relations with Peru and Chile while affording "full protection ... to our citizens and their interests." A special warning was included to maintain the best possible understanding with Prevost and the new minister to Chile, Heman Allen, because it had "unfortunately happened heretofore" that differences had "existed between the agent and the officers in command of naval forces"—differences that had "done injury to our national character and interests."[2]

Adams and Samuel L. Southard, the new secretary of the navy, alarmed at the rift between the diplomatic and naval representatives in the Pacific, attempted to insure co-ordination of purpose and action by providing Allen and Hull with copies of the instructions issued to their opposite numbers. One paragraph of Adams' instructions to Allen read:

> The military operations by sea and by land upon the coasts of Chile and of Peru, have been conducted without due regard to the rights of neutral nations. Many citizens of the United States in pursuit of their lawful commerce, have suffered injuries and losses, reparation and indemnity for which has, in several cases been ineffectually

sought. A Frigate or a ship of the line have been successively stationed, for the last six years, in the Pacific Ocean, for the protection of the Commercial interests of our citizens in those seas, and have, more than once, been the necessary and only effectual protection they could obtain. One consequence of this has been that the commanders of our ships have become obnoxious to those belligerent officers, whose purposes of depredation they have counteracted, and have been made the subject of formal complaint, for the vigour and energy with which they have defended, and, in some instances rescued, the property of their countrymen.[3]

The new minister to Chile, with his family and secretary, were passengers on the *United States* from Norfolk to Valparaiso. During the long voyage the diplomat and the naval officer grew to know and respect each other. The pleasant relationship of the voyage continued in the conduct of official affairs on the station. The friendship extended to their families, for Mrs. Hull and her sister, Miss Jeannette Hart, accompanied the commodore to the Pacific.[4]

After relieving Stewart, Hull began to grapple with the problems of United States merchantmen at Callao, which remained the focal point of trouble. Although the port was under control of the royalists, neutral shipping came and went almost at will because the patriot blockade was haphazardly maintained by Guise's force. Royalist privateers brought in captured prizes, including two Americans, for condemnation proceedings. Other ships in the port were seized by the royalists on various pretexts. The American ship *China*, for example, was condemned for transferring cargo to the brig *Rimac* without a permit. Hull and Tudor joined in protesting the condemnations but to no avail. Tudor wrote Adams that Hull and the royalist commandant were on the worst of terms; Rodil accused the commodore "of insulting him with perpetual threats and other intimidations."[5]

Unlike Stewart the new squadron commander was usually successful in his appeals to the patriots, partly because of better diplomatic relations and partly because of the patriots' improved military situation. However, Hull did not rely entirely on diplomatic representations to protect American interests. He instituted a convoy system between Valparaiso and Guayaquil, which was facilitated by the arrival in July of the *Peacock*, under the command of Master Commandant William Carter. The *Dolphin* and the *Peacock* were used for convoy duty while the *United States* remained in the Callao-Chorillos area, the point of maximum threat. The convoy system served the dual purpose of protecting merchantmen from the raids of royalist privateers and conducting them through the patriot blockade. The *United States* was sometimes used to escort merchantmen whenever any of the blocking force was present. Thus, in September the frigate provided convoy back to Callao for American ships that had gone to Huacho after being denied entrance to Callao by Guise's ships.[6]

One of Hull's first acts was to send Lieutenant Hiram Paulding to Bolívar with a dispatch protesting the blockade and Guise's enforcement of it. Paulding found the Liberator at his headquarters at Huara and was received with marked friendliness. Bolívar promised that the blockade would be confined to Callao and Pisco and would be conducted in accordance with the law of nations. No place would be considered blockaded where there was not an actual force stationed. He agreed that Hull had cause to complain of Guise's actions and pledged that the Peruvian government would hold itself responsible for any just claims that might arise from the admiral's actions. The effect of this last promise was negated somewhat by a statement that Guise must be held personally responsible for any "private offence." Dispatches for Guise, containing instructions along these lines and prohibiting the levy of any duty by naval forces on vessels bound in or out, were entrusted to Paulding for delivery.[7] Bolívar's statements constituted by far the most favorable reaction any American commander had yet received from a patriot official in response to protests on the illegal blockades.

Hull and Bolívar maintained friendly relations. On Washington's Birthday, 1825, the Liberator paid an official visit to the flagship *United States*. On this occasion the yards were manned, the crew exercised at quarters, and a salute of twenty-one guns was fired in his honor as the head of state. Bolívar met and was attentive to the attractive Jeannette Hart, Hull's sister-in-law.[8] The cordiality of the commodore was reflected in the younger officers, who had great admiration for Bolívar and the patriots.

Tudor noted that the irritation exhibited by Spanish officers toward Americans was "increased by the decided part our young officers take with the patriots, and their undisguised ill will for the Spaniards."[9]

The officers of the *United States* and the British ships in the area got along together very well. On the Fourth of July the commanders and some of the lieutenants of the British warships in the harbor dined aboard the *United States* beneath an awning composed of the American and English flags. It may well have been the first joint meeting of British and American officers celebrating that day. Tudor remarked: "The experiment was a delicate one, but succeeded most harmoniously and seemed to give mutual satisfaction"—the fact that the day was Sunday moderated the festivities somewhat.[10]

The Spanish made one last spasmodic effort to regain control of the seas. In September the ship *Asia* and brig of war *Aquiles* arrived from Cádiz and joined three smaller royalist vessels under the guns of Callao.[11] As the Spanish ships stood into the harbor, Guise, in the much smaller *Protector*, offered to do battle but the Spaniards refused the challenge and proceeded to a safe anchorage under the guns of the fort. The Spanish commander excused himself by claiming that he had taken the *United States*, which had weighed anchor to clear the prospective battle area, for an enemy frigate because of her actions. On this occasion the sympathy of the American officers was overwhelmingly for the underdog patriots. As the Spanish ships passed the *United States* the latter was at quarters and according to one of the midshipmen aboard Hull's flagship, "it would have taken little provocation from her to have been complimented with a broad side, from Uncle Isaac."[12]

The two fleets met in an indecisive battle on October 8, after which the Spanish squadron once again took refuge in Callao. Later in the month they put to sea, presumably for the Intermedios. Hull dispatched the *Peacock* to locate the Spaniards and keep a discreet watch on their movements. This was the last movement of the Spanish warships to cause him any concern. After Ayacucho the *Asia* and her squadron left South America for Manila, but some months later the *Asia* surrendered to the patriots at Monterey. So ended the Spanish fleet in the eastern Pacific.[13]

Following the battle of Ayacucho, royalist resistance in most of Peru ceased. By April, 1825, the entire country with the exception of Callao was in the hands of the patriots. At Callao, Rodil obstinately refused to surrender and the port city was laid under strict seige by land and sea. In January the blockade, which had lapsed with the sailing of the Spanish squadron two months previously, was resumed by a Chilean squadron under the command of Blanco Encalada. The arrival of the Chilean squadron had been delayed by a severe storm that damaged the masts of the *O'Higgins* and the *Montezuma*, forcing the squadron into Coquimbo, where repairs were effected with the assistance of carpenters from the *Dolphin*.[14] Because Blanco Encalada maintained a legitimately tight blockade of Callao, Hull made no attempt to circumvent it. He did, however, continue the coastal convoy system because he feared the adventurers who formed a large part of the patriot crews would turn to piracy at the end of hostilities.[15]

Even so, a number of neutral vessels attempted to run the Callao blockade and were captured and sent to Chorillos for admiralty proceedings. Among these were the American vessels *Elizabeth Ann* and *General Brown*, the latter once more the cause of a dispute between the American naval officers and the patriot officials. While she was lying at Chorillos awaiting a hearing, Blanco Encalada ordered half of her crew sent to patriot warships and her sails removed to shore. Lieutenant Beverly Kennon, in command of the *Peacock*, refused to allow this order to be executed by the Chilean prize master, threatening to use force to prevent it. Kennon admitted that the Chileans had the right to hold the *General Brown* for adjudication but maintained that until she had been legally condemned they had no legal right to remove either men or equipment from the ship. He accused the Chileans of being up to their old game of impressment of seamen, and as for the sails, he bluntly, if undiplomatically, told Blanco Encalada that if they were put in the custody of the patriots they could be chalked off as a total loss to the merchantman. Hull backed Kennon in his stand and later incurred the displeasure of the Peruvian government when he claimed the ship was denied a fair hearing because of pressure exerted on the court by Blanco Encalada. The Peruvians countered that Hull, a military officer, was attempting to interfere in matters that were strictly the province of diplomatic representatives.[16]

As time passed, seizures of merchantmen became less frequent. In July, 1825, Hull reported to the Navy Department that he no longer required additional ships for the protection of commerce in South American waters, but looking to the north and west, he requested several small vessels for patrol of the coasts of Mexico and California and for an occasional visit to the Sandwich Islands, way point for ships bound to the Northwest and China.[17]

The *Dolphin*, under command of Percival, who had by now acquired the nickname "Mad Jack," was dispatched on a six-month cruise to the Sandwich and Mulgrave Islands to search for the mutinous crew of the whale ship *Globe*, who had murdered their captain at the Sandwich Islands and fled in the ship to the Mulgraves. While there, the *Dolphin* was to make a general survey of the situation in the central Pacific and recover some of the many Americans who had deserted their ships in the islands. The mission had been ordered in response to memorials from shipowners of Nantucket to the secretary of the navy and the president requesting protection for their ships at the Sandwich Islands. In addition to the search for the *Globe* and deserters, Percival was directed to collect specimens of seeds, plants, vines, and minerals typical of the places visited. He was also to ascertain the attitude of the natives toward the United States and, significantly, to determine future needs for naval vessels in the area.[18]

The dispatching of the *Dolphin* to the Sandwich Islands marked the beginning of a new phase in the mission and operations of the navy in the Pacific. Originally, the navy had been sent into the area to provide protection for United States citizens and their property from the hazards of a savage civil war. Since 1818 one or more vessels had been kept on the west coast of South

America for this purpose, but with the termination of the Wars of Independence and the coming of a restless peace to South America the responsibilities of the Pacific Squadron off Chile and Peru were reduced, if not altogether abolished. Under the prodding of New England shipowners its scope of operations was now being expanded to cover the entire eastern and central Pacific. The United States was looking westward.

Any contention that the United States naval forces in the Pacific were instrumental in helping the patriots gain their independence must be dismissed. Such help as the navy rendered the patriots was mostly in providing technical assistance in converting and repairing their ships, as when the *Ontario*'s crew helped convert the *Windham* from a merchantman to the warship *Lautaro* at Valparaiso in 1818. The *Macedonian* did salvage a derelict barge for San Martín's invasion forces, and the *Constellation* transported patriot troops to quell an uprising at Juan Fernández, but such occasions were rare.

The American commanders were sent into the Pacific with orders to protect the persons and property of United States citizens, especially the extensive fleet of whaling vessels and commercial ships operating on the west coast of South America. This protection was to be afforded "consistently with the laws of nations" and whenever and wherever such protection was needed and could be afforded. At the same time the neutrality of the United States was to be preserved. The protection of commerce and the maintenance of neutrality were not always compatible, as the United States naval commanders off the coasts of Chile and Peru soon learned. Divergent interpretations of the rights and duties of neutrals in time of war inevitably led to disagreements between the American officers and the belligerents.

Prior to 1818, when the patriots wrested control of the seas from the Spanish, most disputes were with the royalists; but with the shift in sea power, the patriots became the greater hazard to neutral shipping. Thus it happened that most disputes over neutral rights were with the patriots rather than the royalists. When differences over the conduct of neutral trade arose, American naval officers felt obliged to support United States merchantmen to the limits of their interpretation of international law and the force available to them.

The recognition of South American independence by the United States in 1822 and the announcement of the Monroe Doctrine in 1823 did not change the problems or the role of the navy in the Pacific because neither changed the conditions that had required the stationing of ships there in the first instance. As Stewart pointed out to Prevost, the recognition of the new states did not mean that the United States was willing to abandon its neutral rights and free movement of commerce in the Pacific.

No question caused the Americans as much trouble as the sweeping declarations of blockades—paper blockades—made by both belligerents. In 1818 the royalists declared the entire coast of Chile under blockade, and in 1819 the Chileans declared the coast of Peru from Guayaquil to Atacama under blockade. From that time until 1826 all or part of the Peruvian coast was under some form of blockade. At no time did either belligerent have sufficient ships to maintain such extensive patrols. In addition, the force stationed to watch a port would disappear for months at a time, yet when they reappeared and found a neutral ship within the proscribed limits it would be captured for violation of blockade, no matter how innocent her cargo. Under the United States concept of international law such blockades were not legal, and the naval commanders refused to recognize them, giving active support to merchant ships intent on evading them.

One of the greatest irritants to the United States commanders was the inordinate delay by the patriots in sending a ship accused of violation of the laws of war before a tribunal for adjudication. Sometimes it would take months for a ship to gain a hearing before an admiralty court. In the meantime, her cargo might decay and often her crew deserted to the patriots; thus, even if she were freed by the courts she would be financially ruined. Downes believed this to be a deliberate policy by Cochrane to destroy American commerce, and it was this reasoning which led him to release the *Louisa* from detention at Huacho in December, 1820.

Another grievance with the patriots arose from their efforts to entice American merchant seamen to desert to their naval ships with promises of high pay, rich prize money, and promotion. The American naval commanders combatted this practice as best they could by protesting the practice to the patriot officials and keeping apprehended deserters in custody for the masters of the merchant ships. The higher echelon of patriot leaders was much more co-operative in ordering the return of deserters to their regular ships than were the patriot ship commanders and minor port officials.

Related to the administration of blockades was the right of neutrals to carry freely the noncontraband property of a belligerent. The United States maintained that enemy goods of a noncontraband nature were free from capture on a neutral ship, whereas the patriots subscribed to the British contention that the presence of any enemy goods made a neutral ship liable to capture. This point was covered in the treaty of 1795 between Spain and the United States but was eliminated in the Adams-Onís Treaty, which became effective in 1821. There was no agreement one way or another with the new patriot governments; thus the question frequently gave rise to dispute. At times the question of ownership of property, especially specie, became important. The patriots claimed that the United States naval forces extended their protection to property claimed as belonging to American citizens, which was, in fact, the property of Spanish nationals or even of the Spanish government.

The Washington administration made the decisions of the commanders in protecting American commerce more difficult by issuing instructions that in one sentence declared the paper blockades of the patriots illegal and in another directed the avoidance of collisions with the patriots on the ideological grounds that the latter were struggling for independence and liberty. This the commanders did to the best of their ability, but when the inevitable conflicts arose they resolved the question in favor of protection of American commercial interests. They were careful to avoid pushing arguments to the point where hostilities were the only solution. Only in three instances—those involving the *Louisa*, *Galen*, and *Canton*—was such action taken. Usually there was an opportunity for referring disputes to diplomatic discussion. In the cases of the *Galen* and *Canton,* Ridgely and Stewart had clear legal grounds for refusing to surrender the merchantmen to the patriots because the merchantmen were still free at the time of the refusal. Downes had no such legal basis for the release of the *Louisa* since that ship was already in the possession of the Chilean Navy when he determined to release her.

Only rarely did the naval officers resort to force. Indeed, their orders forbade interference with a ship once she had been captured; such cases were then required to be handled by the special and commercial agents. But the release of many ships was secured by judicious use of protests to the royalist and patriot officials, and the mere presence of the warships inhibited the seizure of many others. Downes announced it as his policy to prevent the taking of an American ship in his presence but not to interfere once a ship was taken—a policy adhered to in the main by the other commanders, but violated by Downes himself in the case of the *Louisa!*

A few spectacular cases, such as those of the *Louisa* and *Canton,* demonstrate that naval commanders were willing to use force in the protection of American commerce where they considered it justified. But the publicity given such cases has obscured the other services rendered the merchant fleet by the warships. In ports they acted as physical protection from undue molestation and where necessary assisted the masters to maintain discipline by administering punishment to mutinous or recalcitrant crewmen. Between ports they provided convoy. At illegally blockaded ports they escorted the merchantmen in and out of the port through the blockade line. They acted as tenders for the merchantmen, providing the services of artificers for repair work on a reimbursable basis. Similarly, they supplied articles of equipage and even provided officers and crewmen in emergencies. Often the only medical service available was found on the naval vessels. A final service was the provision of a safe depository and transport for monies collected from sale of cargoes.

The carrying of specie aboard the naval vessels became big business. In effect, the naval vessels became floating banks. Alien as this may have been to normal naval duties it was an essential service to American businessmen in Chile and Peru. Without it trade soon would have been stifled for want of a medium of exchange. Moreover, it was universal practice among warships. The British considered the service so important to their merchants on the west coast that they deliberately arranged their warships' schedules so that merchants could depend on dispatching money around the Horn once every four or five months.[19] Downes and succeeding commanders were expressly authorized to bring specie to the United States. The commanders made a handsome profit in this business and used the authorization to the limit to cover transportation of specie for any civilians between South American ports as well as to the United States. Prevost, considering the practice as unneutral and detrimental to the patriots, made repeated appeals to Adams to stop it or at least to tighten the regulations allowing it, but no action was taken to do so until late 1823, when Hull was directed to restrict the service to United States citizens only.

The antagonism between Prevost and the naval commanders over the matter of specie and the legality of blockades in the Pacific was undoubtedly harmful to United States interests in Chile and Peru. In some respects Prevost was a noble figure, in others a tragic one. A doctrinaire democrat, he believed that the establishment of constitutional governments and democratic institutions in South America was far more important than the maintenance of neutral rights of commerce or the protection of private property. In his enthusiasm for the revolutionary cause he abandoned objectivity and looked upon attempts by the naval officers to maintain the rights of neutral trade as so much assistance to the royalists, which, indeed, it was after the patriots gained control of the seas. He was extremely legalistic in his approach to the question of ship seizures, believing no action should be taken until a ship was actually captured and brought in for adjudication, at which time legal representations could be made before the proper authorities. His confidence in the legal system of the patriots was not shared by the naval commanders. They considered it their duty not only to attempt the release of a ship by legal representations and negotiations after she had been taken but also, where possible, to prevent the taking by timely action, thus avoiding long, costly admiralty proceedings for the merchantman.

If the administration placed the naval commanders in an awkward position by its instructions, it gave them full backing when they got into difficulties with the South American governments or the pro-patriot sections of the United States Congress and public. Both Biddle and Stewart received the official backing of the government against complaints of patriot officials and critics at home, although it was considered necessary to subject Stewart to the ordeals of a demeaning court-martial in order to fully satisfy the doubts created in the public mind. In turn, it may be noted that both the administration and its naval arm placed the tangible interests of American commerce above somewhat nebulous ideological considerations. In supporting United States commercial interests they were upholding a long-established policy of freedom for neutral commerce on the seas.

One of the most pleasant aspects of naval operations in the Pacific for the Americans was the cordial relations that existed with the British Navy. The ties of blood and language, and the knowledge of common problems proved surprisingly strong such a short time after the bloodletting of 1812. The harbor that saw the destruction of the *Essex* by the *Phoebe* in 1814 saw a mutual agreement between British and American commanders to maintain discipline aboard the merchantmen of their former enemy. Biddle included British ships in his plans to elude the royalist blockade of Valparaiso. Downes escorted a mixed convoy of British and American merchantmen through the patriot blockade at Callao. Ridgely concluded an agreement with Hardy for mutual protection of their merchantmen. The Britisher Hall was sent by Hardy to Santa María to attempt the rescue of Americans as well as British from Benavides. There may have been bitter commercial rivalry in the Pacific, but Anglo-American naval co-operation blossomed off Chile and Peru during the South American Wars of Independence.

The vigorous, sometimes arbitrary actions of United States naval commanders to preserve the rights of neutral commerce on the west coast of South America during the Wars of Independence gained for them the gratitude of American merchants and shippers in the area. But such actions offended the patriots because most of the clashes over neutral rights occurred with the armed forces or officials of that faction. It may be that they contributed to the growth of the *leyenda imperialista*, which survives to this day to haunt the United States. There is no doubt that the first burst of mutual enthusiasm between the patriots and the North American naval personnel soon deteriorated to an attitude of suspicion and distrust. The causes are multiple.

Most United States naval personnel came to the Pacific friendly to the patriot cause. They believed that the South American revolutions paralleled their own revolution of 1776 and expected the same results in terms of democratic institutions and the achievement of such human rights as liberty, freedom of worship, freedom of speech—in short, the rights guaranteed to United States citizens in the first ten amendments of the Constitution. They quickly learned that there was a wide gap between their concept of democracy and its practice in the South American republics. They were shocked at the poverty and misery they saw among the masses. The general lawlessness and disregard for personal and property rights outraged their sense of moral values. They were disgusted by the venality of officials and the evasion of just financial obligations. Some were appalled by the monopoly of the Catholic church on the religious life of the people, by its opulence in the midst of poverty, and by the worldliness of its priests.

Some officers came to the conclusion that the South Americans were incapable of making a sudden change from the absolutism of the Spanish colonial system to a democratic government with institutions similar to those of the United States because of the ignorance of the masses and the lack of experienced leaders—an opinion shared by some of the more sophisticated patriots themselves, notably San Martín and O'Higgins. The latter believed that his people were not yet ready for democracy. In discussing the failures of representative governments throughout South America with Bland in 1818, O'Higgins told the American: "We have seen that our people are not like yours; they are not used to congresses; therefore congresses have often lost the country...."[20]

The naval commanders invariably formed a more favorable opinion of the royalist leaders than of the patriot high command. Being in an inferior position with respect to sea power, the royalists were forced to make concessions to keep their supply lines open. Viceroy Pezuela and his successor La Serna were well aware that they were dependent on neutral shipping for maintenance of their positions, at first in Lima and later in Upper Peru. Pezuela made deliberate efforts to win the friendship of neutral commanders, especially those of the United States, whom he seemed to favor over the British. The American naval officers found the Spanish officials far easier to get along with than the patriots. The Spanish gave careful and courteous consideration to the representations of the Americans and, where not clearly incompatible with the interests of Spain, acceded to their requests. Thus United States ships were restored to their owners and United States citizens released from the prisons of Callao at the request of the naval officers. The manner of conducting discussions and rendering decisions is an intangible factor but an important one in international relations. The Spanish were much more cosmopolitan and urbane than the patriots in this respect. They gave the impression of making concessions freely and graciously out of respect and friendship for their visitors and the nation they served rather than from any ulterior motive. Their concept of the rights of neutrals coincided much more closely with that of the United States than did that of the patriots and they were punctilious in acknowledging their international obligations. Yet the royalists did not grant concessions for nothing. On at least two occasions Pezuela made Biddle his dupe— once when he caused the naval officer to introduce a spy into the patriot capital on the mission to arrange exchange of prisoners, and again when he prevailed on him to carry his nephew, Colonel Olarria, to Rio de Janeiro.

By contrast, the patriots were often unsure of themselves and were inclined to see an affront in any questioning of their actions. Genuine efforts to reach understandings on questions at issue were often looked upon as interference in their affairs and attempts to hamper their battle for independence. With the dedication of all revolutionaries they were impatient with any viewpoints that did not coincide with their own. The patriots were often shrill in making demands, sullen in granting reasonable requests. True, these qualities were exhibited more often by minor officials than by the top leadership, but unfortunately the naval commanders came to believe that the only way to make themselves heard with any chance of success was by a show of force—a form of persuasion that came easily to the nationalistic veterans of the War of 1812.

The South Americans found the North Americans overbearing—the Spanish word *orgulloso*, meaning haughty and proud, was used more than once to describe the naval commanders. The patriots were angered by the refusal of the American officers to respect the paper blockades of the Peruvian coast and accused them of going beyond support of neutral rights to provide assistance to the Spanish. Likewise, the transportation of specie by the warships was declared to be of more assistance to the Spanish than to neutral merchantmen. The resentment of the patriots was heightened by the failure of the United States to actively support their fight against Spain in the name of democracy. Their expectations were frustrated. When it became apparent that the North American naval forces in the Pacific would not extend aid at the expense of the interests of the United States, their expectations turned to bitterness and resentment—vestiges of which linger to this day.

Abbreviations

The following abbreviations have been used:

ASP   *American State Papers*

DAB   *Dictionary of American Biography*

HAHR   *Hispanic American Historical Review*

LC   Library of Congress, Washington, D.C.

NA:DS   General Records of the Department of State, National Archives, Washington, D.C.

       CI   Instructions to Consuls ("Consular Instructions")

       DIAC   Diplomatic Instructions, All Countries

       ML   Miscellaneous Letters of the Department of State, 1789–1829.

       SA   Special Agents

NA:ND	Naval Records Collection of the Office of Naval Records and Library, National Archives, Washington, D.C.
CL	Letters from Captains ("Captains' Letters")
LTO	Letters Sent to Officers ("Letters to Officers, Ships of War")
MCL	Letters from Commanders ("Master Commandants" through 1837)
MLR	Miscellaneous Letters Received ("Miscellaneous Letters")
OL	Letters from Officers below the Rank of Commander ("Officers' Letters")
PL	Confidential Letters ("Private Letters")
NIP	*United States Naval Institute Proceedings*

Notes

Chapter I

1. Philip Coolidge Brooks, *Diplomacy and the Borderlands, the Adams-Onís Treaty of 1819* (Berkeley, Calif., 1939), p. 86 and *passim*.
2. Arthur Preston Whitaker, *The United States and the Independence of Latin America, 1800–1830* (New York, 1962 [1941]), p. 115 (hereinafter cited as Whitaker, *Independence*).
3. James Monroe, Inaugural Address, Mar. 4, 1817, in James Daniel Richardson, ed., *A Compilation of the Messages and Papers of the Presidents* (Rev. ed.: New York, 1897–1913), II, 573–79 (hereinafter cited as Richardson, *Messages*).
4. Secretary of the Navy (hereinafter cited as SecNav) to Captain Charles Morris, Navy Department, Oct. 16 and 19, 1816, Letters Sent by the Secretary of the Navy to Officers ("Letters to Officers") (hereinafter cited as LTO), XII, in the Naval Records Collection of the Office of Naval Records and Library, National Archives, Washington, D. C. (hereinafter cited as NA:ND). See table on pp. 211–12 for an explanation of the principal abbreviations used in the footnotes.
5. SecNav to Captain James Biddle, Sept. 30, 1817, NA:ND, Private Letters Sent by the Secretary of the Navy to Officers ("Private Letters") (hereinafter cited as PL).
6. Robert Erwin Johnson, *Thence Round Cape Horn* (Annapolis, Md., 1963), p. 3 and *passim* (hereinafter cited as Johnson, *Cape Horn*).
7. Luis Galdames, *A History of Chile*, trans. and ed. Isaac Joslin Cox (Chapel Hill, 1941), pp. 158–85 (hereinafter cited as Galdames, *History*).
8. Bartolomé Mitre, *Historia de San Martín y de la emancipación sudamericana* (Buenos Aires, [1945]), pp. 169–75, 253–54, 328 (hereinafter cited as Mitre, *San Martín*).

9. Galdames, *History*, pp. 194–95; Diego Barros Arana, *Historia jeneral de Chile* (Santiago, 1884–1902), X, 627–28, 630–32; XI, 123 n. 2, 135 (hereinafter cited as Barros Arana, *Historia jeneral*).

10. Mitre, *San Martín*, pp. 517–18; Donald E. Worcester, *Sea Power and Chilean Independence* (Gainesville, Fla., 1962), p. 17 (hereinafter cited as Worcester, *Sea Power*).

11. Alejandro Álvarez, *Rásgos generales de la historia displomática de Chile (1810–1910)* (Santiago, 1911), p. 186.

12. Joseph Byrne Lockey, *Pan-Americanism, Its Beginnings* (New York, 1926), p. 136 and *passim*; Charles Carroll Griffin, *The United States and the Disruption of the Spanish Empire* (New York, 1937), p. 68 and *passim* (hereinafter cited as Griffin, *Disruption*); Whitaker, *Independence*, p. 195.

13. Dexter Perkins, *The Monroe Doctrine, 1823–1826* (Cambridge, Mass., 1932), p. 43; Griffin, *Disruption*, p. 137.

14. Adams to Alexander Everett Hill, Washington, Dec. 29, 1817, in John Quincy Adams, *Writings of John Quincy Adams*, ed. Worthington Chauncey Ford (New York, 1913–17), VI, 280–83 (hereinafter cited as Adams, *Writings*).

15. Frederick L. Paxson, *The Independence of the South American Republics* (Philadelphia, 1903), p. 144.

16. Whitaker, *Independence*, p. 11.

17. Eugenio Pereira Salas, *United States Ships in Chile at the Close of the Colonial Period* (Santiago, [n.d.]), reprinted from the *Andean Monthly* (Jan. and Feb., 1945), p. 6 (hereinafter cited as Pereira Salas, *Ships*); Samuel Eliot Morison, *The Maritime History of Massachusetts, 1783–1860* (Rev. ed.: Boston, 1941), pp. 59–60 (hereinafter cited as Morison, *Maritime History*); Timothy Pitkin, *A Statistical View of the Commerce of the United States* (New York, 1817), p. 230.

18. Morison, *Maritime History*, pp. 61–62; Pereira Salas, *Ships*, pp. 6–8.

19. Monroe to Madison, June 27, [1816], draft copy, Monroe Papers, XXIV, Library of Congress, Washington, D.C. (hereinafter cited as LC).

20. Whitaker, *Independence*, pp. 283–85; H. W. S. Cleveland, *Voyages of a Merchant Navigator* (New York, 1886), p. 168 (hereinafter cited as H. W. S. Cleveland, *Merchant Navigator*); [Jose Toribio Medina], "Prologo" to *Diario de un joven norte-americano detenido en Chile durante el período revolucionario de 1817 a 1819* by [Isaac F. Coffin], translated from the English by J. T. M. (Santiago, 1898), p. 19 (hereinafter cited as Coffin, *Diario*).

21. Joaquín de Pezuela, *Memoria de gobierno* ("Publicaciones de la Escuela de Estudios Hispano-Americanos de Sevilla," No. XXVI [Sevilla, 1947]), pp. 264–65 (hereinafter cited as Pezuela, *Memoria*); Pezuela to Alexandro de Hoxe (Governor and Captain-General of Panama), Lima, Aug. 31, 1818, copy, in Jeremy Robinson Papers, LC.

22. Griffin, *Disruption*, pp. 121–24; Samuel Flagg Bemis, *Latin American Policy of the United States* (New York, 1943), p. 39; Whitaker, *Independence*, pp. 167–88, discusses the work of newspapers and propagandists in creating a favorable attitude for the patriots.

23. *Niles' Weekly Register* (Baltimore, 1811–49), XIII (Jan. 31, 1818), 371–72.

24. John Quincy Adams, *Memoirs of John Quincy Adams, Comprising Portions of His Diary from 1795 to 1848*, ed. Charles Francis Adams (Philadelphia, 1874–77), IV, 56 (hereinafter cited as Adams, *Memoirs*).

25. *Annals of Congress, 1789–1824* (Washington, 1834–56), XXX, 740–43 (hereinafter cited as *Annals Congress*); see also Eugenio Pereira Salas, *La misión Bland en Chile* (Santiago, 1936), p. 9 (hereinafter cited as Pereira Salas, *Bland*).

26. *Annals Congress*, XXXII, 1467, 1474–1646; Whitaker, *Independence*, pp. 243–47; *Niles' Weekly Register*, XIV (Apr. 18 and May 2, 1818) 121–30, 156–65.

27. Griffin, *Disruption*, p. 137.
28. Monroe to Madison, draft copy, June 27, [1816]; Madison to Monroe, Montpelier, July 21, 1816—both in Monroe Papers, XXIV, LC.
29. Whitaker, *Independence*, pp. 152–55. At least two representatives to South America during this period were dismissed because they used their positions to further dubious business transactions, Thomas Lloyd Halsey at Buenos Aires, and Joseph Devereux with a temporary appointment as commercial agent to Chile and Peru. For a detailed account of executive agents' activities see Henry Merritt Wriston, *Executive Agents in American Foreign Relations* (Baltimore and London, 1929).
30. Worthington to Adams, Santiago, Feb. 27, 1818, in *Diplomatic Correspondence of the United States Concerning the Independence of the Latin American Nations*, ed. William R. Manning (New York, 1925), II, 915 (hereinafter cited as Manning, *Correspondence*).
31. Rush to Robinson, Mar. 24, 1817, and Adams to Robinson, Nov. 3, 1817, in Consular Instructions (hereinafter cited as CI), General Records of the Department of State, National Archives, Washington, D.C. (hereinafter cited as NA:DS), II.
32. David Porter to Carrera, Washington, Dec. 13, 1816, in William Miller Collier and Guillermo Feliú Cruz, *La primera misión de los Estados Unidos en Chile* (Santiago, 1926), pp. 223–25 (hereinafter cited as Collier and Cruz, *Primera misión*). Ironically, Carrera, just completing a mission on his own responsibility to the United States, but claiming to represent the Chilean government in exile, was himself a perfect example of the "party" agent.
33. Monroe to Poinsett, Apr. 25, 1817, Manning, *Correspondence*, I, 39–40; Poinsett to Monroe, Charleston, May 7, 1817, Monroe Papers, XXIV, LC.
34. Rush to Morris, Apr. 25, 1817, NA:DS, CI, II; extracts also in Manning, *Correspondence*, I, 38; SecNav to Morris, Apr. 19 and 25, 1817, NA:ND, LTO, XII.
35. Rush to Monroe, June 4, 1817, Monroe Papers, XXIV, LC. See Watt Stewart, "The South American Commission, 1817–1818," *Hispanic American Historical Review* (hereinafter cited as *HAHR*), IX (Feb., 1929), 31–59, for a detailed account of the South American Commission.
36. SecNav to Captain John Rodgers, President of the Navy Board, June 19, 1817, NA:ND, PL; SecNav to John Bullus (Navy Agent, New York), June 20, 1817, *ibid.*; Rodgers to Captain James Biddle, June 21 and 24, 1817, NA:ND, Area 11 File, 1806–1837, Box 2; Rodgers to SecNav, June 20, 1817, NA:ND, Miscellaneous Letters Received by the Secretary of the Navy (hereinafter cited as MLR), 1817, IV.
37. Rush to Caesar A. Rodney and John Graham, July 18, 1817, Manning, *Correspondence*, I, 42–45; Rush to Monroe, July 20, 1817, Monroe Papers, XXIV, LC.
38. SecNav to Biddle, July 21, 1817, NA:ND, LTO, XIII; Biddle to SecNav, New York, July 30, 1817, NA:ND, Letters Received by the Secretary of the Navy from Officers with the Rank of Captain ("Captains' Letters") (hereinafter cited as CL), 1817, III.
39. Rush to John B. Prevost, July 20, 1817; Rush to Worthington, July 24, 1817; Rush to Robinson, July 24, 1817; NA:DS, CI, II; SecNav to Biddle, July 21, 1817 (two letters same date), NA:ND, LTO, XIII.
40. Biddle to SecNav, New York, Aug. 14, 1817, NA:ND, CL, 1817, III; Rush to Rodney, Aug. 23, 1817, NA:DS, CI, II; Rush to Monroe, Sept. 26, 1817, Monroe Papers, XXV, LC.
41. Adams to Caesar A. Rodney, John Graham, and Theodorick Bland, Nov. 21, 1817, NA:DS, CI, II; also Manning, *Correspondence*, I, 47–49; SecNav to Captain Arthur Sinclair, Nov. 27, 1817, NA:ND, PL; Sinclair to SecNav, Near Cape Henry, Dec. 4, 1817, NA:ND, CL, 1817, V.

42. Kenneth Wiggins Porter, *John Jacob Astor, Business Man* (Cambridge, Mass., 1931), I, 240–41 (hereinafter cited as Porter, *John Jacob Astor*).
43. Adams to Prevost, Sept. 29, 1817, and Adams to Biddle, Sept. 29, 1817, NA:DS, CI, II; both are also in NA:DS, Diplomatic Instructions, All Countries (hereinafter cited as DIAC), VIII.
44. SecNav to Biddle, Sept. 30, 1817, NA:ND, PL; James Biddle, "Journal Kept by James Biddle of the *Ontario*, October 4, 1817–Mar. 22, 1819," NA:ND (hereinafter cited as Biddle, "Journal").
45. Adams, *Memoirs*, IV, 14–16; rough draft of questions submitted by Monroe to Heads of Departments, Oct., 1817, Monroe Papers, XXV, LC.
46. SecNav to Captain John D. Henley, Nov. 14 and 18, 1817, NA:ND, PL; Henley to SecNav, Dec. 24, 1817, NA:ND, CL, 1817, V.
47. Collier and Cruz, *Primera misión*, pp. 193, 252; Henry Clay Evans, Jr., *Chile and Its Relations with the United States* (Durham, 1927), pp. 16–18.
48. Morris to SecNav, U.S. Frigate *Congress*, Lynnhaven Bay, Sept. 24, 1817, NA:ND, CL, 1817, IV; Patterson to SecNav, Bay of Saint Louis, Oct. 15, 1816, *ibid.*; Henley to SecNav, U.S.S. *John Adams*, Off Amelia, Dec. 30, 1817, NA:ND, CL, 1817, V; Master Commandant John H. Elton to SecNav, U.S. Brig *Saranac*, Cumberland Sound, Sept. 13, 1817, NA:ND, Letters Received by the Secretary of the Navy from Commanders ("Master Commandants" before 1837) (hereinafter cited as MCL), 1817.
49. Adams, *Memoirs*, IV, 12; Adams to Monroe, Washington, Oct. 3, 1817, Monroe Papers, XXV, LC; Homans to Morris, Navy Department, Sept. 29 and Oct. 7, 1817, NA:ND, LTO, XIII; Charles Morris, "Autobiography," ed. J. R. Soley, *Proceedings of the United States Naval Institute* (hereinafter cited as *NIP*), VI (No. 12, 1880), 191.
50. Nicholas Biddle to Monroe, Philadelphia, Dec. 11, 1817, in Monroe Papers, XXV, LC.
51. Richardson, *Messages*, II, 583.

Chapter II

1. Adams to Prevost, Department of State, Sept. 29, 1817, NA:DS, DIAC, VIII; also in Manning, *Correspondence*, I, 45; Adams to Biddle, Sept. 29, 1817, NA:DS, DIAC, VIII; SecNav to Biddle, Navy Department, Sept. 30, 1817, NA:ND, PL; Biddle to Prevost, U.S.S. *Ontario*, New York, Oct. 2, 1817, and Prevost to Adams, New York, Oct. 3, 1817, NA:DS, Special Agents (hereinafter cited as SA), VI.
2. Prevost to Adams, Oct. 4, 1817, NA:DS, SA, VI; Biddle, "Journal."
3. Biddle to Bullis, New York, Oct. 3, 1817, NA:ND, CL, 1817, IV.
4. List of provisions which the Navy Department was to be requested to procure at Baltimore, dated Nov. 11, 1817, signed by Daniel Brent, Chief Clerk, NA:DS, CI, II. This list was a duplicate of those ordered at New York for the South American Commission when it was scheduled to take passage on the *Ontario*. Brent to Biddle, Oct. 6, 1817, *ibid.*
5. Johnson, *Cape Horn*, p. 1; David Porter, *Journal of a Cruise made to the Pacific Ocean by Captain David Porter in the United States Frigate Essex, in the Years 1812, 1813, 1814* (Philadelphia, 1815), I, 1 and *passim* (hereinafter cited as Porter, *Journal*).
6. Fletcher Pratt, *Preble's Boys* (New York, 1950), pp. 299–300, 308; Charles Oscar Paullin, *Diplomatic Negotiations of American Naval Officers, 1778–1883* (Baltimore, 1912), pp. 122, 224; Adams, *Memoirs*, IV, 307; *Annals Congress*, XXIX, 1798.
7. *Niles' Weekly Register*, XII (May 24, 1817), 200.

8. Horace Kimball, ed., *The Naval Temple* (Boston, 1816), pp. 239–40.
9. Allan Westcott, "Stephen Decatur," *Dictionary of American Biography*, ed. Allen Johnson and Dumas Malone (New York, 1928–37), V, 187–90 (hereinafter cited as *DAB*).
10. Biddle to SecNav, New York, June 27, 1817, NA:ND, CL, 1817, III.
11. Pereira Salas, *Bland*, p. 24; Adams, *Memoirs*, V, 163.
12. Prevost to Adams, Rio de Janeiro, Nov. 25, 1817, NA:DS, SA, VI; Biddle to SecNav, Valparaiso, Jan. 26, 1818, NA:ND, CL, 1818, I.
13. Pezuela, *Memoria*, pp. 120, 170, 227–28.
14. Biddle, "Journal"; David Conner, "Journal of the U.S.S. *Ontario*," LC, entry for Jan. 25, 1818 (hereinafter cited as Conner, "Journal"). Conner's journal is in several fragments, parts of which duplicate each other. He kept a rough journal in chronological order, which was later rewritten in narrative form.
15. Biddle, "Journal." It should be noted that this opinion was rendered over a year after the event.
16. *Ibid.*; Pezuela, *Memoria*, p. 227.
17. Prevost to Adams, Santiago, Feb. 9, 1818, NA:SD, SA, VI.
18. *Ibid.*
19. Conner, "Journal"; Biddle, "Journal."
20. Biddle to San Martín, Jan. 31, 1818, and San Martín to Biddle, Las Tablas, Feb. 1, 1818, in "Copies of Correspondence of James Biddle with Chilean Authorities," NA:ND, Letters from Officers Commanding Expeditions, Jan. 1818–Dec. 1885, I, (c). This series contains copies of Biddle's correspondence with Chilean officials annotated by him. It is apparently a copy of a "supplemental" report made to the secretary of the navy in June, 1819, in answer to attacks appearing in the press (Biddle to SecNav, Philadelphia, June 26, 1818, NA:ND, CL, 1819, III). It bears penciled title, "Cruise of the U.S.S. *Ontario*," and hereinafter will be cited as Biddle, "Cruise," to differentiate it from Biddle's "Journal."
21. Biddle, "Journal"; Conner, "Journal"; Biddle to SecNav, Valparaiso, Feb. 20, 1818, draft (not sent), copied in Biddle, "Cruise."
22. Conner, "Journal"; Luis de la Cruz to Biddle, Santiago, Feb. 5, 1818, and Tomás Guido to Biddle, Santiago, Feb. 7, 1818, copied in Biddle, "Cruise."
23. Biddle to SecNav, Valparaiso, Feb. 20, 1818, draft (not sent), copied in Biddle, "Cruise."
24. *Ibid.*; Biddle, "Journal"; Conner, "Journal."
25. The governor was not always an obstructionist. Jeremy Robinson relates that on one occasion when some ladies were wanted on board the *Ontario* in Valparaiso as a preventive measure against desertion, some were found willing to go out but were stopped by the civil officers. When Biddle remonstrated with the governor at this hindrance, the latter "issued a written order that all the w——s in Valparaiso should repair on board the *Ontario* without delay" (Jeremy Robinson, "Diary," Friday, June 19, 1818, Jeremy Robinson Papers, LC).
26. Biddle to De la Cruz, Valparaiso, Feb. 16, 1818, copied in Biddle, "Cruise."
27. Biddle to SecNav, Valparaiso, Feb. 20, 1818, draft (not sent), copied in Biddle, "Cruise."
28. Conner, "Journal."
29. Coffin, *Diario*, pp. 129–30.
30. *Ibid.*, p. 121.
31. Biddle, "Journal."
32. *Ibid.*; Conner, "Journal"; Biddle to Cabrera, Off Valparaiso, Feb. 14, 1818; Biddle to Cabrera, Valparaiso, Feb. 14, 1818 (2nd letter this date); Cabrera to Biddle, Off Valparaiso, Feb. 14, 1818; Cabrera to Biddle, Off Valparaiso, Feb. 14, 1818 (2nd letter this date); Biddle to SecNav, Feb. 18, 1818; all letters copied in Biddle, "Cruise."

33. Richard J. Cleveland, *Voyages and Commercial Enterprises of the Sons of New England* (New York, 1855) pp. 284–85 (hereinafter cited as Richard Cleveland, *Voyages*); H. W. S. Cleveland, *Merchant Navigator*, p. 168; Whitaker, *Independence*, pp. 283–84.

34. Coffin, *Diario*, p. 45 and *passim*.

35. Francisco Ribas to Thomas Lloyd Halsey, Esq., Concepción, Nov. 18, 1817, Ribas to Cleveland, Concepción, Nov. 20, 1817, Ribas to Biddle, Valparaiso, Feb. 3, 1818, and Ribas to Astor, Santiago de Chile, Mar. 10, 1818, copies, in Jeremy Robinson Papers, LC.

36. Richard Cleveland, *Voyages*, pp. 294, 323 and *passim*; Richard Cleveland to Mrs. Cleveland, Guayaquil, Apr. 10, 1820, quoted in H. W. S. Cleveland, *Merchant Navigator*, pp. 211–12.

37. Conner, "Journal"; Biddle, "Cruise"; Biddle to De la Cruz, Valparaiso, Feb. 27, 1818, and Miguel Zañartu to Biddle, Santiago, Mar. 3, 1818, both copied in Biddle, "Cruise."

38. Pezuela, *Memoria*, pp. 192, 271.

39. Prevost to Adams, Santiago de Chile, Feb. 9, 1818, NA:SD, SA, VI; Conner, "Journal," Feb. 12, 1818, LC.

40. Biddle, "Journal"; Worthington to Adams, Mar. 12, 1818, Manning, *Correspondence*, II, 916.

41. Conner, "Journal."

42. Worcester, *Sea Power*, p. 22. See also Luis Novoa de la Fuente, *Historia naval de Chile* (2nd ed.: Valparaiso, 1944), p. 7 (hereinafter cited as Novoa, *Historia naval*).

43. Conner, "Journal."

44. *Ibid.*

45. Biddle, "Journal"; Henry Hill, *Recollections of an Octogenarian* (Boston, 1884), pp. 125–26 (hereinafter cited as Hill, *Recollections*).

46. Conner, "Journal."

47. Biddle, "Journal."

48. Coffin, *Diario*, p. 83.

49. James Biddle to Nicholas Biddle, Valparaiso, Apr. 11, 1818, Monroe Papers, XXVI, LC.

50. Biddle, "Journal."

51. Francisco Calderón to Excelentisimo senor capitán general y en jefe de las fuerzas unidas, Valparaiso, 31 de marzo de 1818, in *Documentos del archivo de San Martin*, ed. Comisión nacional del centenario (Buenos Aires, 1910), VIII, 183–84. Calderón wrote *Anchiman* instead of *Windham*. Barros Arana explains that the English phrase "The *Windham* East Indiaman" often caused the name to be translated to *Indiaman*, or even *Incliaman* in Spanish documents, *Historia jeneral*, XI, 473 n. 41.

52. Biddle, "Journal"; Conner, "Journal." Conner records the amount as $85,000 in his "Journal."

53. Biddle, "Journal"; Conner, "Journal."

54. San Martín to Biddle, Apr. 18, 1818, copied in Biddle, "Cruise."

55. Jeremy Robinson, "Diary," May 23, 1818, Jeremy Robinson Papers, LC.

56. Prevost to Adams, Santiago, June 20, 1818, NA:DS, SA, VI; Biddle, "Journal."

57. Affidavit of Solomon Townsend and Shubal Burr executed at Valparaiso, Apr. 27, 1818, before Henry Hill, copy, encl., Robinson to Adams, Santiago, June 8, 1818, NA:SD, SA, V.

58. Affidavit of Charles S. Carey, Valparaiso, May 1, 1818, copy, encl., *ibid.*

59. Enclosure to Prevost to Adams, Valparaiso, Apr. 9, 1818, NA:DS, SA, VI; also copy in Biddle, "Journal"; *Niles' Weekly Register*, XIV (July 18, 1818), 358.

60. James Biddle to Nicholas Biddle, Valparaiso, Apr. 11, 1818, Monroe Papers, XXVI, LC.
61. *Ibid.*
62. Nicholas Biddle to Monroe, Andalusia near Philadelphia, Sept. 28, 1818, Monroe Papers, XXVII, LC.
63. Conner, "Journal."

Chapter III

1. Conner, "Journal."
2. Robinson, "Diary," Fri., June 19, [1818], LC.
3. Prevost to Adams, Santiago, June 10, 1818, NA:DS, SA, VI.
4. Pezuela, *Memoria*, pp. 203, 247.
5. Prevost to Pezuela, Lima, Apr. 22, 1818, and Pezuela to Prevost, Apr. 25, 1818, encls., Prevost to Adams, Santiago, June 10, 1818, NA:DS, SA, VI; Biddle to Pezuela, Callao, Apr. 25 and 28, 1818, and Pezuela to Biddle, Apr. 27 and 28, 1818, encls., Biddle to SecNav, Valparaiso, June 12, 1818, NA:ND, CL, 1818, II.
6. Pezuela, *Memoria*, pp. 247, 259.
7. *Ibid.*, pp. 249, 254–55, 258–59.
8. Prevost to Adams, Santiago, June 10, 1818, NA:DS, SA, VI.
9. Pezuela, *Memoria*, p. 259.
10. Biddle to SecNav, Philadelphia, June 26, 1819, NA:ND, CL, 1819, III; Pezuela, *Memoria*, p. 259.
11. Biddle, "Journal."
12. Biddle to Pezuela, Callao, Apr. 25, 1818, and Pezuela to Biddle, Lima, Apr. 27, 1818, copies, encls., Biddle to SecNav, June 12, 1818, NA:ND, CL, 1818, II.
13. Biddle, "Journal."
14. Pezuela to Biddle, Apr. 27, 1818, Biddle to Pezuela, Callao, Apr. 28, 1818, and Pezuela to Biddle, Apr. 28, 1818, copies, encls., Biddle to SecNav, Valparaiso, June 12, 1818, NA:ND, CL, 1818, II.
15. Biddle to SecNav, June 12, 1818, NA:ND, CL, 1818, II; Barros Arana, *Historia jeneral*, XI, 548; Conner, "Journal"; Pezuela, *Memoria*, pp. 260–61.
16. Pezuela, *Memoria*, p. 260.
17. Robinson to Adams, Santiago, June 8, 1818, NA:DS, SA, V.
18. Pezuela, *Memoria*, p. 260.
19. Biddle to Monroe, Philadelphia, Aug. 16, 1819, NA:ND, CL, 1819, IV; Biddle to SecNav, Dec. 9, 1819, *ibid.*, V; Biddle to SecNav, Apr. 2, 1820, NA:ND, CL, 1820, II; Biddle to Adams, Dec. 7, 1819, NA:DS, Miscellaneous Letters of the Department of State, 1789–1829 (hereinafter cited as ML), Nov. 1–Dec. 31, 1819.
20. Biddle, "Journal."
21. Log of U.S.S. *Ontario*, LC.
22. Novoa, *Historia naval*, pp. 7–8.
23. Biddle, "Journal"; Conner, "Journal."
24. Biddle to O'Higgins, May 29, 1818, copy, encl., Biddle to SecNav, Valparaiso, June 12, 1818, NA:ND, CL, 1818, II.
25. Antonio José de Irisarri to Biddle, Ministry of State, May 30, 1818, copy, encl., Biddle to SecNav, Valparaiso, June 12, 1818, NA:ND, CL, 1818, II.
26. *Ibid.*; *Gaceta ministerial de Chile* (Santiago), 6 de junio de 1818 (hereinafter cited as *Gaceta ministerial*), in *Colección de antiguos periódicos chilenos*, ed. Guillermo Filiú Cruz (Santiago, 1951——), V, 50–52 (hereinafter cited as *Antiguos periódicos*); Pereira Salas, *Bland*, p. 26.

27. Biddle to Monroe, Washington, Aug. 16, 1819, NA:ND, CL, 1819, IV; Robinson to Adams, Santiago, June 8, 1818, NA:DS, SA, V.

28. Biddle to SecNav, June 12, 1818, NA:ND, CL, 1818, II; Prevost to Adams, Santiago, June 20, 1818, NA:DS, SA, VI; Conner, "Journal"; Barros Arana, *Historia jeneral*, XI, 549; *Gaceta ministerial*, 13 de junio de 1818, *Antiguos periódicos*, V, 71–72.

29. Biddle to Guido, Santiago, June 5, 1818, and Guido to Biddle, June 7, 1818, copied in Biddle, "Cruise"; Biddle to Monroe, Washington, Aug. 16, 1819, NA:ND, CL, 1819, IV.

30. Biddle to Adams, Philadelphia, Dec. 7, 1819, NA:DS, ML, Nov. 1–Dec. 31, 1819.

31. Conner, "Journal."

32. Pereira Salas, *Bland*, pp. 23–24, 28; Prevost to Adams, Apr. 9, 1818, NA:DS, SA, VI; Jeremy Robinson, "Diary," June 1 and May 31, 1818, LC.

33. Conner, "Journal"; Prevost to Adams, June 20, 1818, NA:DS, SA, VI.

34. Biddle, "Cruise"; Conner, "Journal."

35. *Ibid.*

36. Biddle to Monroe, Philadelphia, Aug. 16, 1819, NA:ND, CL, 1819, IV.

37. Log of the U.S.S. *Ontario*, LC; Biddle to SecNav, Apr. 2, 1820, NA:ND, CL, 1820, II.

38. H. W. S. Cleveland, *Merchant Navigator*, p. 183.

39. Biddle, "Journal"; Biddle to Pezuela, June 29, 1818, copy, encl., Robinson to Adams, Lima, Aug. 31, 1818, NA:DS, SA, V.

40. Cleveland to Astor, Lima, July 25, 1818, quoted in H. W. S. Cleveland, *Merchant Navigator*, pp. 187–91.

41. Robinson to Adams, Lima, Aug. 9, 1818, NA:DS, SA, V.

42. Pezuela, *Memoria*, pp. 281–83.

43. Biddle to Monroe, Aug. 16, 1819, NA:ND, CL, 1819, IV; Biddle to SecNav, Dec. 9, 1819, NA:ND, CL, 1819, V; Biddle to SecNav, Apr. 20, 1820, NA:ND, CL, 1820, II; Biddle to Adams, Dec. 7, 1819, NA:DS, ML, Nov. 1–Dec. 31, 1819; Conner, "Journal."

44. *Annals Congress*, XXXVI, 2156, 2172–73.

45. Biddle to SecNav, Aug. 19, 1818, NA:ND, CL, 1818, III; Biddle, "Journal." Prevost followed Biddle to the Columbia by about six weeks in the British sloop of war *Blossom*, whose commander, Hickey, had orders to formally return possession of the territory to the United States, which was done Oct. 6, 1818 (Prevost to Adams, Monterey, New California, Nov. 11, 1818, NA:DS, SA, VI).

46. Conner, "Journal"; Biddle, "Journal."

47. Biddle, "Journal"; Robinson to Adams, Lima, Dec. 6, 1818, NA:DS, SA, V.

48. Pezuela, *Memoria*, p. 380; Richard Cleveland, *Voyages*, pp. 336–38; H. W. S. Cleveland, *Merchant Navigator*, pp. 191–92.

49. Richard Cleveland, *Voyages*, p. 341.

50. Biddle, "Journal"; George D. Dods to SecNav, July 18, 1817, NA:ND, Letters from Officers below the Rank of Commander (hereinafter cited as OL), 1817, III; Pezuela, *Memoria*, p. 381.

51. Pezuela, *Memoria*, pp. 294–95, 297, 344, 356–57, 362–66, 371–73, 375–76.

52. *Ibid.*, p. 377.

53. Governor of Callao to Biddle, Fort Royal Philip of Callao, Nov. 9, 1818; Biddle to Pezuela, Nov. 9, 1818; and Pezuela to Biddle, Nov. 10, 1818; copied in Biddle, "Cruise."

54. An extract from the viceroy's letter without heading, date, or addressee, is copied in Biddle, "Cruise."

55. Biddle, "Journal"; Conner, "Journal"; Robinson to Adams, Lima, Dec. 6, 1818, NA:DS, SA, V.

Notes to pages 58–64   221

Chapter IV

1. Novoa, *Historia naval*, p. 6; Robinson to Adams, Valparaiso, Jan. 19, 1818, NA:DS, SA, V. The patriot ships were: *San Martin*, 64; *Lautaro*, 54; *O'Higgins*, 50; *Chacabuco*, 22; *Galvarino*, 18; *Araucano*, 16; and *Pueyrredón*, 12. The two frigates were those purchased by Manuel Aguirre in the United States.
2. Bland to Adams, Nov. 2, 1818, extract, Manning, *Correspondence*, II, 949.
3. Worcester, *Sea Power*, pp. 17–18; Barros Arana, *Historia jeneral*, XI, 83–85; Whitaker, *Independence*, p. 235.
4. Acting Secretary of the Navy, John C. Calhoun, to Downes, Nov. 4, 1818, NA:ND, PL.
5. William Laird Clowes et al., *The Royal Navy, a History* (Boston, 1897–1903), VI, 262–63. In 1830 Cochrane was reinstated in the Royal Navy in his proper place on the Navy List. He became a vice-admiral in 1841 and his Order of the Bath was restored in 1847, indicating that he was cleared of complicity in the stock market hoax.
6. Worcester, *Sea Power*, pp. 31, 36.
7. "Maritime operations in the first period of the Independence" [Chile], p. 17. Microfilm copy of an unidentified journal in the Naval Library, Navy Department, Washington, D.C. (hereinafter cited as "Maritime Operations"). There is no record of the author nor the source of this manuscript. It is obviously the translation of an early account that was copied by a person or persons unknown in a journal for use of the Navy Department. Some idea of the date of the original article can be had from a mention of Zenteno, the Chilean minister of war and navy during the independence period, as being alive when the original was written.
8. *Ibid.*
9. Worcester, *Sea Power*, p. 31.
10. F. A. Kirkpatrick, "Establishment of Independence in Spanish America," *Cambridge Modern History* (New York, 1902–12), X, 292, quoted in Worcester, *Sea Power*, p. 31.
11. Hill, *Recollections*, p. 117.
12. Cochrane to Biddle, Dec. 27, 1818, and Biddle to Cochrane, Dec. 28, 1818, copies, Biddle, "Journal."
13. Biddle to Cochrane, Dec. 28, 1818, (two letters this date), and Cochrane to Biddle, Dec. 28, 1818, (two letters), copies, *ibid.* The U. S. Navy regulations promulgated late in 1818 did require "gun for gun" from foreign officials. Art. 14 under "Salutes" stated: "Captains may salute foreign ports with such a number of guns as may have been customary on receiving an assurance that an equal number shall be returned but, without such assurance, they are never to salute."
14. Biddle to O'Higgins, Dec. 29, 1818, *ibid.*
15. Biddle, "Journal"; Biddle to Monroe, Aug. 16, 1819, NA:ND, CL, 1819, IV; Biddle to SecNav, Philadelphia, Apr. 2, 1820, NA:ND, CL, 1820, II. See also: Whitaker, *Independence*, 301–2; Eugenio Pereira Salas, *La actuación de los oficiales navales norte-americanos en nuestras costas (1813–1840)* (Santiago, 1935), pp. 34–35 (hereinafter cited as Pereira Salas, *Actuación*); and *American State Papers, Class VI, Naval Affairs* (Washington, 1834–1861), I, 671–762 (hereinafter cited as *ASP, Naval Affairs*).
16. *Annals Congress*, X, 1482–92; *ASP, Naval Affairs*, I, 510–34, 673–74; Calhoun to Patterson, Oct. 17, 1818, NA:ND, LTO, XIII; Morris, "Autobiography," *NIP*, VI (Nov. 12, 1880), 184. Biddle probably did not have benefit of the 1818 regulations before his return to the United States.
17. Whitaker, *Independence*, pp. 304–5. Whitaker gives a summary of the issues involved in transportation of specie and an account of the shift in United States

policy, which he attributes in part to a fear that Britain's near monopoly on the carrying of specie was harmful to U. S. commerce (p. 304 n. 48).

18. Pezuela, *Memoria*, pp. 284, 387, 396. Osorio was originally directed to proceed around the Horn on the corvette *Sebastiana* but actually proceeded to Spain via Panama. He was transported from Peru to Panama in the American merchant brig *Macedonian*.

19. Biddle, "Journal."

20. Cochrane to Supreme Director, Dec. 31, 1818, copy, encl., Prevost to Adams, Mar. 20, 1819, NA:DS, SA, VI; *Providence Gazette*, May 8, 1819, article "From our correspondent, Buenos Ayres, March 9"; *El Sol de Chile*, 29 de enero de 1819, *Antiguos periódicos*, VIII, 283–84. *El Sol* placed the value of money and Spanish property at 800,000 pesos.

21. Biddle, "Journal."

22. Cochrane to Biddle, Dec. 30, 1818 (2 letters this date); Biddle to Cochrane, Dec. 30, 1818 (2 letters this date); De la Cruz to Biddle, Dec. 30, 1818; Biddle to De la Cruz, Dec. 30, 1818, copied in Biddle, "Cruise."

23. Biddle, "Journal."

24. Log of the U.S.S. *Ontario*, Dec. 31, 1818, LC.

25. Echeverría to Prevost, Mar. 16, 1819, encl., Prevost to Adams, Santiago, Mar. 20, 1819, NA:DS, SA, VI; Robinson to Adams, Valparaiso, Jan. 19, 1819, NA:DS, SA, V; Antonio Álvarez Jonta to San Martín, Valparaiso, Jan. 10, 1819, *Documentos del archivo de san Martín*, VIII, 241–43. Álvarez Jonte, an Argentine, had been assigned by the Logia Lautaro to look out for and advise Cochrane as well as to direct revolutionary propaganda in Peru (Jacinto R. Yaben, *Biográfias Argentinas y Sud-Americanos*, I, 178–81).

26. *Gaceta ministerial*, 23 de enero de 1818, *Antiguos periódicos*, VI, 28–33.

27. Robinson to Adams, Valparaiso, Jan. 19, 1819, NA:DS, SA, V.

28. Worthington to Echeverría, Jan. 4, 1819; Echeverría to Worthington, Jan. 8, 1819, Manning, *Correspondence*, II, 1024–26.

29. Worthington to Adams, State of Chile, Santa Rosa or La Villa de Los Andes, Jan. 26, 1819, *ibid.*, 1026–36. Captain Charles Whiting Wooster was commander of the Chilean ship *Lautaro* and one of the few United States citizens to gain any great distinction in the Chilean naval service. He eventually rose to the rank of rear admiral and was in command of the patriot navy for a brief period but ended his days in poverty in San Francisco. For details of his career and other North Americans in the service of Chile see Worcester, *Sea Power*; Pedro Pablo Figueroa, *Diccionario Biográfico de Extranjeros en Chile* (Santiago de Chile, 1900); and Charles Lyon Chandler, *Inter-American Acquaintances*, (2nd ed.: Sewanee, Tenn., 1917).

30. Prevost to Adams, Santiago, Mar. 20, 1819, NA:DS, SA, VI; Robinson to Adams, Valparaiso, Jan. 19, 1819, NA:DS, SA, V; Worthington to Adams, Santa Rosa, Jan. 26, 1819, and Santiago, Nov. 11, 1818, Manning, *Correspondence*, II, 1022–23, 1026–36.

31. Prevost to Adams, Mar. 20, 1819, NA:DS, SA, VI; Prevost to Echeverría, Mar. 17, 1819, copy, encl., *ibid*.

32. Echeverría to Prevost, Santiago de Chile, original and translation, Mar. 16, 1819, encls., *ibid.*

33. Biddle, "Journal"; Biddle to SecNav, Philadelphia, June 13 and 15, 1819, NA:ND, CL, 1819, III, and Apr. 2, 1820, NA:ND, CL, 1820, II. The Navy Department authorized payment of the $15,000, but the firm claimed an additional $603.48 to cover a 3½ per cent premium on specie and interest from May 17, when the *Ontario* arrived in New York to June 12, the date payment of the $15,000 was authorized. Presumably this was paid, as Biddle informed the department he

considered the claim just and reasonable, since the coin had been expended in the public interest.

34. Biddle to SecNav, U.S.S. *Ontario*, Chesapeake Bay, Apr. 23, 1819, NA:ND, letter of transmittal for the "Journal."
35. Biddle to SecNav, June 26, 1819, NA:ND, CL, 1819, III.
36. Biddle to Messrs. James & Tho. H. Perkins, May 20, 1819, *Charleston Courier*, June 7, 1819, quoting *Boston Daily Advertiser*, May 25, 1819.
37. Biddle to Monroe, Washington, Aug. 16, 1819, NA:ND, CL, 1819, IV.
38. This statement of Robinson's is corroborated in his letter of Jan. 19, 1819, to Adams, NA:ND, SA, V.
39. Comments of Homans appended to Biddle to Monroe, Aug. 16, 1819, NA:ND, CL, 1819, IV.
40. Adams to John M. Forbes, July 7, 1820, NA:DS, CI, II; also Manning, *Correspondence*, I, 133–34; Prevost to Adams, Santiago, Jan. 6, 1821, NA:DS, SA, VI.
41. Robert Walsh, jr., to N. Biddle, [n.d.], Nicholas Biddle Papers, III, 1812–15, LC. This letter bears no heading nor date and is erroneously filed with the correspondence for the year 1813.
42. De la Serna to Biddle, Spanish legation in the United States, Philadelphia, Oct. 8, 1819, encl., Biddle to SecNav, Nov. 27, 1819, NA:ND, CL, 1819, V.
43. *Annals Congress*, XXXVI, 1696.
44. Biddle to SecNav, Apr. 2, 1820, NA:ND, CL, 1820, II.
45. SecNav to the Honorable the SPEAKER of the House of Representatives, Apr. 8, 1820, *ASP, Naval Affairs*, I, 672.
46. *Annals Congress*, XXXVI, 651, 2156, 2172–73.
47. Nicholas Biddle to Monroe, Andalusia near Philadelphia, June 14, 1821, Monroe Papers, XXX, LC.
48. SecNav to Captain Biddle, Mar. 26, 1822, NA:ND, PL.
49. Adams, *Memoirs*, V, 164–65.

Chapter V

1. Stewart to SecNav, U.S. Ship *Franklin*, Leghorn, Aug. 15, 1818, NA:ND, CL, 1818, III.
2. *Gaceta ministerial*, 7 de noviembre de 1818, *Antiguos periódicos*, V, 245; *El Argos de Chile*, ibid., VIII, 64.
3. Adams to Rush, Department of State, Washington, May 20, 1818, Adams, *Writings*, VI, 319–27; Adams to Gallatin, May 19, 1818, *ibid.*, pp. 312–13; Adams to George Washington Campbell, June 28, 1818, *ibid.*, pp. 366–80.
4. Adams to Gallatin, May 19, 1818, *ibid.*, pp. 312–13.
5. *Niles' Weekly Register*, XIV (Mar. 7, Apr. 11, May 12, and June 20, 1818), 31, 116, 167, 293; Pezuela, *Memoria*, pp. 372, 373, 376; see also Whitaker, *Independence*, p. 253.
6. Sinclair to SecNav, U.S. Frigate *Congress*, Hampton Roads, July 9, 1818, NA:ND, CL, 1818, III.
7. Adams to Rush, July 30, 1818, NA:DS, DIAC, VIII; Adams, *Memoirs*, IV, 155–56.
8. Robinson to Adams, Lima, Aug. 12, 1818, NA:DS, SA, V; Joseph Allen to Robinson, Ship *Maro*, Callao, Aug. 20, 1818, encl., Robinson to Adams, Lima, Aug. 31, 1818, *ibid.*
9. Robinson to Adams, Aug. 12, 1818, NA:DS, SA, V.
10. Prevost to Adams, Santiago, Feb. 9, 1818, NA:DS, SA, VI.

11. Worthington to Adams, Santiago, Feb. 27, 1818, Manning, *Correspondence*, II, 915.
12. Hon. S. Smith to SecNav, Baltimore, May 13, 1818, NA:ND, MLR, 1818, III. Writers of the period frequently used "China Sea," "South Seas," and even "India Seas" to refer to any part of the Pacific Ocean.
13. Adams, *Memoirs*, IV, 91–92.
14. SecNav to Bainbridge, May 30, 1818, NA:ND, LTO, XIII.
15. SecNav to Captain John Downes, Navy Department, June 16, 1818, *ibid.*
16. Porter, *Journal*, I, 4 and *passim*.
17. Hill, *Recollections*, pp. 134–35, 140.
18. SecNav to Downes, June 16, 1818, NA:ND, LTO, XIII; Downes to SecNav, June 23, 1818 NA:ND, CL, 1818, II; Bainbridge to SecNav, Boston, July 30, 1818, NA:ND, CL, 1818, III (Bainbridge incorrectly gave the chaplain's name as Uriah); John C. Calhoun to Monroe, War Department, Sept. 4, 1818, Monroe Papers, LC; SecNav to Doctor John Locke, Oct. 28, 1818, NA:ND, LTO, XIII.
19. SecNav to Downes, Sept. 2, 1818, NA:ND, PL.
20. *Ibid.*
21. Benjamin Homans, "By order of the President of the United States," to Downes, Sept. 2, 1818, NA:ND, PL. This order follows immediately after the secretary's order of the same date in the department order book. It is very peculiar that Homans should issue instructions in this manner although he frequently gave orders in the name of the secretary of the navy. The most likely explanation is that the secretary had signed his instructions in advance of the date of issue and the president, desiring amplification, directed Homans to issue them "By Order" in Crowninshield's absence.
22. Downes to SecNav, Off Cape Henry, Oct. 9, 1818, NA:ND, CL, 1818, IV.
23. SecNav to Doctor John Locke, Oct. 28, 1818, NA:ND, LTO, XIII; Downes to SecNav, Nov. 5, 1818, NA:ND, CL, 1818, IV.
24. Acting SecNav, J. C. Calhoun, to Downes, Nov. 4, 1818, NA:ND, PL.
25. Charles Gauntt, "Private Remarks of Lieutenant Chas. Gauntt, of the U.S. Ship Macedonian, John Downes, esqr., Commander, made during a cruise in the Pacific Ocean in the Years 1818, 19, 20, 21" (Unpublished private journal, NA:ND), p. 16 (hereinafter cited as Gauntt, "Private Remarks").
26. Downes to SecNav, Valparaiso, Jan. 28, 1819, NA:ND, CL, 1819, I.
27. Gauntt, "Private Remarks," p. 31; Downes to SecNav, Jan. 28, 1819, NA:ND, CL, 1819, I; Prevost to Adams, Santiago, Apr. 15, 1819, NA:DS, SA, VI.
28. Gauntt, "Private Remarks," p. 7; Charles J. Deblois, "Private Journal kept on board the U. S. Frigate Macedonian, John Downes, Esqr., Commander, on a Cruise from Boston, Massachusetts, to the Pacific Ocean, &c, &c, by C. J. Deblois, Captns Clerke, Said Frigate, in the years 1818 1819" (Unpublished private journal, NA:ND), entry for Jan. 30, 1819, and *passim* (hereinafter cited as Deblois, "Private Journal").
29. Hill, *Recollections*, p. 139.
30. Gustavo Opazo Maturana, "Lady Cochrane en Chile," *Boletín de la Academia Chilena de la Historia* (Santiago), X (Segundo trimestre de 1943), 9–17.
31. Deblois, "Private Journal," Apr. 15, 1819.
32. *Ibid.*, Feb. 2, 1819.
33. *Ibid.*, Feb. 4, 1819.
34. *Ibid.*, Feb. 2, 1819.
35. *Ibid.*, Feb. 22, 1819; Gauntt, "Private Remarks," pp. 33–36.
36. Deblois, "Private Journal," Jan. 31 and Feb. 27, 1819.
37. "Maritime Operations," p. 17.
38. Deblois, "Private Journal," Mar. 3, 1819.
39. *Ibid.*, Feb. 27, Mar. 2 and 4, 1819.

40. *Ibid.*, Feb. 3, 1819.

41. John Downes, "Narrative of a Cruise made by the United States Frigate Macedonian, John Downes, Esqr. Commander," NA:ND, CL, 1821, III (hereinafter cited as Downes, "Narrative Report"). This is Downes's narrative report of the principal events of the cruise submitted to the secretary of the navy from Boston under date of June 19, 1821. Most of the events narrated in this document were the subject of earlier and more detailed letter reports. This narrative is invaluable, however, as a concise, chronological account of the entire cruise. See also Deblois, "Private Journal," Feb. 22, 1819; Pereira Salas, *Actuación*, pp. 21–22 n. 3.

42. Downes, "Narrative Report"; Downes to SecNav, Valparaiso, Mar. 10, 1819, NA:ND, CL, 1819, I.

43. Deblois, "Private Journal," Jan. 28, Jan. 31, and Feb. 1, 1819.

44. Downes to Governor of Valparaiso, Mar. 12, 1819, copy in Deblois, "Private Journal," Mar. 12, 1819; *ibid.*, Apr. 5 and 23, 1819.

45. Log of the U.S.S. *Macedonian*, Fri., Apr. 16, 1819; Deblois, "Private Journal," Apr. 16, 1819; Gauntt, "Private Remarks," p. 41.

46. Deblois, "Private Journal," Mar. 11, 1819.

47. Gauntt, "Private Remarks," pp. 36–37.

48. Deblois, "Private Journal," Feb. 15, 1819.

49. Downes, "Narrative Report"; Log of the U.S.S. *Macedonian*; Deblois, "Private Journal," Mar. 13, 1819.

50. Charles Oscar Paullin, "Duelling in the Old Navy," *NIP*, XXXV (Dec., 1909), 1155–97. This is a study of the practice of dueling in the early nineteenth century and gives the details of some of the more famous naval duels, including the Perry-Heath and Barron-Decatur affairs; it lists some eighty-two duels from 1798 to 1850, including the ones herein discussed. Little was done to discourage or punish duelers and it was not until 1862 that there was a regulation making the practice an offense against the laws of the navy. Paullin states that during the first fifty years of the old navy, the mortality of naval officers resulting from duels was two-thirds of that resulting from naval wars. In 1845 Downes served as senior officer of a nine-man board to determine how dueling in the naval service could be stopped.

51. Deblois, "Private Journal," Mar. 2, 1819; Gauntt, "Private Remarks," p. 36; Downes to SecNav, Mar. 10, 1819, NA:ND, CL, 1819, I. There is no mention of the cause of the quarrel.

52. Deblois, "Private Journal," Mar. 3 and 4, 1819.

53. *Ibid.*, Mar. 9, 10, and 16, 1819.

54. Charles C. Jones, Jr., *The Life and Services of Commodore Josiah Tattnall* (Savannah, 1878), pp. 24, 26. It was Tattnall who as commander of the U.S. East Indian Squadron in 1859 gave assistance to the British at Pei-ho in spite of his neutral status, excusing this action by the remark that "blood is thicker than water."

55. Downes, "Narrative Report"; Hill, *Recollections*, p. 137.

56. Downes to SecNav, Valparaiso, Apr. 6, 1819, NA:ND, MLR, 1819, III; SecNav to Downes, June 25, 1819, NA:ND, LTO, XIII. In November, 1819, the bills were sent to Morris, then preparing to take over the deceased Perry's mission to Buenos Aires. Morris was instructed to get cash or provisions for the bills, but he had no better success than Downes (SecNav to Morris, Nov. 3, 1819, NA:ND, LTO, XIII; Morris to SecNav, Buenos Ayres, Feb. 15, 1820, NA:ND, CL, 1820, I).

57. Supreme Director to Jeremaí Robinson, Invitation to Banquet for Downes, 4 p.m., [April] 11, Jeremy Robinson Papers, IV, LC; Prevost to Adams, Santiago, Apr. 15, 1819, NA:DS, SA, VI.

58. Deblois, "Private Journal," Apr. 4, 9, and 11, 1819.

59. Secretary of State, Chile (Joaquín de Echeverría), to Downes, Santiago, Apr. 17, 1819; Downes to Secretary of State, Chile, Valparaiso, Apr. 20, 1819, copies, encls., Downes to SecNav, Valparaiso, Oct. 20, 1819, NA:ND, CL, 1819, IV.

60. Worcester, *Sea Power*, pp. 37–40; Barros, Arana, *Historia jeneral*, XII, 220–33; Pezuela, *Memoria*, pp. 411–12; *Gaceta ministerial*, 24 de abril de 1819, *Antiguos periódicos*, VI, 168–70.

61. Carlton Savage, ed., *Policy of the United States Toward Maritime Commerce in War* (Washington, 1934), I, 2, 17, 37 (hereinafter cited as Savage, ed., *Maritime Commerce in War*). The article providing for free goods in free ships in the treaty of 1795 with Spain was modified by the treaty of 1819 to the extent that it was effective only in the case of governments that also recognized its validity (*ibid.*, p. 42; Adams to Onís, Oct. 31, 1818, Adams, *Writings*, VI, 455–62).

62. Commercial treaties were concluded with Chile in 1832 and with Peru in 1836 (Savage, ed., *Maritime Commerce in War*, I, 44).

63. *Ibid.*, pp. 24, 118.

64. Robert D. Powers, "Blockade: For Winning without Killing," *NIP*, LXXXIV (August, 1958), 61–66.

65. Quoted in *ibid.*, p. 62.

66. Madison to Monroe, Jan. 5, 1804, quoted in Savage, ed., *Maritime Commerce in War*, I, 248–49.

67. *Ibid.*, pp. 36, 118.

68. Monroe to Onís, Mar. 20, 1816, NA:DS, Notes to Legations, II; see also Manning, *Correspondence*, I, 26.

69. Prevost to Adams, July 3, 1819, NA:DS, SA, VI.

70. Prevost to Downes, Santiago, Apr. 20, 1819, copy, encl., Prevost to Adams, Santiago, May 16, 1819, *ibid.*

71. The merchant brig *Macedonian*, owned by Perkins & Co. of Boston and captained by Eliphalet Smith, is often confused with the warship *Macedonian* since both of them operated on the west coast of South America at the same time. There was little doubt about the legality of the seizure of the *Montezuma*, as she was carrying contraband of war. The seizure of Captain Smith's specie, however, was different. In April, 1819, Chilean raiders from Cochrane's ships seized $80,000 being transported overland under Spanish guard. Another $60,000 put aboard the French schooner *Gazelle* for safekeeping by Smith's agent was seized at Ancon. Smith claimed that the specie was the private property of the owners of the *Macedonian*, paid to him by the Philippine Company from the lawful sale of the brig's cargo. The Chileans claimed that the money was Spanish property being smuggled out of the country. The case became a question for negotiation between the United States and Chilean governments. It was eventually settled by the Chileans agreeing to pay $104,000 plus interest. Two years later an almost identical case involving the same parties occurred in southern Peru. The latter case became a matter for international arbitration and was not settled until 1858. See John Bassett Moore, ed., *History and Digest of the International Arbitrations to which the United States Has Been a Party* (Washington, 1898), II, 1449–68 (hereinafter cited as Moore, *International Arbitrations*), for a brief summary of the first case and a complete account of the arbitration of the second case.

72. Prevost to Adams, Sept. 13, 1819, NA:DS, SA, VI.

73. Downes to The Supreme Director of Chile, Valparaiso, Apr. 23, 1819, copy, encl., Downes to SecNav, Valparaiso, Oct. 20, 1819, NA:ND, CL, 1819, IV.

74. Downes to Viceroy of Peru, at Sea, May 23, 1819 and Downes to H. E., the Viceroy of Mexico, Acapulco, Aug. 23, 1819, copies, encls., *ibid.*

75. Downes to SecNav, Panama, Jan. 5, 1820, NA:ND, CL, 1820, I.

76. *Ibid.*

77. Log of the U.S.S. *Macedonian*; Deblois, "Private Journal," May 5–14, 1819; Gauntt, "Private Remarks," pp. 42–45; Downes, "Narrative Report."

78. Whitaker, *Independence*, p. 308; see also Pereira Salas, *Actuación*, p. 44; and Deblois, "Private Journal," May 14, 1819. The usual fee for the commanding officer for this service was 2½ per cent. Deblois estimated that Downes would get a commission of $3,690, or a thumping six per cent on the $66,000 he claimed was received from the *Thomas*. Deblois was highly critical of his captain for assisting "smugglers" and said that some of the officers thought Downes would get into difficulty with the U. S. government for taking the specie on board.

79. Hill, *Recollections*, pp. 135–36.

80. SecNav to Downes, Aug. 27, 1819, NA:ND, PL.

81. Downes, "Narrative Report." The amount is arrived at as follows: the "considerable" amount from the *Thomas* in May, 1819, estimated by Deblois at $66,000; "about" $480,000 at Lima on Dec. 5, 1819, part for Panama, part for the brig *Macedonian* at San Blas, and part for the U.S.; "about" $490,000 at San Blas on Feb. 23, 1820, for Panama; $500,000 from shore and $130,000 from the British ship *Thais* at Mollendo on Jan. 13, 1821. $1,000,000 was landed at Rio de Janeiro on May 13, 1821, on the homeward trip.

82. Downes to SecNav, Valparaiso, Oct. 20, 1819, NA:ND, CL, 1819, IV.

83. Log of the U.S.S. *Macedonian*; Downes, "Narrative Report"; Downes to Viceroy of Mexico, Acapulco, Aug. 23, 1819, copy, encl., Downes to SecNav, Oct. 20, 1819, NA:ND, CL, 1819, IV.

Chapter VI

1. Gauntt, "Private Remarks," p. 68.

2. Log of the U.S.S. *Macedonian*.

3. Deblois, the chronicler of the ship's social affairs and small gossip, stopped writing his journal in July, having become sick with tuberculosis. He was sent home on a "sick ticket" across the Isthmus of Panama in December. Downes to SecNav, Panama, Dec. 27, 1819, NA:ND, CL, 1819, V.

4. Downes to Supreme Director of Chile, Oct. 29, 1819, copy, encl., Downes to SecNav, Valparaiso, Aug. 22, 1820, NA:ND, CL, 1820, III.

5. Echeverría to Downes, Oct. 29, 1819; Echeverría to Prevost, Santiago, Nov. 11, 1819; and Prevost to Echeverría, Buenos Aires, Jan. 9, 1820, copies, encls., Prevost to Adams, Buenos Aires, Jan. 10, 1820, NA:DS, SA, VI; Decree, signed by O'Higgins and Zenteno, Santiago, July 27, 1820, copy, encl., Downes to SecNav, Valparaiso, Aug. 22, 1820, NA:ND, CL, 1820, III.

6. Hill, *Recollections*, pp. 141–42.

7. Log of U.S.S. *Macedonian*; Gauntt, "Private Remarks," pp. 69–70.

8. Downes, "Narrative Report."

9. Antonio José de Irisarri to Chilean Minister of State, Department of Foreign Relations, London, Aug. 10, 1819, in *Archivo de don Bernardo O'Higgins*, ed., Ricardo Donoso, *et al.* (Santiago de Chile, 1946–48), III, 42 (hereinafter cited as *Archivo O'Higgins*).

10. *Ibid.*, p. 44.

11. Pezuela to Downes, Lima, June 1, 1819; Downes to Pezuela, Callao, Nov. 18, 1819, copies, encls., Downes to SecNav, Panama, Jan. 5, 1820, NA:ND, CL, 1820, I.

12. Downes to Pezuela, Nov. 22, 1819; Pezuela to Downes, Nov. 22, 1819, copies, encl., *ibid.*

13. Pezuela, *Memoria*, p. 415 and *passim*.

14. Downes to SecNav, Panama, Dec. 27, 1819, NA:ND, CL, 1819, V. This letter reports drawing of bills of exchange for $12,000, $3,000, and $15,000 in favor of George Bier. Premiums of 5 per cent were received on the first two and 2½ per cent on the last.

15. Gauntt, "Private Remarks," pp. 68, 73. An intriguing interlineation is made in Gauntt's journal for Dec. 6, over "Baron" Kavanaugh's name. Obviously added at a later date it states simply: "Turned out to be no Baron."

16. Pezuela, *Memoria*, pp. 513, 573–75.

17. *Ibid.*, p. 562; Downes, "Narrative Report."

18. Downes to SecNav, Panama, Jan. 10, 1820, NA:ND, CL, 1820, I; Gauntt, "Private Remarks," p. 77.

19. Gauntt, "Private Remarks," pp. 85–86.

20. Downes to SecNav, Valparaiso, Aug. 22, 1820, NA:ND, CL, 1820, III.

21. Gauntt, "Private Remarks," p. 86; Downes, "Narrative Report."

22. Hill, *Recollections*, p. 144; Log of the U.S.S. *Macedonian*.

23. Gauntt, "Private Remarks," pp. 85–86.

24. Deblois, "Private Journal," Apr. 3, 1819.

25. Gauntt, "Private Remarks," p. 93. It is probable that Gauntt's sympathy for the Carreras was shared by most naval officers through the influence of Porter, who was an avowed friend of the Carreras from the days of the *Essex* and the *patria vieja*. See Collier and Cruz, *Primera misión*. The only indication known to this writer that O'Higgins may have been conscious of any pro-Carrera sentiment among North Americans is found in Worthington to Adams, Santiago, July 4, 1818, Manning, *Correspondence*, II, 930–39. In this letter Worthington states that the government of Chile "view almost every citizen of the United States with peculiar jealousy, supposing them to be more or less attached to the party of the Carreras."

26. Downes to Supreme Director of Chile, Valparaiso, Oct. 29, 1819, encl., Downes to SecNav, Aug. 22, 1820, NA:ND, CL, 1820, III.

27. Downes to Supreme Director, Coquimbo, Feb. 21, 1821, copy, encl., Downes to SecNav, Off Boston Light, June 19, 1821, NA:ND, CL, 1821, III.

28. Quoted in Irisarri to O'Higgins, London, Jan. 1, 1820, *Archivo O'Higgins*, IV, 267–68.

29. Irisarri to Echeverría, London, Aug. 16 and 23, 1819, *ibid.*, III, 61–72; Irisarri to O'Higgins, London, Jan. 1, 1820, *ibid.*, IV, 263–71.

30. Downes to SecNav, Valparaiso, Aug. 22, 1820, NA:ND, CL, 1820, III.

31. Downes to Supreme Director of Chile, Valparaiso, Aug. 8, 1820; José Ignacio Zenteno to Downes, Office of Marine, Aug. 10, 1820, copies, encls., *ibid.*

32. Decree, dated Aug. 20, signed by Bernardo O'Higgins and Ignacio Zenteno, copy, encl., *ibid.*

33. Downes, "Narrative Report."

34. *Ibid.*; Downes to SecNav, Coquimbo, Aug. 31, 1820, NA:ND, CL, 1820, III; Gauntt, "Private Remarks," p. 94. The details of the seizure of the *Warrior* as reported by Downes do not agree with Pereira Salas' account (*Actuación*, p. 50), which states that the *Warrior* was taken by Cochrane off Coquimbo on August 25, three days before Downes's arrival at the northern port, that her crew were distributed among the ships of the expeditionary force, and that she herself was sent to Valparaiso, with hostages, for adjudication.

35. Downes, "Narrative Report."

36. *Ibid.*

37. Barros Arana, *Historia jeneral*, XIII, 88–89; Gauntt, "Private Remarks," p. 97; Pezuela, *Memoria*, p. 781.

38. Gauntt, "Private Remarks," p. 97; Downes, "Narrative Report."

39. Downes to SecNav, Off Callao, Nov. 20, 1820, NA:ND, CL, 1820, IV.

Notes to pages 112–20   229

40. Thomas, Earl of Dundonald, G.C.B. [Lord Cochrane], *Narrative of Services in the Liberation of Chili, Peru, and Brazil, from Spanish and Portuguese Domination* (London, 1859), I, 90.
41. Gauntt, "Private Remarks," p. 102.
42. Downes to SecNav, Off Callao, Nov. 20, 1820, NA:ND, CL, 1820, IV.
43. Pezuela, *Memoria*, pp. 797–98; Gauntt, "Private Remarks," pp. 100–1; Searle to Hardy, *Hyperion*, Callao, Nov. 8, 1820, and Hardy to Croker, *Creole*, Off Buenos Aires, Dec. 22, 1820, in *The Navy and South America, 1807–1823, Correspondence of the Commanders-in-Chief on the South American Station*, ed. Gerald Graham and R. A. Humphreys (London, 1962), pp. 322–23 (hereinafter cited as Graham and Humphreys, *Navy, Correspondence*).
44. Downes to Viceroy of Peru, Off Callao, Nov. 8, 1820, copy, encl., Downes to SecNav, Off Callao, Nov. 20, 1820, NA:ND, CL, 1820, IV.
45. Downes to Viceroy, Nov. 8, 9, 10, 11, 16, and 19 (two), 1820, copies, encls., Downes to SecNav, Off Callao, Nov. 20, 1820, *ibid.*
46. Viceroy to Downes, Nov. 9, 10, 14, 15, 17, and 19, 1820, copies, encls., *ibid.*; Pezuela, *Memoria*, pp. 797–98.
47. Downes to Viceroy, Nov. 19, 1820, and Viceroy to Downes, Nov. 19, 1820, copies, encls., Downes to SecNav, Off Callao, Nov. 20, 1820. The *Rampart* was refitted with the help of the *Macedonian*'s carpenters and artificers.
48. Log of the U.S.S. *Macedonian*; Downes, "Narrative Report"; Gauntt, "Private Remarks," p. 103.
49. Downes, "Narrative Report"; Gauntt, "Private Remarks," pp. 106–7.
50. Downes to SecNav, Off Paita, Dec. 10, 1820, NA:ND, CL, 1820, IV; Downes, "Narrative Report"; Log of the U.S.S. *Macedonian*.
51. Downes, "Narrative Report"; Downes to SecNav, Off Boston Light, June 19, 1821, NA:ND, CL, 1821, III; Downes to San Martín, Huacho, Dec. 26, 1820, copy, encl., *ibid.*; Gauntt, "Private Remarks," pp. 108–10.
52. Downes to San Martín, Dec. 26 and 28 (two letters), 1820, and San Martín to Downes, Dec. 27, 1820, copies, encls., Downes to SecNav, June 19, 1821, NA:ND, CL, 1821, III; Downes, "Narrative Report"; Gauntt, "Private Remarks," p. 110.
53. Downes to Supreme Director of Chile, Coquimbo, Feb. 21, 1821, copy, encl., Downes to SecNav, June 19, 1821, NA:ND, CL, 1821, III.
54. Downes to Prevost, Coquimbo, Feb. 24, 1821, copy, encl., *ibid.*
55. Barros Arana, *Historia jeneral*, XIII, 549 n. 4.
56. Prevost to Adams, Santiago, May 2, 1821, NA:DS, SA, VI.
57. Downes, "Narrative Report."
58. *Ibid.*; Downes to SecNav, Off Boston Light, June 19, 1821, NA:ND, CL, 1821, III.
59. Gauntt, "Private Remarks," p. 115; Hill, *Recollections*, pp. 145–56; Basil Hall, *Extracts from a Journal Written on the Coasts of Chili, Peru, and Mexico, in the years, 1820, 1821, 1822* (1st ed.: Edinburgh, 1824), I, 50.
60. Downes to Prevost, Valparaiso, Mar. 11, 1821, and Prevost to Downes, Santiago, Mar. 12, 1821, copies, encls., Prevost to Adams, May 2, 1821, NA:DS, SA, VI.
61. Prevost to Adams, Santiago, Jan. 6, 1821, NA:DS, SA, VI; Echeverría to Prevost, Ministry of State, Jan. 5, 1821, copy, encl., *ibid.*
62. Ridgely to Downes, Valparaiso, Mar. 16, 1821; Prevost to Downes, Santiago, Mar. 16, 1821; Downes to Ridgely, Mar. 16, 1821; Downes to Prevost, Mar. 18, 1821, copies, encls., Downes to SecNav, Off Boston Light, June 19, 1821, NA:ND, CL, 1821, III.
63. Downes to SecNav, Off Boston Light, June 19, 1821, NA:ND, CL, 1821, III; Gauntt, "Private Remarks," p. 123.

Chapter VII

1. Gardner W. Allen, "Charles Goodwin Ridgely," *DAB*, XV, 595–96.
2. James Fenimore Cooper, *Lives of Distinguished Naval Officers* (Philadelphia, 1846), I, 91–92 (hereinafter cited as Cooper, *Naval Officers*).
3. Livingston Hunt, "Trial of Lieutenant Ridgely for Murder," *NIP*, LVI (Nov., 1930), 985–90.
4. Charles G. Ridgely to SecNav, New York, June 28, 1819, and Ridgely to SecNav, Baltimore, July 8, 1819, NA:ND, CL, 1819, III.
5. Ridgely to SecNav, Coquimbo, May 16, 1821, NA:ND, CL, 1821, II; Ridgely to SecNav, Valparaiso, Nov. 2, 1821, NA:ND, CL, 1821, V.
6. Ridgely to SecNav, Baltimore, May 3, 1820, NA:ND, CL, 1820, II; Sinclair to SecNav, Norfolk, May 10, 1820, *ibid.*; SecNav to Ridgely, May 12, 1820, LTO, XIII.
7. SecNav to Ridgely, June 11, 1820, NA:ND, PL.
8. *Ibid.*
9. Arthur Preston Whitaker, "John Murray Forbes," *DAB*, VI, 506–7; Adams to Forbes, July 5, 6, and 7, 1820, NA:DS, CI, II; Adams to Prevost, July 10, 1820, NA:DS, CI, II; also Manning, *Correspondence*, I, 130–37.
10. SecNav to John H. Forbes, Esq., July 14, 1820, NA:ND, PL.
11. Ridgely to SecNav, At Sea, Aug. 11, 1820, NA:ND, CL, 1820, III; Ridgely to SecNav, Valparaiso, Mar. 7, 1821, NA:ND, CL, 1821, I; Charles G. Ridgely, "Journal of Charles G. Ridgely, Captain in the U. S. Navy, from 8th May 1815 till—[Mar. 30, 1821]. Now on board the United States Frigate Constellation," unpublished journal, Manuscripts Division, LC, entry for Jan. 25, 1821 (hereinafter cited as Ridgely, "Journal").
12. Ridgely to Lt. [John H.] Clack, At Sea, Nov. 1, 1820; Ridgely to SecNav, Rio de Janeiro, Nov. 24, 1820, and Dec. 14, 1820; all in NA:ND, CL, 1820, IV.
13. Ridgely, "Journal."
14. Ridgely to SecNav, Valparaiso, Mar. 7, 1821, NA:ND, CL, 1821, I. Cambreleng became deranged and died aboard the *Macedonian* before she sailed from Valparaiso. Over a year later, at the urging of the secretary of the navy, Smith Thompson, Ridgely reluctantly agreed to drop the charges against Randolph and Hall because of the difficulty of assembling witnesses. See Ridgely to SecNav, Baltimore, Dec. 20 and 28, 1822, NA:ND, CL, 1822, III; Feb. 2, 1823, NA:ND, CL, 1823, I.
15. Ridgely to SecNav, Valparaiso, Mar. 7, 1821, NA:ND, CL, 1821, I; Raines to Ridgely, Ship *Surry*, Sidney, Aug. 1, 1821, copy, encl., Ridgely to SecNav, Valparaiso, Nov. 2, 1821, NA:ND, CL, 1821, V. See *The Mariner's Chronicle* (New Haven, 1834), pp. 398–402; and R. Thomas, ed., *Interesting and Authentic Narratives of the Most Remarkable Shipwrecks, Fires, Famines, Calamities, Providential Deliverances and Lamentable Disasters on the Seas, in Most Parts of the World* (Hartford, 1834), pp. 323–25, for contemporary accounts of the incredible story of the sinking of the *Essex*. The former is the account of Captain Pollard of the *Essex*. The latter mentions the hiring of Captain Raines to stop at Ducie Island but credits the act to Downes rather than to Ridgely.
16. Ridgely to SecNav, Valparaiso, Mar. 7, 1821, NA:ND, CL, 1821, I.
17. *Ibid.*; Ridgely, "Journal."
18. Ridgely to SecNav, Coquimbo, May 16, 1821, NA:ND, CL, 1821, II.
19. *Ibid.*
20. *Ibid.*
21. Hardy to O'Higgins, *Augusta*, schooner, Off Buenos Ayres, Sept. 27, 1820, Graham and Humphrey, *Navy, Correspondence*, pp. 311–13.

22. Extract of Instructions to Captain Searle relative to blockade, [Dec. 11, 1820], *ibid.,* pp. 318-19.
23. Ridgely, "Journal"; Ridgely to SecNav, Coquimbo, May 16, 1821, NA:ND, CL, 1821, II.
24. Ridgely to SecNav, Coquimbo, May 16, 1821, NA:ND, CL, 1821, II.
25. *Ibid.*
26. Barros Arana, *Historia jeneral,* XIII, 166-71, 186-88, 193-95; Mitre, *San Martín,* pp. 700, 719, 722.
27. Mitre, *San Martín,* pp. 731-39.
28. Extracts from Ridgely's "Journal," encl., Ridgely to SecNav, Valparaiso, Nov. 2, 1821, NA:ND, CL, 1821, V.
29. Pezuela, *Memoria,* pp. 847-49; Barros Arana, *Historia jeneral,* XIII, 177 n.
41. Another passenger from Chile to England on board the *Andromache* was Lady Cochrane. The distaff sides of the Pezuela and Cochrane families formed a lasting friendship during the trip to England.
30. Pezuela, *Memoria,* p. 851.
31. It is possible that Ridgely and La Serna discussed the predicament of Pezuela and the *General Brown* at Lima but there is nothing in Ridgely's correspondence to support such a belief.
32. SecNav to Ridgely, Nov. 7, 1820, NA:ND, LTO, XIV; Ridgely to SecNav, Valparaiso, Nov. 2, 1821, NA:ND, CL, 1821, V.
33. Extracts from Ridgely's "Journal"; Thomas Sackville Forster to Ridgely, June 7, 1821; copy of Cochrane's order of Nov. 8, 1820, copies, encls., Ridgely to SecNav, Valparaiso, Nov. 2, 1821, NA:ND, CL, 1821, V.
34. Ridgely to Forster, June 7, 1821; Forster to Ridgely, June 11, 1821; Ridgely to Forster, June 12, 1821, copies, encls., *ibid.*
35. Pezuela, *Memoria,* p. 852; Pezuela to Ridgely, June 7, 1821, translation, and Ridgely to Pezuela, June 8, 1821, copies, encls., Ridgely to SecNav, Nov. 2, 1821, NA:ND, CL, 1821, V.
36. La Serna to Ridgely, Lima, June 8, 1821; Ridgely to La Serna, Callao, June 7, 1821; extract from Ridgely's "Journal," copies, encls., Ridgely to SecNav, Nov. 2, 1821, NA:ND, CL, 1821, V. When the peace negotiations first began, the English commodore, Hardy, was also invited by La Serna, through Captain Spencer of the *Owen Glendower,* to guarantee any treaty entered into between the latter and San Martín (Hardy to Croker, *Superb,* Valparaiso, July 28, 1821, in Graham and Humphreys, *Navy, Correspondence,* pp. 341-44, 342 n. 1).
37. Pezuela, *Memoria,* p. 853.
38. Ridgely to San Martín, June 15, 1821; San Martín to Ridgely, June 15, 1821; and extracts from Ridgely's "Journal," copies, encls., Ridgely to SecNav, Valparaiso, Nov. 2, 1821, NA:ND, CL, 1821, V.
39. Pezuela, *Memoria,* p. 854; John Heffernan (supercargo of the *General Brown*) to Ridgely, On board the United States Frigate *Constellation,* At Sea, July 29, 1821, copy, encl., Ridgely to SecNav, Valparaiso, Nov. 2, 1821, NA:ND, 1821, V.
40. Pezuela, *Memoria,* pp. 858-59. Ridgely made no mention of this arrangement in his reports to the Navy Department. He must have known of the presence of such high-ranking ladies on his ship and have had some knowledge of the reason for their presence. Of course, it is possible he was given some other plausible explanation by the conspirators.
41. *Ibid.,* pp. 854-58, 861; Extracts from Ridgely's "Journal," copy, encl., Ridgely to SecNav, Valparaiso, Nov. 2, 1821, NA:ND, CL, 1821, V.
42. Extracts from Ridgely's "Journal," copy, encl., Ridgely to SecNav, Nov. 2, 1821, NA:ND, CL, 1821, V.

43. Barros Arana, *Historia jeneral*, XIII, 279–81; Clements R. Markham, *A History of Peru* (Chicago, 1892), p. 250 (hereinafter cited as Markham, *History*).
44. Cochrane to Ridgely, Blockaded Port of Callao, July 12, 1821, copy, encl., Ridgely to SecNav, Nov. 2, 1821, NA:ND, CL, 1821, V.
45. Extracts from Ridgely's "Journal"; Ridgely to Cochrane, July 14, 1821; Cochrane to Ridgely, July 14, 1821, copies, encls., *ibid*.
46. Extracts from Ridgely's "Journal," copy, encl., *ibid*.
47. *Ibid*.
48. Hardy to Croker, *Creole*, Valparaiso, June 26, 1821, Graham and Humphreys, *Navy, Correspondence*, pp. 338–40; Barros Arana, *Historia jeneral*, XIII, 555.
49. Captain Basil Hall to Hardy, Mollendo, June 14, 1821, and Cochrane to Hardy, *General San Martin*, June 17, 1821, Graham and Humphreys, *Navy, Correspondence*, pp. 333–34, 336–37.
50. Extract from Ridgely's "Journal," copy, encl., Ridgely to SecNav, Nov. 2, 1821, NA:ND, CL, 1821, V.
51. *Ibid*.; Ridgely to Heffernan, At Sea, July 28, 1821, and Heffernan to Ridgely, July 29, 1821, copies, encls., *ibid*.
52. Extracts from Ridgely's "Journal," and Capt. E. Smith to Ridgely, Arequipa, June 17, 1821, copies, encls., *ibid*.
53. Extracts from Ridgely's "Journal"; E. Smith to Ridgely, Arequipa, June 17, 1821; Declaration of E. Smith to Michael Hogan, Arequipa, May 21, 1821; and Ridgely to Supreme Director of Chile, Santiago, Oct. 10, 1821, copies, encls., Ridgely to SecNav, Valparaiso, Nov. 2, 1821, NA:ND, CL, 1821, V; Moore, *International Arbitrations*, II, 1449–52.
54. Ridgely to SecNav, Valparaiso, Nov. 2, 1821, NA:ND, CL, 1821, V.
55. Ridgely to Supreme Director of Chile, Santiago, Oct. 10 and 14, 1821; Zenteno to Ridgely, Santiago, Oct. 12, 1821; and Echeverría to Ridgely, Santiago, Oct. 17, 1821, copies, encls., *ibid*.
56. Protests of Captain James Sheffield, Master, Brig *Hersilia* of Stonington, and William S. Lane, Chief Mate, Brig *Ocean* of Boston, sworn before Michael Hogan, Agent for Commerce and Seamen on part of the United States of America for Ports of Chili, Valparaiso, Sept. 2, 1821, copies, encls., *ibid*.
57. Captain Basil Hall to Ridgely, Valparaiso, Oct. 30, 1821, copy, encl., *ibid*.
58. Ridgely to Vicente Benavides, Valparaiso, Sept. 30, 1821, and Ridgely to Supreme Director of Chile, Valparaiso, Oct. 31, 1821, copies, encls., *ibid*.
59. Report, Survey Board to Ridgely, Valparaiso, Oct. 3, 1821, encl., *ibid*.
60. *Ibid*.
61. *Ibid*.
62. Barros Arana, *Historia jeneral*, XIII, 489 n. 21; "Maritime Operations," p. 92; Markham, *History*, p. 251; Worcester, *Sea Power*, p. 71.
63. Mitre, *San Martin*, p. 123.
64. Worcester, *Sea Power*, p. 72; "Maritime Operations," pp. 93–94.
65. Ridgely to SecNav, Nov. 2, 1821, NA:ND, CL, 1821, V.
66. *Ibid*.
67. Affidavit of Latham Cross, Master of the Brig *Persia* of New Bedford, Valparaiso, Oct. 15, 1821, and extract from the journal of Reuben Swain, master of the ship *Washington*, Oct. 15–16, 1821, copies, encls., *ibid*.; Michael Hogan to Adams, Valparaiso, extract in Manning, *Correspondence*, II, 1058–59; Barros Arana, *Historia jeneral*, XIII, 623–24.
68. Michael Hogan to Adams, Valparaiso, Nov. 4, 1821, Manning, *Correspondence*, II, 1059–60; Prevost to Adams, Lima, Dec. 17, 1821, NA:DS, SA, VI; also Manning, *Correspondence*, III, 1729–31.

69. Prevost to Adams, Lima, Feb. 6, 1822, NA:DS, SA, VI; also Manning, *Correspondence*, III, 1731–34.
70. Prevost to Adams, Lima, Mar. 4, 1822, NA:DS, SA, VI; also extract in Manning, *Correspondence*, III, 1734–35.
71. Testimony of Charles G. Ridgely in "Proceedings of Courts-Martial, Correspondence, Etc., Relating to the Conduct of Commodore Charles Stewart, on the Pacific Station, and of that of Lieutenants Joshua R. Sands and William M. Hunter" (hereinafter cited as "Stewart [Sands] [Hunter]–Court-Martial"), *ASP, Naval Affairs*, II, 487–610.
72. SecNav to Ridgely, Mar. 22, 1821, NA:ND, PL. These instructions were repeated in June, 1821, by SecNav to Ridgely, June 28, 1821, NA:ND, LTO, XIV.
73. Ridgely to SecNav, Rio de Janeiro, June 14, 1822, NA:ND, CL, 1822, IV.
74. James Paroissien to Robinson, Santiago, Mar. 3, 1822, Jeremy Robinson Papers, V, LC.
75. Ignacio Manning to Robinson, Pacific Ocean, Off Ancon, July 17, 1821, Jeremy Robinson Papers, V, LC.

Chapter VIII

1. SecNav to Stewart, Sept. 8, 1821, NA:ND, PL.
2. SecNav to Conner, Apr. 2, July 18, and Sept. 13, 1821, NA:ND, LTO, XIV.
3. Fletcher Pratt, *Preble's Boys* (New York, 1950), pp. 32, 318; George van Deurs, "A Commodore's Namesake," *NIP*, LXXXI (June, 1955), 678–84. Stewart was close enough to Monroe to correspond with him directly without going through the secretary of the navy. A letter to the president from Stewart, aboard his flagship *Franklin*, in the Harbor of Syracuse, [n.d.], containing recommendations on discipline has the following notation on the envelope: "Copies of letters from Commo. Stewart relative to suspension of the commanders in the Mediterranean, received from the President of the United States and which have not been communicated to the Secretary of the Navy" (in NA:ND, CL, 1819, III).
4. Stewart to SecNav, U.S. Ship *Franklin*, Gibraltar, July 22, 1819, NA:ND, CL, 1819, III; General Order, Stewart to Commanding Officers, U.S. Ship *Franklin*, Gibraltar, July 8, 1819, NA:ND, CL, 1819, III.
5. Cooper, *Naval Officers*, I, 251–52.
6. Stewart to Forsyth, Gibraltar, July 14, 1819, and Forsyth to Stewart, Madrid, July 23, 1819, copies, encls., Stewart to SecNav, Gibraltar, July 29, 1819, NA:ND, CL, 1819, III; Stewart to SecNav, Gibraltar, Feb. 19, 1820, NA:ND, CL, 1820, I.
7. Stewart to SecNav, New York, Sept. 17, 1821, NA:ND, CL, 1821, IV.
8. Stewart to SecNav, Off New York, Oct. 1 and 10, 1821, NA:ND, CL, 1821, V.
9. SecNav to Stewart, Sept. 8, 1821, NA:ND, PL.
10. SecNav to Stewart, May 8, 1821, NA:ND, LTO, XIV; Stewart to SecNav, May 17, NA:ND, CL, 1821, II.
11. SecNav to Stewart, June 9, 1821, NA:ND, LTO, XIV; Art. 24–"Regulations for the Promotion of Discipline, Cleanliness, Etc."–in "Rules, Regulations, and Instructions, for the Naval Service," *ASP, Naval Affairs*, I, 519.
12. "Stewart–Court-Martial," pp. 487–610.
13. Log of the U.S.S. *Franklin*, July 31, 1821–Sept. 14, 1824, NA:ND, III, entries for Jan. 29, 1822–Feb. 7, 1822.
14. "Stewart–Court-Martial," pp. 492, 494, 499, 504, 515, 517, 541–42; Stewart to Prevost, Callao, May 9, 1823, *ibid.*, p. 564; LeRoy, Bayard & Co. to SecNav, New York, Aug. 23, 1825, *ibid.*, p. 582; "Extract from statement of Lieutenant

Wm. A. Weaver," *New York Gazette*, Mar. 30, 1824, reprinted in *Charleston Courier*, Apr. 10, 1824. Since U.S. warships were under orders to contact merchantmen wherever possible and to convoy them whenever necessary, such a meeting as that described does not necessarily imply any improper motives or skulduggery.

15. Stewart to Conner, Mar. 16, 1822, and Conner to Stewart, Apr. 3, 1822, copies, encls., Stewart to SecNav, May 3, 1822, NA:ND, CL, 1822, I.

16. Stewart to SecNav, Mar. 23, 1822, NA:ND, CL, 1822, I; *Niles' Weekly Register*, XXII (July 13, 1822), 320; Lieutenant Thomas S. Hammersley, "Journal Kept on Board the United States Ship Franklin of '74 guns, Charles Stewart, Esquire, Commander," unpublished journal, covering the period 1821-24 on board the *Franklin*, Manuscript Division, LC (hereinafter cited as Hammersley, "Journal").

17. "Stewart–Court-Martial," pp. 547, 593.

18. Stewart to SecNav, Mar. 23, 1822, NA:ND, CL, 1822, I.

19. Johnson, *Cape Horn*, p. 30.

20. Stewart to SecNav, May 5, 1822, NA:ND, CL, 1822, I.

21. *Ibid*.

22. *Ibid*.

23. "Stewart–Court-Martial," pp. 517-18.

24. Adams to Stewart, Sept. 4, 1821; Stewart to Supreme Director of Chile, Valparaiso, Apr. 16, 1822, *ibid*., pp. 553, 568-69.

25. Stewart to Prevost, Callao, May 9, 1823, *ibid*., p. 564; Platt H. Crosby, document bearing the heading "These facts relative to the Franklin's Cruize in the Pacific were written in May last" (hereinafter cited as Crosby, "Facts relative to the Franklin's Cruize"), in "Cruise of U.S.S. Franklin, Commodore Charles Stewart, in the Pacific, 1821-24," NA:ND, Letters of Commanders of Expeditions, I, (b) (hereinafter cited as "Cruise of U.S.S. *Franklin*"). This last is a collection of letters and documents assembled from various sources bearing on the *Franklin's* cruise in the Pacific. It was obviously assembled for use in connection with Stewart's court-martial for misconduct while in command of the Pacific Station. Many of the documents are found in the report of Proceedings of Court-Martial of Commodore Stewart, in ASP, *Naval Affairs*, II, 487-610, and the latter will be cited where the letter or document appears in both sources.

26. "Stewart–Court-Martial," pp. 505, 517; Pezuela, *Memoria*, pp. 387, 541.

27. Pereira Salas, *Actuación*, p. 63; Crosby, "Facts Relative to the Franklin's Cruize."

28. Moore, *International Arbitrations*, II, 1449-68.

29. "Stewart–Court-Martial," pp. 493, 495, 500, 517, 546-47.

30. Prevost to Stewart, Santiago, Jan. 26, 1824 [1823], and Stewart to Prevost, Callao, May 9, 1823, "Stewart–Court-Martial," pp. 563-64.

31. Stewart to Marquis of Truxillo, supreme delegate of the government of Lima, Harbor of Callao, Aug. 9, 1822, and Stewart to Valdivieso, Callao Harbor, Aug. 20, 1822, *ibid*., pp. 571-73.

32. Whitaker, *Independence*, pp. 308-9 n. 62.

33. Crosby, "Facts relative to the Franklin's Cruize."

34. Ramírez to Stewart, Arequipa, Feb. 25, 1822, translation, and Stewart to Ramírez, United States Ship *Franklin*, Off Quilca, Apr. 20, 1822, "Stewart–Court-Martial," pp. 569-70.

35. "Stewart–Court-Martial," p. 517; Stewart to Conner, May 6, 1822, *ibid*., p. 558.

36. "Proceedings of a Court-Martial in the case of Lieutenant David Conner," ASP, *Naval Affairs*, I, 1073-79. The court-martial did Conner's career no harm. He later became commander of the Pacific Squadron. At the outbreak of the

Mexican War in 1846 he was commander of U.S. naval forces in the Gulf of Mexico.

37. Stewart to SecNav, May 5, 1822, NA:ND, CL, 1822, I; SecNav to Stewart, Sept. 8, 1821, NA:ND, PL.

38. "Stewart–Court-Martial," pp. 492, 495, 543–44, 548, 593; Agreement signed by Samuel Chandler (Master of the *Pearl*) and Charles Stewart, dated June 10, 1822, copy, *ibid.*, p. 565; Stewart to Henry, Arica, June 22, *ibid.*, p. 521; Stewart to SecNav, Valparaiso, Jan. 5, 1823, *ibid.*, p. 567.

39. *Ibid.*, pp. 492, 494–98, 511, 516, 544, 593.

40. *Ibid.*, pp. 495, 498, 544, 593; SecNav to Stewart, Feb. 26, 1825, NA:ND, LTO, XV; Stewart to SecNav, Philadelphia, Mar. 1, 1825, NA:ND, CL, 1825, II.

41. "Stewart–Court-Martial," pp. 490, 496, 512.

42. *Ibid.*, p. 495.

43. *Ibid.* pp. 517–18; LeRoy, Bayard & Co. to SecNav, Aug. 23, 1825, *ibid.*, p. 582.

44. *Ibid.*, pp. 492–93, 499, 501, 514, 546.

45. Juan García del Río and Diego Paroissien to Echeverría, Santiago, Mar. 14, 1822, "Cruise of the U.S.S. *Franklin*."

46. Echeverría to Del Río and Paroissien, Santiago, Mar. 15, 1822; Del Río and Paroissien to Minister of State, Chile, Santiago, Mar. 18, 1822, "Cruise of the U.S.S. *Franklin*"; Stewart to Prevost, Valparaiso, Jan. 19, 1823, "Stewart–Court-Martial," p. 563; affidavit of John O'Sullivan, commander and supercargo of the ship *Canton* of N. Y., before W. M. Hunter, First Lieutenant, U. S. Ship *Franklin*, Dec. 1, 1822, *ibid.*, pp. 578–79; affidavit of Horatio G. Ward before José María de la Rosa, Sept. 16, 1822, *ibid.*, p. 579; affidavit of Wm. January, first officer of ship *Canton*, before W. M. Hunter, First Lieutenant of Ship *Franklin*, Dec. 1, 1822, *ibid.*, p. 579.

47. "Stewart–Court-Martial," pp. 492, 494, 499, 504; Stewart to SecNav, Valparaiso, Jan. 5, 1823, *ibid.*, pp. 567–68.

48. Stewart to SecNav, Valparaiso, May 5, 1822, NA:ND, CL, 1822, I; Stewart to Prevost, Valparaiso, Jan. 19, 1823, "Stewart–Court-Martial," p. 563.

49. Barros Arana, *Historia jeneral*, XIII, 555; Hardy to Croker, *Creole*, Callao Bay, Nov. 14, 1821, Graham and Humphreys, *Navy, Correspondence*, pp. 349–50.

50. Prevost to Adams, Lima, Apr. 24, 1823, copy, in "Cruise of the U.S.S. *Franklin*"; also in Manning, *Correspondence*, III, 1739–41, and NA:DS, SA, VI.

51. Hammersley, "Journal"; "Stewart–Court-Martial," pp. 492–94, 495, 517; Stewart to Captain William Prunier, Off Quilca, July 12, 1822, *ibid.*, pp. 580–81; Stewart to SecNav, Jan. 5, 1823, *ibid.*, pp. 567–68.

52. "Stewart–Court-Martial," pp. 493, 495, 499, 588; Wm. Hunter and Thos. S. Hammersley to Stewart, U.S. Ship *Franklin*, Harbor of Arica, June 10, 1822, *ibid.*, p. 565.

53. Stewart to SecNav, Valparaiso, Jan. 5, 1823; Prunier to Stewart, Quilca, July 9, 10 (2 letters), 1822; Stewart to Prunier, U.S. Ship *Franklin*, Off Quilca, July 9, 1822; Prunier to Tomás Guido, Minister of War and Marine, *Belgrano*, July 13, 1822, translation—all in "Stewart–Court-Martial," pp. 567–68, 579–82.

54. Stewart to Prunier, U.S. Ship *Franklin*, Off Quilca, July 11, 1822, *ibid.*, p. 580.

55. Prunier to Stewart, *Belgrano*, July 11, 1822, translation, and Stewart to Prunier, July 12, 1822, *ibid.*, pp. 580–81.

56. Prunier to Guido, July 13, 1822, translation, *ibid.*, pp. 581–82.

57. *Ibid.*, pp. 586–87.

58. Stewart to SecNav, Jan. 5, 1823, *ibid.*, pp. 567–68.

59. Stewart to Marquis of Truxillo, supreme delegate of the government of Lima, Harbor of Callao, Aug. 9, 1822, *ibid.*, p. 571; Stewart to Valdivieso, Callao

Harbor, Aug. 20 and Sept. 26, 1822, *ibid.*, pp. 572–73; Valdivieso to Stewart, Lima, Aug. 13 and Sept. 10, 1822, translations, *ibid.*, pp. 599–600.

60. Stewart to Valdivieso, Callao Harbor, Aug. 20, 1822, *ibid.*, pp. 572–73.
61. Valdivieso to Stewart, Lima, Sept. 10, 1822, translation, *ibid.*, pp. 599–600.
62. Stewart to Valdivieso, Off Callao, Sept. 26, 1822, *ibid.*, p. 573.
63. Stewart to SecNav, Jan. 5, 1823, *ibid.*, pp. 567–68.
64. Valdivieso to Stewart, Lima, Sept. 10, 1822, translation, and Stewart to Valdivieso, Callao, Sept. 18, 1822, "Cruise of the U.S.S. *Franklin*"; Prevost to Stewart, Santiago, Jan. 26, 1824 [1823], "Stewart–Court-Martial," pp. 563–64; Crosby, "Facts relative to the Franklin's Cruize." Both Prevost and Crosby stated that the arms landed at the Valparaiso customs house by the *Canton* were smuggled aboard the *Pearl* in some unexplained manner and were either landed by the *Pearl* at Arica or transferred to the *Canton* at sea and subsequently landed from that vessel. Little credence can be placed in Crosby's account as it is all based on hearsay and contains many errors of fact, such as listing Ward as the supercargo of the *Pearl* rather than the *Canton*. He appears to have been blinded with hatred or jealousy of Smith.
65. Stewart to Conner, Callao, Sept. 5, 1822, copy, "Stewart–Court-Martial," p. 558; *ibid.*, pp. 500, 515, 548. Lang, or Long, is not identified other than as an Englishman. His money was taken aboard at Quilca (p. 500).
66. *Ibid.*, p. 498.
67. *Ibid.*, p. 548.
68. *Ibid.*, pp. 493–94, 498, 510, 515, 516, 590.
69. *Ibid.*, pp. 497, 500, 504, 515, 518.
70. *Ibid.*, pp. 509–10.
71. Crosby, "Facts relative to the Franklin's Cruize."
72. "Stewart–Court-Martial," pp. 493–94, 510.
73. *Ibid.*, pp. 493, 510, 515, 591; Crosby, "Facts relative to the Franklin's Cruize."
74. Mitre, *San Martin*, pp. 1144–49.
75. Hammersley, "Journal," Sept. 29 to Oct. 23, 1822.
76. "Stewart–Court-Martial," pp. 493, 499, 502, 506–7, 518, 551–52; Countess of Valle Ermosa [*sic*] to Mrs. Stewart, [n.d.], translation, *ibid.*, p. 566; Answers to interrogatories by Delia Tudor Stewart, "Hunter–Court-Martial," p. 609; Statement of Lieutenant William M. Hunter, Washington, Aug. 16, 1825, *ibid.*, p. 610.
77. Stewart to SecNav, Valparaiso, Oct. 21, 1823, "Stewart–Court-Martial," pp. 565–66.
78. *Ibid.*, pp. 493, 499, 502, 506–7, 518, 551–52; "Hunter–Court-Martial," pp. 605, 606. On his return to the United States in 1824, Stewart preferred charges against Hunter for neglect of duty in not reporting the presence of Madrid on board to him. The court acquitted Hunter but the trial served as a useful vehicle to get the testimony of Mrs. Stewart on record, as she was not considered as a competent witness at her husband's trial. If any blame attaches to Stewart in this event it is his readiness to sacrifice his subordinates to protect himself.
79. Hammersley, "Journal."
80. Stewart to SecNav, Valparaiso, Jan. 5, 1823, "Stewart–Court-Martial," pp. 567–68.
81. Prevost to Adams, Santiago, Jan. 11, 1823, NA:DS, SA, VI; also in "Cruise of the U.S.S. *Franklin*."
82. Stewart to Prevost, Valparaiso Harbor, Jan. 2, 1823, "Stewart–Court-Martial," p. 562.
83. Stewart to Prevost, Valparaiso, Jan. 19, 1823, *ibid.*, p. 563.
84. Prevost to Stewart, Santiago, Jan. 5, 1823, *ibid.*, p. 562.
85. *Ibid.*
86. Stewart to Prevost, Valparaiso, Jan. 19, 1823, *ibid.*, p. 563.

87. Ibid.
88. Hammersley, "Journal"; Prevost to Adams, Lima, Mar. 13, 1823, NA:DS, SA, VI; Log of the U.S.S. *Franklin*.
89. Prevost to Adams, Santiago, Jan. 24, 1823, NA:DS, SA, VI; Worcester, *Sea Power*, pp. 76–77.
90. Prevost to Adams, Santiago, Jan. 31, 1823, NA:DS, SA, VI; Barros Arana, *Historia jeneral*, XIII, 817–34.
91. Log of the U.S.S. *Franklin*, III, Mar. 24, 1823, NA:ND.
92. Stewart to Prevost, Callao, May 9, 1823, and Prevost to Stewart, Lima, May 12, 1823, "Stewart–Court-Martial," pp. 564–65.
93. Prevost to Adams, Lima, May 1, 1823, with encl., Prevost to Valdivieso, Apr. 29, 1823; Prevost to Adams, May 15, 1823, with encl., Prevost to Valdivieso, May 6, 1823; Prevost to Adams, June 12, 1823; all in NA:DS SA, VI.

Chapter IX

1. Mitre, *San Martín*, pp. 1158–71; Markham, *History of Peru*, pp. 260–70.
2. Prevost to Adams, Lima, Apr. 24, 1823, Manning, *Correspondence*, III, 1739–40; Charles Wilkes, Jr., "Journal on Board the Ship O'Cain of Boston, Charles Wilkes, Jr., Capt. Comd. March 25th–Valparaiso Bay," unpublished private journal kept by Midshipman Wilkes after his transfer from the *Franklin* to the *O'Cain*, NA:ND, Logs, Journals, and Diaries of Officers of the United States Navy at Sea, Mar., 1776–June, 1908.
3. Log of the U.S.S. *Franklin*, III, Mar. 3, 1823, NA:ND.
4. R. Alvarado to Stewart, Head-Quarters at Callao, June 29, 1823, "Stewart–Court-Martial," p. 600.
5. Stewart to Sucre, Callao Harbor, June 30, 1823, *ibid.*, pp. 573–76.
6. Sucre to Stewart, Head-Quarters at Callao, July 8, 1823, *ibid.*, pp. 601–2.
7. Stewart to Sucre, Callao Bay, July 14, 1823, *ibid.*, pp. 574–75.
8. Certificate of Nationality of the schooner *Robinson Crusoe* signed by Charles Stewart, Commander in Chief of U. States Naval forces the Pacific Ocean, dated March 21, 1823, copy, encl., Prevost to Adams, June 29, 1823, in "Cruise of the U.S.S. *Franklin*."
9. Prevost to Valdivieso, Lima, June 4, 1823, and Valdivieso to Prevost, Lima, June 7, 1823, copies, encls., Prevost to Adams, Lima, June 12, 1823; Prevost to Adams, Lima, June 29, 1823; Prevost to Adams, Lima, Aug. 31, 1823–all in "Cruise of the U.S.S. *Franklin*"; Crosby, "Facts relative to the Franklin's Cruize."
10. John Miller, *Memorias del general Miller al servicio de la República del Peru*, traducidas al castellano por el general Torrijos (Madrid, [1918]), II, 45–88 (hereinafter cited as Miller, *Memorias*); Stewart to SecNav, Valparaiso, Nov. 20, 1823, in "Cruise of the U.S.S. *Franklin*."
11. Leonard Sistare to Hogan, Arica, Nov. 4, 1823, copy, in "Cruise of the U.S.S. *Franklin*"; "Extract from the Schooner Adonis's log Book, commencing 1st November, 1823," *ibid*.
12. Stewart to SecNav, Callao Harbor, June 26, 1823, *ibid.*; Prevost to Adams, Lima, July 10 and 21, 1823, Manning, *Correspondence*, III, 1743–45.
13. Miller, *Memorias*, II, 63–64.
14. Log of U.S.S. *Franklin*, III, Sept. 27, 1823, NA:ND.
15. Stewart to Antonio de Quintanilla, Callao Harbor, July 28, 1823; Quintanilla to Stewart, San Carlos, Oct. 25, 1823; and S. Williams to Stewart, Valparaiso, Nov. 10, 1823–all copies, encls., Stewart to SecNav, Nov. 20, 1823, in "Cruise of the U.S.S. *Franklin*."

16. Stewart to Valdez, Jan. 15, 1824, copy, in "Cruise of the U.S.S. *Franklin*."
17. "Stewart—Court-Martial," p. 497.
18. Hammersley, "Journal"; Valdez to Stewart, Yura, Jan. 7, 1824, and Stewart to Valdez, Quilca, Jan. 15, 1824, "Stewart—Court-Martial," pp. 575–76, 601–2.
19. Valdez to Stewart, Yura, Jan. 7, 1824, and Stewart to Valdez, Quilca, Jan. 15, 1824; Stewart to La Serna, Quilca, Jan. 16, 1824, and La Serna to Stewart, Cuzco, Feb. 4, 1824; Rafael Pero to Stewart, Quilca, Feb. 5, 1824, and Stewart to Pero, At Sea, Feb. 6, 1824—all in "Stewart—Court-Martial," pp. 575–77, 601–3.
20. Stewart to Hull, Callao Bay, Apr. 27, 1824, copy, and Stewart to SecNav, At Sea, May 5, 1824, in "Cruise of the U.S.S. *Franklin*."
21. Miller, *Memorias*, II, 117.
22. SecNav to Stewart, June 4, 1823, NA:ND, LTO, XV.
23. "Stewart—Court-Martial," p. 497; Stewart to Conner, Quilca, Jan. 22, 1824, *ibid.*, p. 560.
24. Mitre, *San Martín*, pp. 1181–82; Prevost to Adams, Truxillo, Mar. 13, 1824, Manning, *Correspondence*, III, 1747–48.
25. Stewart to Hull, Valparaiso, Mar. 13, 1824, copy, and Stewart to SecNav, At Sea, May 5, 1824, in "Cruise of the U.S.S. *Franklin*"; "Stewart—Court-Martial," p. 497.
26. Mitre, *San Martín*, pp. 1183, 1186; Prevost to Adams, Mar. 13, 1824, Manning, *Correspondence*, III, 1747–48.
27. P. Bowers (master, merchant ship *Providence*) to Stewart, Lima, Mar. 20, 1824, copy, "Cruise of the U.S.S. *Franklin*"; Miller, *Memorias*, II, 105.
28. Captain Gardner (*Sabine*) to Captain Shepard (brig *Post-Captain*), Puná, Feb. 20, 1824, extract in *Charleston Courier*, June 4, 1824; Miller, *Memorias*, II, 102–4.
29. José de Espinar to General of the Army of the Center, Henríquez Martínez, General Secretary's office, Head Quarters, Pativilca, Feb. 10, 1824, copy, encl., Stewart to SecNav, New York, Sept. 6, 1824, NA:ND, CL, 1824, III. The underlining was made by the same person who made the copy, probably Stewart. There are several derogatory notes on Bolívar made in the same hand.
30. Aaron W. Williams and Timothy Ropes, Jr., [master and supercargo of the brig *Herald*], to Commodore Charles Stewart or the Commanding Officer of any U.S. Vessel of War, Callao Roads, Mar. 3, 1824; Hiram Putnam [master of the ship *China*] and masters of four American ships to Stewart, Callao Bay, Mar. 1, 1824—copies, both in "Cruise of the U.S.S. *Franklin*."
31. P. Bowers, Master and Supercargo, Ship *Providence, et al* [masters and supercargoes of five American ships at Callao], to Stewart, [not dated]; Aaron W. Williams and Timothy Ropes, [master and supercargo of the brig *Herald*], to Commodore Charles Stewart or the Commanding Officer of any U.S. Vessel of War, Callao Roads, Mar. 3, 1824; P. Bowers to Stewart, Lima, Mar. 20, 1824—copies, all in "Cruise of the U.S.S. *Franklin*."
32. Henry L. De Koven to Stewart, Ship *America*, May 1, 1824, copy, encl., Stewart to Hull, Callao Bay, May 1, 1824, in "Cruise of the U.S.S. *Franklin*." The name of the *America*'s master is variously spelled—De Koven, De Coven, or Decoven.
33. Hammersley to Stewart, Callao Bay, Apr. 27, 1824, copy, encl., Stewart to Hull, Callao Bay, May 1, 1824, copy, in "Cruise of the U.S.S. *Franklin*."
34. Stewart to General José Rámon Rodil, Governor, Commander in Chief at Callao, Mar. 28, 1824, and Rodil to Stewart, Callao, Apr. 9, 1824, copies, in "Cruise of the U.S.S. *Franklin*"; Tudor to Adams, Lima, June 7, 1824, Manning, *Correspondence*, III, 1752–54; Prevost to Adams, Truxillo, May 6, 1824, NA:DS, SA, VI. Another brother of Mrs. Stewart was Frederic Tudor, who made a fortune shipping ice to South America and the Caribbean and was known as the "ice

King." William Tudor was finally granted an *exequatur* by the patriot government when Bolívar returned to Lima in December, 1824.

35. Hull to SecNav, Valparaiso, Apr. 1, 1824, NA:ND, CL, 1824, I; Gardner Weld Allen, ed., *Papers of Isaac Hull, Commodore United States Navy* (Boston, 1929), p. 43 (hereinafter cited as Allen, *Hull*); "Stewart—Court-Martial," p. 497.

36. Stewart to Heman Allen, Callao Bay, Apr. 19, 1824, copy, in "Cruise of the U.S.S. *Franklin*"; Hull to SecNav, Callao Bay, May 4, 1824, NA:ND, CL, 1824, II; Percival to SecNav, U.S. Schooner *Dolphin*, Callao Bay, Apr. 30, 1824, NA:ND, OL, 1824, III; Conner to SecNav, New York, Aug. 30, 1824, NA:ND, OL, 1824, VI; Stewart to SecNav, At Sea, May 5, 1824, in "Cruise of the U.S.S. *Franklin*"; Log of the U.S.S. *Franklin*.

37. Stewart to SecNav, At Sea, May 5, 1824, in "Cruise of the U.S.S. *Franklin*."

38. Valdivieso to Minister of State and Foreign Relations, the United States of North America, Lima, Mar. 29, 1823, translation; José María Salazar to The Secretary of State and Foreign Relations, Philadelphia, Sept. 6, 1823; Valdivieso to Prevost, Lima, May 18, 1823, translation, encl., Prevost to Adams, May 27, 1823—all copies, in "Cruise of U.S.S. *Franklin*."

39. Prevost to Adams, Lima, May 27, 1823, in "Cruise of the U.S.S. *Franklin*."

40. Prevost to Adams, Santiago, Oct. 9, 1822, Jan. 20 and Oct. 28, 1823; Lima, May 15 and Aug. 31, 1823; Callao, June 29, 1823—all in "Cruise of the U.S.S. *Franklin*"; Prevost to Adams, Truxillo, May 5, June 9, and Aug. 5, 1824, in NA:DS, SA, VI; Prevost to Thomas Morris, Truxillo, May 15, 1824, NA:DS, SA, VI; unsigned note, "note on Capt. Stewart's Cruise, Note A," encl., Prevost to Adams, Truxillo, Mar. 13, 1824, duplicate, NA:DS, SA, VI; Adams to Prevost, Dec. 16, 1823, and Brent to Prevost, Dec. 24, 1823, NA:DS, CI, II.

41. Bernardo Rivadavia, Minister of Government and Foreign Relations of the United Provinces of South America, to Caesar A. Rodney, United States Minister at Buenos Aires, Buenos Aires, Feb. 12, 1824, translation, Manning, *Correspondence*, I, 635–36; see also Whitaker, *Independence*, pp. 311–12. There is no explanation for the phrase "near the authorities of his Catholic Majesty." It is likely that this was allowed to slip in by the originator or translator through habit and that what was actually meant was the patriot government.

42. Crosby, "Facts relative to the Franklin's Cruize," encl., Prevost to Adams, Lima, Aug. 31, 1823, in "Cruise of the U.S.S. *Franklin*." Three copies of Crosby's accusations are bound with the documents of the "Cruise of the U.S.S. *Franklin*." A copy was sent to Henry Clay by Richard Alsop. See Whitaker, *Independence*, p. 158 n. 36 and p. 309 n. 62.

43. Crosby, "Facts relative to the Franklin's Cruize." The prohibition on visits by patriot officials is probably exaggerated. General Miller records that he and Guido were frequent visitors on board the *Franklin*.

44. Robinson to Adams, Valparaiso, July 25 and Aug. 15, 1822, and Santiago, Dec. 14, 1822, in NA:DS, SA, V; Robinson to Adams, Valparaiso, Jan. 9, 1822 [1823], in "Cruise of the U.S.S. *Franklin*."

45. Robinson to Adams, Santiago, Apr. 29, 1822, in "Cruise of the U.S.S. *Franklin*." Several words in this passage are obscured by the binding or are illegible.

46. Adams to Minister of State and Foreign Relations of Peru, Washington, Dec. 12, 1823, Manning, *Correspondence*, I, 219–20.

47. Adams to Prevost, Dec. 16, 1823, NA:DS, CI, II; Prevost to Doctor José Sanchez Carrion, Minister General of Peru, Truxillo, June 14, 1824, copy, encl., Prevost to Adams, Truxillo, Aug. 5, 1824, NA:DS, SA, VI.

48. Adams to Minister of State and Foreign Relations of Peru, Washington, Dec. 12, 1823, Manning, *Correspondence*, I, 219–20.

49. *Ibid.*

50. Adams to Prevost, Dec. 16, 1823, NA:DS, CI, II.
51. *Ibid.*
52. *Ibid.* The letter of Guido referred to had been intercepted by *montoneras* in 1819 and forwarded to the State Department. Prevost had claimed ignorance of its meaning. See Guido to Supreme Director of the United Provinces of Buenos Aires, Santiago, Sept. 30, 1819, copy, and Prevost to Adams, Santiago, Jan. 6, 1821, in NA:DS, SA, VI; Adams to Prevost, July 10, 1820, in NA:DS, CI, II.
53. Adams to Salazar, Dec. 5, 1823, copy, in "Cruise of the U.S.S. *Franklin.*"
54. Adams, *Memoirs,* VI, 218.
55. Stewart to Latimer, Philadelphia, Sept. 30, 1824, and Latimer to Stewart, Philadelphia, Oct. 5, 1824, encls., Stewart to SecNav, Oct. 5, 1824, NA:ND, CL, 1824, III.
56. Latimer to SecNav, Philadelphia, Nov. 28, 1824, NA:ND, OL, 1824, III.
57. SecNav to Stewart, Nov. 16, 1824, NA:ND, LTO, XV; Adams, *Memoirs,* VI, 429.
58. Stewart to SecNav, Nov. 20 and 25, and Dec. 4, 1824; Jan. 17 and 24, Feb. 4 and 14, Mar. 5 and 27, June 5 and 22, July 5, 8 and 19, and Aug. 8, 1825—NA:ND, CL, 1824, IV, and 1825, I, II, III, IV, and V; SecNav to Stewart, Nov. 16, 22, and 29, and Dec. 1, 1824; Jan. 18 and 25, Feb. 9 and 25, Mar. 23, May 25, July 12 and 13, and Aug. 5, 1825—NA:ND, LTO, XV, XVI; Adams to Prevost, Jan. 20, 1825, NA:DS, CI, II; *Niles' Weekly Register,* XXIX (Oct. 15, 1825), 102. *Niles' Weekly Register* reported that Prevost died at a lonely posthouse on the road to Cuzco. A Mr. Clark who went from Lima to claim the body found that it "had been thrown out of the hut and left exposed on the desert Cordilleras, it being denied a grave because that he was a heretic!"
59. "Stewart—Court-Martial," p. 491; SecNav to Barron, Mar. 24, 1821; SecNav to Alexander Murray, Mar. 20, 1821; and SecNav to Stewart, Mar. 20, 1821—all in NA:ND, LTO, XV; *Niles' Weekly Register,* XXII (April 6, 1822), 82.
60. "Stewart—Court-Martial," pp. 489–91.
61. *Ibid.*, pp. 505, 507, 512.
62. *Ibid.*, 505–6, 507, 512–13. Underlining added.
63. *Ibid.*, pp. 519–21.
64. *Ibid.*, p. 520.

Chapter X

1. Mitre, *San Martín,* pp. 1188–1201; Tudor to Adams, Lima, Aug. 24, Sept. 27, Oct. 17, Nov. 11, and Dec. 7, 1824, and Prevost to Adams, Chancay, Nov. 9, 1824, in Manning, *Correspondence,* III, 1758–73. The battle of Ayacucho did not stop all fighting in South America. Isolated garrisons at Chiloé and Callao held out for more than a year before they surrendered to the patriots.
2. SecNav to Hull, Dec. 24, 1823, NA:ND, LTO, XV.
3. Adams to Heman Allen, Nov. 23, 1823, NA:DS, DIAC, X; extract in "Cruise of the U.S.S. *Franklin.*"
4. Allen, *Hull,* p. 43.
5. Tudor to Adams, Lima, Aug. 24, Sept. 18, and Oct. 17, 1824, and Feb. 25, 1825, Manning, *Correspondence,* III, 1758–61, 1764–66, 1768–71, 1778–79; Hull to SecNav, Callao Bay, Oct. 2, 1824; NA:ND, CL, 1824, III.
6. Hull to SecNav, Callao Bay, Oct. 2 and Nov. 2, 1824, NA:ND, CL, 1824, III and IV; Hull to SecNav, Callao Bay, Jan. 23, 1825, NA:ND, CL, 1825, I; Carter to SecNav, Aug. 5, 1824, NA:ND, OL, 1824, VI.

7. Paulding to Hull, Callao, July 15, 1824, in Allen, *Hull*, pp. 45–47; Tudor to Adams, Lima, July 11, 1824, Manning, *Correspondence*, III, 1755–57. In a letter to Guise (Huamachuco, 28 de abril de 1824), Bolívar had hinted at friction between himself and Guise but had entreated the latter to maintain command of the squadron and continue the blockade. See Vincente Lecuna, *Cartas del Libertador*, IV, 140–44.

8. Johnson, *Cape Horn*, p. 35; Allen, *Hull*, p. 52.

9. Tudor to Adams, Lima, Nov. 11, 1824, Manning, *Correspondence*, III, 1772–73. One officer who went contrary to the general opinion of Bolívar was Midshipman Stephen Rowan, who recorded in his private journal that it was the opinion of many leading statesmen [in Peru?] that Bolívar desired to make himself emperor of Peru. He also recorded that Bolívar's private character was "infamous."

10. Tudor to Adams, Lima, July 11, 1824, Manning, *Correspondence*, III, 1755–57. The British vessels were the ship *Cambridge*, the frigate *Tartar*, and the sloop *Fly*.

11. Worcester, *Sea Power*, p. 81.

12. Tudor to Adams, Lima, Sept. 18, 1824, Manning, *Correspondence*, III, 1764–66; Midshipman Andrew H. Foot to a friend, William A. Brown, U.S. Frigate *United States*, Callao, Sept. 5, 1824, NA:ND, Area 9 file, 1814–1910, Box No. 1.

13. Tudor to Adams, Lima, Oct. 17, 1824, Manning, *Correspondence*, III, 1768–71; Hull to SecNav, Callao Bay, Nov. 2, 1824, NA:ND, CL, 1824, IV; Prevost to Adams, Chancay, Nov. 9, 1824, Manning, *Correspondence*, III, 1771–72; Hull to SecNav, Chorillos, Aug. 1, 1825, NA:ND, CL, 1825, V.

14. Barros Arana, *Historia jeneral*, XIV, 424–25, 509. Rodil held out until Jan., 1826. Another royalist stronghold, Chiloé, also capitulated in Jan., 1826.

15. Hull to SecNav, Callao Bay, Jan. 23, 1825, NA:ND, CL, 1825, I.

16. Lieutenant Beverly Kennon to Hull, U.S.S. *Peacock*, Chorillos, Apr. 11, 1825, NA:ND, CL, 1825, II; Hull to SecNav, Chorillos, Sept. 6 and 26, 1825, NA:ND, CL, 1825, VII.

17. Hull to SecNav, Chorillos, July 30 and Aug. 11, 1825, NA:ND, CL, 1825, V.

18. SecNav to Hull, Apr. 29, May 24, and June 24, 1825, NA:ND, LTO, XVI; Hull to SecNav, Chorillos, Aug. 11, 1825, NA:ND, CL, 1825, V; Hull to Percival, Chorillos, Aug. 14, 1825, copy in "Cruise of the United States, 1825," NA:ND, Letters From Officers Commanding Expeditions, 1818–1885, I, (e).

19. Hardy to Thomas Brown, *Creole*, Rio de Janeiro, Aug. 30, 1823, Graham and Humphreys, *Navy, Correspondence*, pp. 372–74. See Whitaker, *Independence*, pp. 300–10, for a resumé of the role of the navy in handling specie in South America.

20. Report of Theodorick Bland to Adams, Nov. 2, 1818, extract, Manning, *Correspondence*, II, 946–1005.

Bibliography

I. Primary Sources

A. MANUSCRIPTS

1. Collections in the National Archives, Washington, D.C.

   Naval Records Collection of the Office of Naval Records and Library (Record Group 45).
   Area 9 File, 1776–1910. A collection of fifty boxes of loose letters and other documents concerning the navy and the Pacific Ocean area east of longitude 180°, assembled from official and private sources. Largely duplication of material found elsewhere, but contains some fresh private letters.
   Area 11 File, 1775–1909. Seven boxes of loose papers comprising correspondence with other executive departments of the government, including the White House offices. It is largely duplication of material found elsewhere.
   Confidential Letters Sent ("Private Letters"), 1813–22, 1840, 1843–79. Office of the secretary of the navy. Copies of confidential letters originating in the secretary of the navy's of-

fice. Contains sailing orders; special instructions; and matters of a private and confidential nature, which it was not desired to make public at the time of origin.

Letters from Captains ("Captains' Letters"), 1805–61, 1866–85. Office of the secretary of the navy. Letters from captains containing reports of operations, activities, and all matters affecting their commands. This is the most important single source for studies of naval activities in periods covered.

Letters from Commanders ("Master Commandants" through 1837, thereafter "Commanders' Letters"), 1804–86. Office of the secretary of the navy. Covers same matter as "Captains' Letters" for lesser commands. Since most master commandants were under orders of a senior captain, their reports were usually made through the superior officer and are found as enclosures to the captains' letters.

Letters from Officers below the Rank of Commander ("Officers' Letters"), 1802–84. Office of the secretary of the navy. Letters from junior officers, routine requests for commissions, change of duty, furloughs, and similar matters. Of little value except as a check on the activities of an individual officer.

Letters from Officers Commanding Expeditions, 1818–85. Office of the secretary of the navy. Volume I contains correspondence relating to the cruises of the *Cyane, Franklin, Ontario, Peacock*, and *United States*. Part (b), concerning the *Franklin* (1822–24), contains approximately five hundred pages of correspondence of Commodore Charles Stewart, Special Agent John B. Prevost, and Jeremy Robinson with the secretaries of state and navy and various South American officials. It was obviously assembled for use in connection with the court-martial of Stewart in 1825 for alleged misconduct while in command of the Pacific Station from 1822 to 1824. Many of the documents contain condemnations of Stewart while many are favorable to him. Part (c) relates to the cruise of the *Ontario* in the Pacific in 1818 and contains copies of correspondence of Captain James Biddle with various South American officials, both royalist and patriot. Biddle added his comments or explanations. The correspondence is by no means exhaustive, having been selected by him for submission to the secretary of the navy to refute press charges that he had committed unneutral acts against the patriots while

Bibliography

in the Pacific. Part (e) is a collection of about one hundred pages of instructions issued in 1825 by Commodore Isaac Hull to officers of the Pacific squadron from his flagship, the frigate *United States*, and copies of his correspondence with United States consuls and local officials in Peru and Chile. Largely duplicates material from other sources.

Letters Sent to Federal Executive Agents, 1798–1866. Office of the secretary of the navy. Copies of letters sent to the president, secretary of state, secretary of war, and secretary of the treasury, mostly concerning routine administrative matters. After 1824 all executive letters were consolidated into one "Executive Letters" book.

Letters Sent to Officers ("Letters to Officers, Ships of War"), 1798–1886. Office of the secretary of the navy. Copies of letters and instructions to commanding officers of squadrons and ships and to other officers of all ranks; replies to their reports of operations; circulars; general orders; court-martial orders and precepts; letters relating to the discipline and assignment of officers; and general matters of a nonclassified nature. This is an important source for naval operations and information on naval personnel.

Miscellaneous Letters Received ("Miscellaneous Letters"), 1801–84. Office of the secretary of the navy. Letters received from all classes of correspondents except naval officers. Includes all letters from private persons and firms, and covers such subjects as employment, inventions, claims, recommendations for commissions, and inquiries about naval personnel.

Logbooks and Journals Kept by Naval Personnel Attached to Vessels at Sea, 1776–1908.

Journal and Correspondence of Captain James Biddle, commanding the U.S.S. *Ontario* on a Cruise from New York to the Columbia River and back to Norfolk, October 4, 1817–April 23, 1819 (Microfilm copy). This document is actually a memorandum report on the cruise of the *Ontario* submitted by Biddle at its termination and is not a journal in the true sense. It contains copies of correspondence between Biddle and Lord Cochrane concerning failure of Biddle to render a salute at Valparaiso in December, 1818.

Private Journal kept on board the U.S. Frigate *Macedonian*, John Downes, Esqr. Commander, on a Cruise from Boston,

Massachusetts, to the Pacific Ocean, &c, &c, by C. J. Deblois, Captns Clerke, Said Frigate, in the Years 1818 1819 (Microfilm copy). Unpublished private journal of the captain's clerk of the *Macedonian* during the first year of her cruise to the Pacific. Contains outstanding descriptions of shipboard life, descriptions of ports visited, and observations on the people and social conditions. Unfortunately, the journal does not cover the entire period of the *Macedonian*'s cruise since the writer was returned to the United States because of ill-health in December, 1819.

Private Remarks of Lieutenant Chas. Launtt, of the U.S. Ship *Macedonian*, John Downes, esqr., Commander, made during a cruise in the Pacific Ocean in the years 1818, 19, 20, 21 (Microfilm copy). Unpublished private journal of a lieutenant aboard the *Macedonian*. Primarily concerned with navigational and technical data but contains much valuable material concerning United States shipping on the west coast of South America, the relations of the navy to such shipping, protection and assistance provided, relations of the *Macedonian* with the patriot and royalist forces, the blockades, and details of the patriot and royalist naval forces. Some scientific data and descriptions of social conditions.

Journal on Board the Ship *O'Cain* of Boston, Charles Wilkes, jr. Capt. Comd. March 25th, 1863–Valparaiso Bay. Journal kept by the future explorer when he was detailed to take command of the whaler *O'Cain* after the death of her regular master off the coast of Chile. It is almost entirely navigational and technical data.

Records of the Bureau of Naval Personnel (Record Group 24).
Ship's Logs, 1801–1942.
Log of the U.S.S. *Constellation*, July 5, 1819–January 25, 1825.
Log of the U.S.S. *Franklin*, July 31, 1821–September 14, 1824.
Log of the U.S.S. *Macedonian*, March 20, 1819–December 29, 1820.

Records of the Office of the Judge Advocate General (Navy) (Record Group 125).
Records of General Courts-Martial and Courts of Inquiry of the Navy Department, 1799–1867 (Microfilm copy). These

case files are the official records of the trial and punishment of officers and enlisted men of the Navy and Marine Corps. A complete dossier contains the precept appointing the court, charges and specifications of charges, the plea of the defendant, testimony, exhibits, the findings of the court, the sentence if the defendant is found guilty, and endorsements of the secretary of the navy and the president. The records are in such poor condition that they may be viewed on microfilm only. The important parts of the trial of Commodore Stewart (Case No. 434, microfilm roll 19, series M 273) are reproduced in *American State Papers, Naval Affairs*, II, 487–610.

General Records of the Department of State (Record Group 59) (Microfilm copy).

Diplomatic Instructions, 1791–1906. Letters sent to diplomatic representatives of the United States. The first twelve volumes are to all countries. Instructions to ministers in South America start with Vol. IX but some instructions to special agents are in preceding volumes.

Instructions to Consuls, 1801–1906. Instructions and correspondence to consular representatives and agents performing consular duties. For the period 1801–34 the letters are copied chronologically without regard to place. Vol. II (1817–28) contains much correspondence on the South American Commission and instructions to agents in Argentina, Chile, and Peru.

Miscellaneous Letters, 1789–1906. Letters received by the Department of State from all sources with exception of diplomatic and consular dispatches or notes from foreign legations and consulates. The letters for the years 1789–1820 are briefed in the *Calendar of the Miscellaneous Letters Received by the Department of State from the Organization of the Government to 1820* (Washington, 1897). Remaining volumes are well indexed but are of little value unless the name of correspondents and approximate dates of the communications are known.

Notes to Foreign Legations, 1793–1834. Correspondence from the Department of State to foreign diplomatic representatives in the United States. Vols. II and III cover the independence period of Latin America and contain letters of

Secretaries Robert Smith, James Monroe, Richard Rush, John Quincy Adams, and Henry Clay. Many letters are signed by John Graham, chief clerk of the department and his successor, Daniel Brent.

Special Agents, 1794–1906.

Jeremy Robinson, 1817–23 (Vol. V). Letters written by Robinson from Chile and Peru, where he had gone after his commission as agent for commerce and seamen for Peru and Chile was revoked. Robinson had no official status at the time of writing and his credibility is lessened by his obvious attempts to obtain a new appointment in South America, but he provides much interesting background material on people, places, and politics in South America.

John B. Prevost, 1817–25 (Vol. VI). Dispatches from Chile, Peru, Argentina, and the Pacific Northwest, describing political and military events, the country, people, and commerce of the various regions. Prevost was militantly pro-patriot and his dispatches are replete with criticism of the royalists and the United States naval commanders, whom he accused of actions inimical to the patriot cause. The volume contains some letters from his son, Stanhope Prevost, who held an acting appointment as vice-consul at Lima.

2. Collections in the Manuscript Division, Library of Congress, Washington, D.C.

Papers of James Monroe, 1758–1839. 37 vols.
Collected letters of James Monroe, letters received, drafts of letters sent, notes for cabinet meetings. Many concern South America, the Wars of Independence, recognition of the new states, diplomatic representation, and the protection of United States commerce.

Nicholas Biddle Papers, 1775–1846. 113 vols.
Biddle's correspondence is primarily concerned with financial matters connected with the Bank of the United States. There are a few items concerned with South America and an occasional mention of his brother, Captain James Biddle.

Papers of Jeremy Robinson. 6 portfolios, 1808–32; a letter book, 1831–32; and 8 small journals, 1817–23. The journals include Robinson's diary, accounts of travel, and detailed descriptions of South American cities and customs. Valuable for background material on personalities and the political and military situations in Chile and Peru during the period 1818–23; frequent mention of the navy and naval officers. Robinson must be viewed as an opportunist whose reports were colored by his personal interests.

Log books and journals kept by officers on board naval vessels, accounts and miscellaneous volumes and papers relating to the United States navy.

> Log and journal of the U.S.S. *Ontario*, James Biddle, captain on a passage from Valparaiso to Lima, April 13, 1818–Feb. 19, 1819, with some fragments from the year 1817.
>
> Journal of the U.S.S. *Ontario*, kept by Lieutenant David Connor, fragments, 1817–19.
>
> Log of the U.S.S. *Ontario*, fragments, April 13, 1818–February 19, 1819.
>
> Journal Kept on Board the United States Ship *Franklin*, of 74 Guns, Charles Stewart, Esquire, Commander, Lieutenant Thomas S. Hamersley [Hammersley], U.S. Navy 1821, 1822, 1823, 1824.
>
> Journal of Charles G. Ridgely, Captain in the U.S. Navy, from 8th May 1815 till–[March 30, 1821], Now on board the United States Frigate *Constellation*.

3. Navy Department Library, Navy Department, Office of the Chief of Naval Operations, Naval History Division, Washington, D.C.

Maritime Operations in the First Period of Independence [Chile]. [n.d.], Microfilm. Handwritten journal containing a very poor and literal translation of an unidentified Chilean account of naval operations during the Wars of Independence. The material is repetitious of various historical works but does contain some fresh accounts of the manning and outfitting of the *Lautaro*; also some interesting insights into the troubles encountered in manning the Chilean Navy, the inducements offered foreigners, and the animosities created by the differentials between the Chileans and the foreigners.

B. PUBLIC OR OFFICIAL DOCUMENTS

American State Papers, Class VI, Naval Affairs. 4 vols. Washington: Gales and Seaton, 1834–61.

Annals of Congress, 1789–1824. 42 volumes. Washington: Gales and Seaton, 1834–56.

Richardson, James Daniel (comp.). *A Compilation of the Messages and Papers of the Presidents.* 20 vols. Rev. ed. New York: Bureau of National Literature, 1897–1913.

C. NEWSPAPERS AND PERIODICALS

El Argos de Chile, May 23, 1818–November 19, 1818, Santiago de Chile, in *Colección de antiguos periódicos chilenos.* 9 vols. Santiago de Chile: Biblioteca Nacional, 1951——; VIII, 1–75.

Charleston Courier, 1803–73.

Colección de antiguos periódicos chilenos. 9 vols. Santiago de Chile: Biblioteca Nacional, 1951——.

Gaceta ministerial de Chile, May 2, 1818–July 29, 1820, Santiago de Chile, in *Colección de antiguos periódicos chilenos.* 9 vols. Santiago de Chile: Biblioteca Nacional, 1951——, V–VII.

Niles' Weekly Register. 76 volumes. Baltimore, 1811–49.

Providence Gazette, 1762–1825.

El Sol de Chile, July 3, 1818–February 12, 1819, Santiago de Chile, in *Colección de antiguos periódicos chilenos,* 9 vols. Santiago de Chile: Biblioteca Nacional, 1951——, VIII, 179–290.

D. MEMOIRS, DIARIES, AND CORRESPONDENCE

Adams, John Quincy. *Memoirs of John Quincy Adams, Comprising Portions of His Diary from 1795 to 1848,* ed. Charles Francis Adams. 12 vols. Philadelphia: J. B. Lippincott and Company, 1874–77.

———. *Writings of John Quincy Adams,* ed. Worthington Chauncey Ford. 7 vols. New York: The Macmillan Company, 1913–17.

Allen, Gardner Weld (ed.). *Papers of Isaac Hull.* Boston: The Boston Athenaeum, 1929.

Archivo de don Bernardo O'Higgins, ed. Ricardo Donoso et al. 4 vols. Santiago de Chile: Editorial Nascimento and Imprenta Universitaria, 1946–48.

Cartas del Libertador. 12 vols. Vols. I–XI edited by Vicente Lecuna. Caracas and New York: Lit. y Tip. del Comercio and Commercial Press, Inc., 1929–48. Vol. XII edited by Manuel Pérez Vila for the John Boulton Foundation. Caracas: John Boulton Foundation, Impreso por Italgráfica C.A., 1959.

Cleveland, Richard J. *Voyages and Commercial Enterprises of the Sons of New England*. New York: Leavitt & Allen, 1855.
[Coffin, Isaac Foster]. *Diario de un joven norte-americano detenido en Chile durante el periodo revolucionario de 1817 á 1819*. Traducido del ingles por J. T. M. Santiago de Chile: Imprenta Elzeviriana, 1898.
Documentos del archivo de San Martín, 12 vols. Comisión nacional del centenario. Buenos Aires: Museo Mitre, Impr. de Coni hermanos, 1910–11.
Graham, Gerald S., and R. A. Humphreys (eds.). *The Navy and South America, 1807–1823, Correspondence of the Commanders-in-Chief on The South American Station*. London: The Navy Records Society, 1962.
Hall, Basil. *Extracts from a Journal Written on the Coasts of Chili, Peru, and Mexico, in the Years, 1820, 1821, 1822*. 2 vols. 1st ed. Edinburgh and London: Archibald Constable and Co., Edinburgh; and Hurst, Robinson, and Co., London, 1824.
Hill, Henry. *Recollections of an Octogenarian*. Boston: D. Lathrop and Company, 1884.
Manning, William Ray (ed.). *Diplomatic Correspondence of the United States Concerning the Independence of the Latin American Nations*. 3 vols. New York: Oxford University Press, 1925.
Miller, John. *Memorias del general Miller, al servicio de la República del Perú*. 2 vols. Traducido al castellano por el general Torrijos. Madrid: Editorial-América, [1918?].
Morris, Charles. "The Autobiography of Commodore Charles Morris, U.S.N.," ed. James Russell Soley. *Proceedings of the United States Naval Institute*, VI (No. 12, 1881), 112–219.
Pezuela y Sánchez Muñoz de Velasco, Joaquín de la. *Memoria de gobierno*. Edición y prólogo de Vicente Rodríguez Casado y Guillermo Lohmann Villena. Publicaciones de la Escuela de Estudios Hispano-Americanos de Sevilla, No. XXVI. Sevilla: Talleres Tipográficos Editorial Católica Española, S.A., 1947.
Porter, David. *Journal of a Cruise made to the Pacific Ocean by Captain David Porter in the United States Frigate Essex, in the Years 1812, 1813, and 1814*. 2 vols. Philadelphia: Bradford and Inskeep, 1815.
Thomas, Earl of Dundonald, G.C.B. [Lord Cochrane]. *Narrative of Services in the Liberation of Chili, Peru, and Brazil, from*

Spanish and Portuguese Domination. 2 vols. London: James Ridgeway, 1859.

II. Secondary Works

A. GENERAL WORKS

Barros Arana, Diego. *Historia jeneral de Chile.* 16 vols. Santiago de Chile: Various publishers, 1884–1902.

Bemis, Samuel Flagg. *John Quincy Adams and the Foundations of American Foreign Policy.* New York: Alfred A. Knopf, 1949.

———. *The Latin American Policy of the United States.* New York: Harcourt, Brace and Company, 1943.

Brooks, Philip Coolidge. *Diplomacy and the Borderlands, the Adams-Onís Treaty of 1819.* Berkeley: University of California Press, 1939.

Galdames, Luis. *A History of Chile.* Translated and edited by Isaac Joslin Cox. Chapel Hill: The University of North Carolina Press, 1941.

Griffin, Charles Carroll. *The United States and the Disruption of the Spanish Empire, 1810–1822.* New York: Columbia University Press, 1937.

Herring, Hubert. *A History of Latin America.* Rev. ed. New York: Alfred A. Knopf, 1961.

Johnson, Robert Erwin. *Thence Around Cape Horn.* Annapolis, Maryland: United States Naval Institute, 1963.

Kirkpatrick, Frederick Alexander, "Establishment of Independence in South America," *The Cambridge Modern History,* ed. A. W. Ward, G. W. Prothro, and Stanley Leathes. 13 vols. New York and London: The Macmillan Company and Macmillan & Co., Ltd., 1902–12, X, 280–309.

Lockey, Joseph Byrne. *Pan-Americanism, Its Beginnings.* New York: The Macmillan Company, 1926.

The Mariner's Chronicle: Containing Narratives of the Most Remarkable Disasters at Sea, Such as Shipwrecks, Storms, Fires and Famines: also Naval Engagements, Piratical Adventures, Incidents of Discovery, and other Extraordinary and Interesting Occurrences. New Haven: George W. Gorton, 1834.

Markham, Clements R. *A History of Peru.* Chicago: Charles J. Sergel and Company, 1892.

Bibliography

Mitre, Bartolomé. *Historia de San Martín y de la emancipación sud-americana.* [Buenos Aires]: Edición Peuser, [1945].

Paxson, Frederic L. *The Independence of the South American Republics.* Philadelphia: Ferris & Leach, 1903.

Perkins, Dexter. *The Monroe Doctrine, 1823-1826.* Cambridge: Harvard University Press, 1932.

Thomas, R. *Interesting and Authentic Narratives of the Most Remarkable Shipwrecks, Fires, Famines, Calamities, Providential Deliverances, and Lamentable Disasters on the Seas, in Most Parts of the World.* Hartford: Silas Andrus & Son, 1835.

Whitaker, Arthur Preston. *The United States and the Independence of Latin America, 1800-1830.* New York: Russell & Russell, Inc., 1962 [1941].

B. MONOGRAPHS AND SPECIAL STUDIES

Álvarez, Alejandro. *Rasgos generales de la historia diplomática de Chile (1810-1910).* Santiago de Chile: Imprenta, Litografía y Encuadernación "Barcelona," 1911.

Chandler, Charles Lyon. *Inter-American Acquaintances.* 2nd ed. Sewanee: The University of Sewanee, Tennessee, 1917.

Clowes, William Laird, et al. *The Royal Navy, A History from the Earliest Times to the Present.* 7 vols. Boston and London: Little, Brown and Company, and Marston and Company, 1897-1903.

Collier, William Miller, and Guillermo Feliú Cruz. *La Primera misión de los Estados Unidos en Chile.* Santiago: Imprenta Cervantes, 1926.

Evans, Henry Clay, Jr. *Chile and Its Relations with the United States.* Durham: Duke University Press, 1927.

Hunt, Livingston. "The Trial of Lieutenant Ridgely for Murder," *United States Naval Institute Proceedings,* LVI (November, 1930), 985-90.

Moore, John Bassett (ed.). *History and Digest of the International Arbitrations to which the United States Has Been a Party.* 6 vols. Washington: Government Printing Office, 1898.

Morison, Samuel Eliot. *The Maritime History of Massachusetts, 1783-1860.* Boston: Houghton Mifflin Company, 1941.

Neumann, William L. "United States Aid to the Chilean Wars of Independence," *Hispanic American Historical Review,* XXVII (May, 1947), 204-19.

Novoa de la Fuente, Luis. *Historia naval de Chile.* 2nd ed. Valparaiso: Imprenta de la Armada, 1944.
Paullin, Charles Oscar. *Diplomatic Negotiations of American Naval Officers, 1778–1883.* Baltimore: The Johns Hopkins Press, 1912.
———. "Duelling in the Old Navy," *United States Naval Institute Proceedings,* XXXV (December, 1909), 1155–97.
———. "Naval Administration Under the Naval Commissioners," *United States Naval Institute Proceedings,* XXXIII (June, 1907), 597–641.
Pereira Salas, Eugenio. *La actuación de los oficiales navales norteamericanos en nuestras costas (1813–1840).* Santiago: Prensas de la Universidad de Chile, 1935.
———. *La misión Bland en Chile.* Santiago: Imprenta Universitaria, 1936.
———. *United States Ships in Chile at the Close of the Colonial Period.* Santiago, Chile: The Chile-United States Cultural Institute, [n.d.].
Pitkin, Timothy. *A Statistical View of the Commerce of the United States of America: Its Connection with Agriculture and Manufactures: and an Account of the Public Debt, Revenues, and Expenditures of the United States.* 2nd ed. New York: James Eastburn & Co., 1817.
Powers, Robert D. "Blockade: For Winning Without Killing," *United States Naval Institute Proceedings,* LXXXIV (August, 1958), 61–66.
Savage, Carlton (ed.). *Policy of the United States Toward Maritime Commerce in War.* 2 vols. Washington: United States Government Printing Office, 1934.
Stewart, Watt. "The South American Commission, 1817–1818," *Hispanic American Historical Review,* IX (February, 1929), 31–59.
Wriston, Henry Merritt. *Executive Agents in American Foreign Relations.* Baltimore: The Johns Hopkins Press, 1929.
Worcester, Donald E. *Sea Power and Chilean Independence.* "University of Florida Monographs, Social Sciences," No. 15, Summer, 1962. Gainesville: University of Florida Press, 1962.

C. BIOGRAPHIES

Allen, Gardner Weld. "Charles Goodwin Ridgely," *Dictionary of American Biography,* ed. Allen Johnson and Dumas Malone.

21 vols. New York: Charles Scribner's Sons, 1928-37, XV, 595-96.
Bolton, Charles K. "William Tudor," *Dictionary of American Biography*, ed. Allen Johnson and Dumas Malone. 21 vols. New York: Charles Scribner's Sons, 1928-37, XIX, 48-49.
Cooper, James Fenimore. *Lives of Distinguished Naval Officers*. 2 vols. Philadelphia: Carey and Hart, 1846.
Cleveland, H. W. S. *Voyages of a Merchant Navigator*. New York: Harper & Brothers, 1886.
Frost, John. *American Naval Biography*. Philadelphia: E. H. Butler, 1844.
Jones, Charles C., Jr. *The Life and Services of Commodore Josiah Tattnall*. Savannah: Morning News Steam Printing House, 1878.
Opazo Maturana, Gustavo. "Lady Cochrane en Chile," *Boletín de la Academia Chilena de la Historia*, X (Segundo trimestre de 1943, No. 25), 9-17.
Porter, Kenneth Wiggins. *John Jacob Astor, Business Man*. 2 vols. Cambridge: Harvard University Press, 1931.
Pratt, Fletcher. *Preble's Boys: Commodore Preble and the Birth of American Sea Power*. New York: William Sloan Associates, 1950.
Van Deurs, George. "A Commodore's Namesake," *United States Naval Institute Proceedings*, LXXXI (June, 1955), 678-84.
Westcott, Allan. "Stephen Decatur," *Dictionary of American Biography*, ed. Allen Johnson and Dumas Malone. 21 vols. New York: Charles Scribner's Sons, 1928-37, V, 187-90.
Whitaker, Arthur Preston, "John Murray Forbes," *Dictionary of American Biography*, ed. Allen Johnson and Dumas Malone. 21 vols. New York: Charles Scribner's Sons, 1928-37, VI, 506-7.

D. REFERENCE WORKS

Figueroa, Pedro Pablo. *Diccionario biográfico de estranjeros en Chile*. Santiago de Chile: Imprenta Moderna, 1900.
Johnson, Allen, and Dumas Malone (eds.). *Dictionary of American Biography*. 21 vols. New York: Charles Scribner's Sons, 1928-37.
Neeser, Robert Wilden. *Statistical and Chronological History of the United States Navy, 1775-1907*. 2 vols. New York: The Macmillan Company, 1909.

Yaben, Jacinto R. *Biografías argentinas y sudamericanas.* 5 vols. Buenos Aires: Editorial "Metrópolis," 1938–40.

E. BIBLIOGRAPHICAL AIDS

A Brief Guide to U.S. Naval History Sources in the Washington, D.C. Area. Washington: Navy Department, Office of the Chief of Naval Operations, Naval History Division, 1957.

Calendar of Correspondence of James Monroe. Department of State, *PD4380, House Documents,* Vol. M3, No. 620. Washington: Department of State, 1893.

Guide to Materials on Latin America in the National Archives, Vol. I. National Archives Publication No. 62-3. Washington: General Services Administration, National Archives and Records Service, The National Archives, 1961.

List of National Archives Microfilm Publications, 1961. National Archives Publication No. 61-12. Washington: The National Archives, National Archives and Records Service, General Services Administration, 1961.

Calendar of the Miscellaneous Letters Received by the Department of State from the Organization of the Government to 1820. Washington: Government Printing Office, 1897.

Index

A

Abercrombie, Midshipman John B., USN, 90
Acapulco, 99
Adams, John Quincy, Secretary of State, opposes recognition of South American states, 6; revokes Robinson's commission, 10; appoints Prevost agent to Chile and Peru, 12; instructions to Biddle, 12; interviews Captain Morris on South American affairs, 14; replies to Chilean complaints against Biddle, 72; compares services of Biddle and Prevost, 75; cabinet discussion on sending armed forces to South America, 79; distrust of Prevost, 123–24; requests Stewart assist settlement of brig *Macedonian* claims, 153; backs Stewart, rebukes Prevost, 188–89; states U.S. policy on blockade, 189–90; reply to Colombian minister on Peru's complaints, 190; instructions to Heman Allen, 195–96; mentioned, 52, 68, 119, 171, 177, 188, 205
Adonis, U.S. merchantman, 158, 177, 179
Aguila, Chilean brig-of-war, 58
Aguirre, Manuel Hermenegildo, 59
Aguirre bills of exchange, attempts to collect, 82, 86, 92, 124, 225
Allen, Heman, 195–96
Amanda, U.S. merchantman, 105, 179
Amelia Island, 3, 9, 13, 14
America, U.S. merchantman, 151, 183, 184
Amphion, British man-of-war, 21, 24, 32
Ancon, 111, 137, 138, 141, 160
Andes, Chilean privateer, 88
Andromache, British man-of-war, 53, 54, 65, 69, 88, 101, 103, 131, 231
Aquiles, Spanish brig-of-war, 198
Arab, U.S. merchantman, 178
Araucano, Chilean brig-of-war, 166
Arauco, 118, 126, 129, 140
Archimedes, French whale ship, 92
Arequipa, 138, 139, 144, 159
Arica, 98, 139, 154, 156, 157, 159, 160, 161, 162, 165, 167, 172, 177, 188, 189
Asia, Spanish man-of-war, 198
Astor, John Jacob, 7, 12, 29, 51, 69, 70
Atacama, 93, 202
Ayacucho, battle of, 194, 198, 199

B

Balcarce, General Antonio Gonzales, 48–49

[257]

Barron, Captain James, USN, 191, 192
Beaver, U.S. merchantman, 7, 21, 28–30, 40, 42, 49, 51–54, 64, 73, 105
Belgrano, Peruvian man-of-war, 161, 176, 186, 193
Benavides, Vicente, 119, 140, 206
Biddle, Captain James, USN, commands Ontario, 11; associated with Prevost in reclamation of Columbia River territory, 12–13; sailing orders, 12–13, 16; relations with Prevost, 12–13, 16, 31, 37, 39–40, 49, 68–69; character and career, 17–19; Spanish blockade squadron at Valpariso, 20–21, 28–30, 38, 42–43; protests desertions of U.S. seamen to patriot privateers, 22–23, 36; relations with patriot high command, 23; quarrel with governor of Valparaiso, 23–25; efforts on behalf of Beaver and Canton, 29–30, 51, 53–54; claims on behalf of Enterprise, 30–31; fear of royalist success at Valparaiso, delays departure, 31–34; plans to rescue U.S. and British ships, 32–34; assistance to patriots in purchase and outfitting of Windham as warship, 34–35; on recognition of Chile, 38; relations with Pezuela, 41–45, 52, 54–57, 64–65, 208; sponsors cartel mission to Chile, 41–49; co-operation of British, 43, 50; at Columbia River, 53; meets commander of Russian warship Kutusoff at Monterey, 53; quarrel with Cochrane, 58, 61–67; carries specie on board Ontario, 63; Spanish passengers on board on visit to Valparaiso, 63–64; fears search by Chilean naval forces, departs Valparaiso, 65–66; Chilean repercussions, 67–68; Chilean complaint of his conduct, 68–69; informal defense in U.S. press, 69–70, 72; answers to Chilean charges, 70–72; exonerated by Navy and State Departments, 72; object of congressional inquiry, 73; backed by administration, 74–75, 206; compared to Prevost by Adams, 75; witness at Stewart's court-martial, 192–93; mentioned, 96, 99. See also Prevost, Ontario

Biddle, Nicholas, banker (brother of James Biddle), 15, 17, 38, 72, 75
Biddle, Captain Nicholas, USN, 17
Blanco Encalada, Admiral Manuel, 59, 60, 141, 199
Bland, Judge Theodorick, 12, 47, 48–49, 59, 78, 207
Blockades, by royalists, of Chilean coast (1817), 20; relaxed by Pezuela, 43; by patriots, Guayaquil to Atacama (1819), 93; primary cause of friction between U.S. and belligerent commanders, 94–95, 102, 171, 202; paper blockades, 95; disagreement between Prevost and U.S. naval commanders over, 96–97, 143, 171–73; Downes refuses to recognize as legal, 97–98, 109; Irisarri cautions Chilean government against, 109; British attitude toward, 109, 128, 137; by patriots, Iquique to Guayaquil (1820), 110; rigorously enforced at Callao, 129; Cochrane's instruction on capture of merchantmen under protection of neutral warships, 131–32; new blockade at Callao (1821), 136; of 1820, shortened to Ancon to Pisco, (June, 1821), 137; U.S. commanders ordered avoid conflict over, 144–45, 150; by patriots, of Intermedios, 15°–22°30′S (Oct., 1821), 160; Stewart declares patriot blockades illegal, 162, 175–76; of Intermedios, redefined, 14°–22°20′S (March, 1823), 175; by patriots, Chancay to Pisco, except Callao (June, 1823), 175; of Intermedios, resumed as patriots driven out (Sept.–Nov., 1823), 177; Chancay to Pisco, ended (July, 1823), 178; by patriots, entire coast from Callao to Cobija (Feb., 1824), 181; Adams states U.S. policy on, 188–90; of Callao, haphazardly maintained (1824), 196; Bolívar promises to conduct according to international law, 197; of Callao, allowed to lapse, resumed and enforced by Blanco Encalada (Jan., 1825), 199; respected by Hull, 199
Blossom, British man-of-war, 220
Bolívar, Simón, 4, 106, 143, 175, 177, 181, 182, 194, 197, 241
Bowers, P., 183

Index

Bowles, Commodore William, British naval officer, 21, 24, 50, 128
Brackenridge, Henry M., 11
Buckskin, *Macedonian*'s tender, 114
Buenos Aires, 10, 11, 12, 16, 40, 59, 67, 72, 119, 124, 141, 186, 190
Burr, Shubal, 35

C

Cabrera, Capitán de Navío Tomás, 20, 21, 28, 29
Calderón, Francisco, 23, 24, 34, 35, 217
Callao, 5, 8, 20, 29, 38–56 *passim*, 64, 65, 78, 92, 93, 100–15 *passim*, 129–46 *passim*, 154, 156, 160–87 *passim*, 194–99 *passim*, 206, 208
Cancha Rayada, battle of, 32, 34
Canterac, General José, 174, 178, 194
Canton, China, 29, 164
Canton, U.S. merchantman, 7, 21, 28–30, 40, 42, 49, 51, 53, 64, 73, 105, 111, 114, 151, 153–54, 158–63, 165–66, 173, 176, 186, 188, 191, 192, 193, 203–4, 236
Cape Disappointment, 53
Cape Horn, 7, 12, 13, 17, 20, 21, 79, 80, 82, 118, 135, 150, 151, 156, 205
Carrera, José Miguel, 5, 10–11, 215
Carrera family, 49, 228
Cartel mission to Chile, 41–49
Carter, Master Commandant William, USN, 197
Casares, Marquesa of, 134
Castlereagh, Robert Stewart, 109
Cerro Colupo, 175
Cevallos, Colonel Rafael de, 131
Chacabuco, battle of, 5, 8, 125
Chacabuco, Chilean man-of-war, 66, 93
Chancay, 135, 175, 178
Chandler, Samuel, 157
Chauncey, U.S. merchantman, 177
Chesapeake, U.S. merchantman, 110, 118, 128–29, 146
Chile, liberated by patriots, 4–5; U.S. trade with, 7; opens ports, 7; conditions in, 26–28, 37–38, 84–86, 88, 92, 145, 170; repels royalist expedition, 31–34; Peruvian cartel mission, 46–49; lack of facilities for sea power, 59; threat of search of British and U.S. ships for Spanish specie, 65; published accounts of Biddle-Cochrane correspondence, 67; makes formal complaint against Biddle, 68; hope for recognition by U.S., 76; commands Southeast Pacific, 95; protests transportation of specie as an unneutral act, 98; resentful of British and U.S. disregard of their blockade, 104; invasion of royalist Peru in 1820, 108, 110–11; Irisarri warns government against preferential treatment of British, 109; resentment over *Louisa* affair, 117; revolt against O'Higgins, 170; provisional government, 173. *See also* Blockades, Chilean Navy, Cochrane, O'Higgins, San Martín
Chilean Navy, started by San Martín and O'Higgins, 5; encourages deserters from merchantmen, 22–24, 35–36; impressment of seamen, 36–37; purchases of ships, 32, 34–35, 59; conversion of *Lautaro* (ex-*Windham*) to warship, 35–36; assistance by U.S. navy, 35, 110, 199, 201; growth, 55, 58–59, 222; gains control of Southeast Pacific, 55, 93, 95; Cochrane becomes commander in chief, 59; training, 59–60; jealousy between native and foreign crewmen, 60; patterned after British, 60–61; attack on Callao 65, 93; blockade force, Callao and Peru coast, 93, 102–3, 115, 130–31, 135–37; amphibious assault on Peru, 110, 111; capture of *Esmeralda*, 111–12; Cochrane-San Martín rift, 141; defections to Peruvian Navy, 141; leaves Peruvian waters, 142; Chilean government fears loss of fleet, 145; Cochrane resigns, 173; deterioration of fleet, 173; resumes blockade of Callao (Jan., 1825), 199. *See also* Blockades, Cochrane
Chiloé, 105, 111, 145, 154, 175, 178, 179, 180
China, U.S. merchantman, 183, 196
Chorillos, 113, 136, 137, 197, 199
Clack, Lieutenant John H., USN, 124
Clay, Henry, 9, 73, 74
Cleveland, Richard J., 29, 30, 51, 54
Clorinde, French man-of-war, 167
Cobbett, Captain Henry, Chilean Navy, 135
Cobija, 160, 181
Cochrane, Lady Katherine, 59, 83, 85, 92
Cochrane, Lord Thomas, commander in chief Chilean Navy, 58–59; in-

stills British discipline and ideals, 60; complex character of, 61; quarrel with Biddle, 62–68; attacks and blockades Callao (1819), 93; amphibious attack against Peru, invests Callao, 110–11; applies British principles to neutral commerce, 94, 137; taking of American ships as prizes, 96, 110–11, 115, 127; captures *Esmeralda*, 111–12; and Downes, 97, 102–4, 107–9, 114–15, 117, 202; British protests, 128, 137; instructions on capture of ships under protection of foreign men-of-war, 131–32; returns to Callao with entire fleet (1821), 135; and Ridgely, 136–37, 144–45, 152; seizes brig *Macedonian*'s specie and merchandise, 138–39, 153, 226; break with San Martín, 141; leaves Peru with fleet, 142; leaves Chile to command Brazilian Navy, 173; mentioned, 84, 116, 151, 221, 222. See also Blockades, Chilean Navy

Coffin, Francis, 51, 114
Coffin, Isaac, 27, 29
Coig, Capitán de Fragata Luis, Spanish Navy, 55
Columbia River territory, 4, 12–13, 15, 17, 37, 49, 50, 53, 220
Columbus, U.S. whale ship, 115
Concepción, 33, 151
Condarco, José Antonio Álvarez, 32, 59
Congress, United States, debate on recognition of South American states, 8–9; investigation of Biddle, 73–75, 206; strengthens neutrality act (1818), 77
Congress, USS, 11, 12–13, 78
Conner, David, U.S. naval officer, 19, 21, 24, 25–27, 49, 148, 156, 168, 185, 217, 234
Constellation, USS, at Valparaiso, 118, 125–27, 139–43, 144–45; departed New York, 123; at Coquimbo, 127–29, 143; off Santa María, 129; at Rio de Janeiro, 124–25, 145; at Callao, 130–34, 135–38, 143; at Huacho, 135; at Ancon, 138, at Mollendo, 138–39, 143–44; to Juan Fernández, 143; to Guayaquil, 143; departs for home, arrives Sandy Hook, 145; mentioned, 115, 118, 122, 124, 146, 148, 152, 153, 201. See also Ridgely
Conway, British man-of-war, 118, 140

Coquimbo, 5, 21, 91–92, 110–11, 118, 126–27, 128–29, 143, 199
Cora, U.S. merchantman, 167–68
Cossack, U.S. merchantman, 99
Creole, British man-of-war, 140
Crompton, Thomas, 44–45, 46, 47, 49
Crosby, Platt H., 155, 166, 167–68, 187, 192, 236
Cross, Latham, 142
Crowninshield, Benjamin, U.S. Secretary of the Navy, 11, 14, 21
Cruz, Peruvian man-of-war, 161

D

Deblois, Charles J., 81–82, 84, 88, 89, 90, 108, 227
De Koven, Henry L., 183–84
De la Cruz, Luis, 23, 24–25, 31, 62, 65, 82, 87
Del Río, Juan García, 159, 165
De Puy, Cornelius, 151
Deserters, 22–24, 35–37, 54–55, 101, 115–16, 127, 200, 203
Diana, U.S. whale ship, 126
Dods, Midshipman George D., USN, 54
Dolphin, USS, 148, 150–51, 156, 158, 166, 168, 173, 184, 185, 186, 197, 199, 200
Downes, Captain John, USN, ordered command of *Macedonian*, 79; career and character, 79–80; sailing orders, 80–81, 123; attempts to collect Aguirre bills of exchange, 82, 86, 92; and Lady Cochrane, 83; claims from sale of *Montezuma*, 86; assists U.S. shipping, 86–87, 89, 106, 118; protests attack on Lieutenant Percival, 87; takes responsibility for discipline of British and U.S. merchant seamen, 88; cordial relations with patriots, 92, 100; and Prevost, 96–99, 117, 119, 120; determined to prevent seizures of American ships, 97, 111; and Cochrane, 97–98, 102–3, 107–9, 114–15, 202; declares patriot blockade illegal, 97, 108–9, 110; carrying of specie, 98, 106, 205, 227; protests capture of *Traveller* and *Cossack* to viceroy of Mexico, 99; protests preferential treatment of British in Chile, 101–2; and Pezuela, 104–5, 106, 113–14; gives asylum to escaped English and Irish prisoners at Panama, 107; protests attacks on *Buckskin* and

Index

Rampart, 113-14; convoys British and U.S. ships through blockade at Callao, 114-15, 206; liberation of the *Louisa*, 115-18, 204; and San Martín, 116, 138; and Ridgely, 118, 119-20, 122; witness at Stewart trial, 192; mentioned, 127, 150, 225. See also Blockades, *Ontario*
Dueling, 90-91, 124, 125, 225

E

Echeverría, Joaquin de, 66-70, 119
Eliza Barker, U.S. whale ship, 56, 104
Ellen Maria, U.S. merchantman, 90, 105, 106
Elton, Master Commandant John H., USN, 14
Enterprise, U.S. merchantman, 30, 49
Esmeralda, Spanish man-of-war, 31, 46, 111-12, 135
Essex, U.S. whale ship, 126, 230
Essex, USS, 14, 17, 86, 90, 105, 206, 228
Essex Junior, USS, 79

F

Fly, British man-of-war, 182
Forbes, John M., 72, 123-24
Forster, Captain Robert, Chilean Navy, 130, 131-32
Franklin, USS, relief of *Constellation*, 144; Stewart ordered to command, 148; departs New York, 150; arrives Juan Fernández, 151; at Valparaiso, 151-60, 170-73, 178-79, 181; at Arica, 160-61; at Quilca, 161-63, 169-70, 173, 178, 179-81; at Callao, 163-68, 173, 178, 181-85; at Juan Fernández, 173; at Iquique, 173; homeward bound, 185; arrives New York, 190. See also Stewart
Frederick, U.S. merchantman, 179
Freeman, Captain, Peruvian Navy, 183-84
Freire, General Ramón, 170

G

Galen, U.S. merchantman, 138, 146, 203, 204
Galvarino, Chilean man-of-war, 85-86, 88, 115
Gauntt, Lieutenant Charles, USN, 81
General Brown, U.S. merchantman, 130-35, 138, 146, 199, 231
Globe, U.S. whale ship, 200

Golconda, U.S. whale ship, 115
Gordon, Midshipman Alexander G., USN, 90-91
Governor Shelby, U.S. merchantman, 8, 51
Graham, John, 11
Griswold, Daniel S., 125
Guarmey, 98
Guayaquil, 5, 79, 93, 98, 105, 110, 143, 145, 163, 166, 177, 196, 202
Guido, Tomás, 23, 32, 35, 36, 48, 178, 190, 239
Guise, Captain George Martin, Peruvian Navy, 141, 176, 181-84, 197, 199, 241

H

Hall, Captain Basil, British Navy, 140, 206
Hammersley, Lieutenant Thomas S., USN, 161, 170, 179, 184
Hardy, Commodore Sir Thomas, British Navy, 103, 128, 137, 140, 206, 231
Hart, Jeannette, 196, 197
Heffernan, John, 135, 138
Henley, Captain John, USN, 13-14
Henry, Lieutenant Henry, USN, 157-58, 161, 166, 169
Herald, U.S. merchantman, 182-83
Hero, U.S. whale ship, 119, 140
Hersilia, U.S. merchantman, 139
Hickey, Captain James, British Navy, 50, 220
Hicks, master of the *Louisa*, 115-16
Hill, Henry, 36-37, 61, 79, 80, 82, 91, 99, 102, 107-8, 127
Hogan, Michael, 139, 157, 191
Homans, Benjamin, chief clerk of U.S. Navy Department, 14, 72, 224
Huacho, 115, 116, 118, 134, 135, 183, 197, 202
Huara, 116, 130, 197
Hull, Captain Isaac, USN, relief of Stewart, 181, 185; arrives Callao, 184; sympathetic to patriots, 194; sailing orders, special provisions re specie and relations with U.S. diplomatic representative, 195; institutes convoy system between ports, 196; friendly relations with Bolívar, 197; orders *Peacock* keep watch on diminished Spanish fleet, 198; respects patriot blockade of Callao, 199; reports no need for additional ships off South

America, 200; sends *Dolphin* to Sandwich Islands, 200. *See also* Blockades, United States
Hyperion, British man-of-war, 111–12, 115, 128

I

Independencia, Chilean man-of-war, 103, 130
Iquique, 110, 173, 175
Irisarri, Antonio José de, 47, 103–4, 109

J

Jay Treaty of 1794, 94
Johnson, Samuel B., USMC, 99
Juan Fernández Island, 30, 120, 142–43, 151, 157, 159, 173

K

Kennon, Lieutenant Beverly, USN, 199–200
Kutusoff, Captain, Russian Navy, 53

L

Lane, William S., 140
La Serna, José de, viceroy of Peru, 129; negotiations with San Martín, 130, 133; asks Ridgely guarantee terms of armistice, 133; orders restoration of all U.S. ships taken by privateers, 180; mentioned, 106, 130, 184, 186, 194, 208, 231
Latimer, Lieutenant William K., USN, 89, 190–91
Lautaro, Chilean man-of-war (ex-*Windham*), 35–37, 38, 41, 46, 59, 93, 115, 116, 201
Laws of the Indies, 22, 28, 29, 94
Levant, U.S. merchantman, 37, 70
Lima, 10, 13, 20, 24, 25, 31–53 *passim*, 63, 65, 68, 69, 74, 81, 92–113 *passim*, 126–39 *passim*, 152–84 *passim*, 191, 208
Livonia, British merchantman, 90
Louisa, U.S. merchantman, 115–18, 138, 203–4

M

Macedonian, Peruvian man-of-war (ex-U.S. brig *Macedonian*), 183–84
Macedonian, U.S. merchant brig, 55, 96, 105, 106, 123, 138, 153–54, 163–64, 173, 222, 226

Macedonian, USS, ordered to Pacific, 79; Downes ordered to command, 79; sailing orders, 80–81; delayed by gale damage in Atlantic, 81; departs Norfolk, 82; at Valparaiso, 82–91, 92, 101–2, 107–10, 118–20; at Coquimbo, 91–92, 110–11, 118; visits Arica, Guarmey, Trujillo, Túmbez, Guayaquil, 92, 98; receives specie off Arica, 98; at San Blas, 99, 107; at Acapulco, 99; at Callao, 102–6, 111–14; at Panama, 106, 107; assistance to patriots, 110, 201; at Samanco and Paita, 115; at Huacho, 115–16; at Mollendo, 118; leaves Pacific, 120; arrives U.S., 120; mentioned, 75, 122, 125, 226. *See also* Blockades, Downes
Mackau, Baron, French Navy, 167
Madrid, Spanish officer, stowaway on board *Franklin*, 169–70
Maipú, battle of, 34, 35, 37, 40, 41
Maipú, patriot privateer, 54, 105
Maria Isabel, Spanish man-of-war, 55, 60, 77
Martinez, General Henríquez, 182
Maury, Lieutenant John M., USN, 80, 89
Miller, Colonel William, 139, 178, 239
Mollendo, 118, 138, 143, 153, 156, 162, 178
Monroe, James, 3–5, 7, 9–10, 11, 15, 17, 19, 95
Monteagudo, Bernardo, 117–18, 165
Monterey, 53, 199
Morris, Captain Charles, USN, 11, 14, 63, 225

N

Nixon, Lieutenant Zachariah W., USN, 110, 158

O

O'Cain, U.S. whale ship, 175
Ocean, U.S. whale ship, 90, 140
Ochavarriague y Blanco, Félix de, 42, 44–49, 50, 51, 52, 69, 71
O'Higgins, Bernardo, 5, 31, 32, 47, 49, 111, 118, 128, 139, 145, 152, 170, 173, 207, 228
O'Higgins, Chilean man-of-war, 93, 103, 199
Olarría, Spanish colonel, 64, 73, 208
Onís, Chevalier Luis de, 8, 40
Ontario, USS, Biddle to command, to transport South American Commis-

Index

sion, 11; orders changed to Pacific, 12; new sailing orders, 12-13; departs New York, 16; arrives Valparaiso, 20; encounters Spanish blockade squadron 20, 28-29, 38; at Valparaiso, 21-38, 45-51, 58-66; at Callao, 39-45, 51-52, 53-57; at Columbia River, 53; at Monterey, 53; departs Valparaiso, homeward bound, 66; arrives Annapolis, 69; mentioned, 67, 68, 70, 73, 74, 104, 201. *See also* Biddle

Osorio, General Mariano, 5, 55, 64, **222**

O'Sullivan, John, 151, 159, 186, 191

Owen Glendower, British man-of-war, 135, 140, 231

P

Paita, 115

Panama, 8, 105, 106, 107, 156, 157

Panther, U.S. merchantman, 111, 114, 115

Paroissien, Diego, 159, 165

Patterson, Captain Daniel F., USN, **13**, 14, 63, 64, 72

Paulding, Lieutenant Hiram, USN, 80, 197

Peacock, USS, 196, 197, 198, 199

Pearl, U.S. merchantman, 157, 160, 161, 173, 176, 236

Percival, Lieutenant John, USN, 87, 88, 185, 200

Pero, Colonel Rafael, 180

Persia, U.S. whale ship, 142-43

Peru, last royalist stronghold, 4; patriot plans to capture by sea, 5; royalist attempts to reconquer Chile defeated at Maipú, 31-35; cartel mission to Chile via *Ontario*, 41-49; military weakness of royalists, dependent on foreign shipping, 55, 105; patriots begin amphibious assault, declare blockade of coast, 110-11; Viceroy Pezuela deposed, replaced by La Serna, 129; patriots capture Lima, royalists hold Callao, 136; independence proclaimed, San Martín named Protector, 136; Callao falls to patriots (Sept., 1821), 140; rift between San Martín and Cochrane, 141; Chilean Navy leaves Peru, 142; resignation of San Martín, reorganization of government, 165; assault on royalists in Upper Peru through Intermedios, 168-69; royalists recapture Lima, patriots withdraw to Callao (June, 1823), 174; royalists abandon Lima (July, 1823), 174; Bolívar given command of patriot forces with dictatorial power, 174-75; new patriot attack on Upper Peru through Intermedios (1823), forced to withdraw, 174, 177; patriot mutiny at Callao, royalists occupy Callao and Lima (1824), 181; patriot government maintained at Trujillo, 181; mistreatment of U.S. shipping at Callao, 181-83, 184; patriot government makes formal complaint against Stewart, 185-86; royalists evacuate Lima, retain Callao (Sept., 1824), 194; royalists defeated at Ayacucho (Dec., 1824), 194; Bolívar disavows conduct of Callao blockade, 197; Spanish efforts to regain control of seas fail, 198; Spanish fleet leaves South America, 198. *See also* Blockades, Bolívar, Cochrane, La Serna, Peruvian Navy, San Martín, Pezuela

Peruvian Navy, squadron formed under Guise, 141; blockade force at Intermedios, 160-62; U.S. brig *Macedonian* confiscated, converted to man-of-war, 164-65; transports expedition to Intermedios (1822), 168-69; harassment of U.S. merchantmen, 176-77, 182-84; blockades Callao after mutiny of patriot garrison (1824), 181, 196; ordered by Bolívar to take neutral merchantmen at Callao, 182; battle with Spanish ships, Callao (Oct., 1824), 198-99. *See also* Blockades, Guise

Peru, U.S. whale ship, 89

Peruviano, U.S. schooner, attached to Pacific Squadron, 157, 158, 166, 173, 179, 184

Pezuela, Joaquín de, viceroy of Peru, purchase of arms from U.S., 8; orders blockade of Chile, 20; and Prevost, 40-42; sends secret agents to Chile on *Ontario*, 44; and Biddle, 42-45, 52, 54-57, 64-65, 69-71, 208, 231; and Downes, 104-5, 111, 113-14, concessions to U.S. merchantmen, 105; deposed, 129, 131; escape from Peru aboard the *General Brown*, 131-32, 134-35, 146; asylum aboard *Constel-*

lation, 132; meets San Martín aboard *Constellation*, 133
Pezuela, Spanish man-of-war, 46
Pisco, 43, 111, 137, 141, 145, 160, 175, 178, 197
Poinsett, Joel R., 11
Porter, Commodore David, USN, 10, 14, 17, 79, 86, 166, 191
Prevost, Judge John B., appointed special agent to Chile and Peru, 12; and Biddle, 12–13, 25, 39, 49, 68, 72, 96, 119; instructions to, 16; career, 19; recommends permanent naval force in pacific, 22, 78; recommends recognition of Chile, praises effects of *Ontario*, 37; pro-patriot, 40, 96, 124, 205–6; agrees to cartel mission to Chile, ignored in negotiations, 41–42; and Downes, differences between, 96–97, 99, 118, 119–20; views on patriot seizures of U.S. ships, 96–97; opposes transportation of specie by U.S. warships, 99, 119; and Ridgely, 122, 139, 143; visits Guayaquil on board *Constellation*, 143; and Stewart, 152, 165, 166, 170–73, 176–77, 186, 202; with patriot government at Trujillo, 184; censured by Adams, 189–90, 240; death, 191, 240; reclaimed Columbia River territory, 220; mentioned, 17, 21, 31, 35, 43, 48, 51, 92, 95, 123, 160, 173, 192, 195
Prieto, Colonel Joaquín, 140
Privateers, 9, 13, 14, 22, 43, 60, 78, 158, 175, 178–81, 185, 196, 197
Protector, Peruvian man-of-war, 176, 177, 183, 196
Providence, U.S. merchantman, 182, 183
Prueba, Spanish man-of-war, 145
Prunier, Captain William, Peruvian Navy, 161, 162, 163, 165, 188
Punchauca, 130, 133

Q

Quilca, 154, 159–81 *passim*, 186
Quintanilla, Antonio de, 178
Quintanilla, Spanish privateer, 158, 178–81

R

Ramírez, General Juan, 155, 156
Rampart, U.S. merchantman, 111, 113–14

Rebecca, British merchantman, 88, 90, 111
Recognition of South American states, 9, 37, 38, 49, 76, 78, 145–46, 202
Ribas, Francisco, 30
Ridgely, Captain Charles Goodwin, USN, and Downes, 119–20, 122; career and character, 121–22; and Prevost, 122, 139; ordered to command *Constellation*, 123; sailing orders, 123; special instructions re slave vessels, specie, 123; maintenance of discipline, 124–25; arranges for rescue of survivors of whale ship *Essex*, 126; and the *Chesapeake*, *Warrior*, 126, 128–29; adverse opinion of patriots, 127; and Cochrane, 127, 136, 141–42; reciprocal arrangements with British for protection of shipping, 127–28, 140, 206; Ridgely and the *General Brown*, 130–35, 138, 146, 231; gives Pezuela asylum, 133, 146; declines guarantee of armistice, 133; and the *Galen*, 135–39, 146, 204; and San Martín, 138, 143–44; and Eliphalet Smith, 138, 143–44; transports patriot troops to Juan Fernández, 142; specie, 143–44; cautioned to avoid conflict over blockades, 144–45; summary of cruise, 145–47; witness at Stewart's trial, 192; mentioned, 150, 152. *See also* Blockades, *Constellation*
Rio de Janeiro, 10, 23, 63, 64, 70, 80, 120, 123, 124, 135, 145, 208
Riva Agüero, José de la, 174, 175
Rivadavia, Bernardo, 186
Robinson Crusoe, U.S. merchantman, 157, 176–77
Robinson, Jeremy, 10, 12, 39, 48–49, 51, 53, 66, 68, 71, 78, 146, 187–88, 217
Rodil, General José Ramón, 181, 184, 196
Rodney, Caesar A., 11, 12, 186
Rodney, Midshipman John, USN, 12
Royal Decree of 1797, Spanish, not applicable to Pacific ports, 7
Rush, Richard, 10, 11, 148

S

Sacramento, Peruvian man-of-war, 161
Salutes, gun, U.S. Navy regulation of 1818 concerning, 221
Samanco, 115
San Blas, 98, 99, 107

Index

Sandwich Islands, 53, 92, 157, 200
San Martín, Chilean man-of-war, 62, 66, 93, 136, 137
San Martín, José de, invades Chile, 5; plan to conquer Peru by sea, 5, 108; promises to stop patriot enticements of U.S. seamen to desert, 22–23; defense of Chile, victory at Maipú, 31–34; amphibious attack on Peru, 108, 110, 129–30; Downes and the *Louisa*, 116–17, 138; negotiations with La Serna, 130, 133; and Ridgely, 133; visits *Constellation*, meets Pezuela aboard, 133; enters Lima, establishes independent government, 135–36; Protector of Peru, 136; Callao surrenders to, 140; break with Cochrane, 141, 145, 152; declares blockade of Intermedios coast, 160; resigns as Protector, leaves Peru, 165; mentioned, 35, 44, 48, 59, 127, 153, 171, 187, 207. *See also* Chile, Cochrane, O'Higgins, Peru
Santa Cruz, General Andrés, 174, 177
Santa María, 120, 126, 129, 151
Santiago, 5, 10, 21–36 *passim*, 46, 47, 48, 49, 52, 65, 67, 86, 92, 108, 125, 139, 152, 159, 165, 170, 173
Sarah, British merchantman, 160
Searle, Captain Thomas, British Navy, 128
Sheffield, James P., 139
Shirreff, Captain William Henry, British Navy, 50, 88, 131
Simpson, Captain, Chilean Navy, 136
Sinclair, Captain Arthur, USN, 12, 14, 122–23
Sistare, Captain Leonard, 177
Smith, Eliphalet, 96, 124, 138–39, 143–44, 155–56, 158–59, 169, 186, 187, 192, 226
Sola, Pablo Vicente, 53
Somers, Lieutenant Richard, USN, 122, 148
South American Commission, 11–12, 13, 15, 16, 17, 77, 78
Southard, Samuel L., U.S. Secretary of the Navy, 191, 195
Specie, transportation of, common practice in British and U.S. navies, 63, 205; U.S. Navy regulations on, 63; sanctioned by Acting Secretary of the Navy Calhoun (1818), 63, 64, 72; by U.S. commanders in Pacific, 63, 65, 69, 70–71, 98, 99, 106, 118, 130, 143–44, 154, 166–68, 185, 192, 203, 204–5, 227; protested by patriots as unneutral act, 98–99, 203; opposed by Prevost, 99, 119, 205; seizures of, by patriots, 98, 123–24; 138–39, 226; special instructions on, to U.S. commanders in Pacific, 99, 123, 195; U.S. fear of British monopoly, 221–22; premium on, at New York, 222
Spry, Captain John, Chilean Navy, 85, 88, 89
Stewart, Captain Charles, USN, ordered to command Pacific Squadron, 148; career and character, 148–49, 233; sailing orders, 150; instructions to avoid use of force in protection of neutral rights, 150; merchant ship *Canton* under protection, 151, 154, 158–63; disagreements with Prevost, 152, 153, 165, 170–73, 202; low opinion of patriots, 152, 164–65, 184; relations with Eliphalet Smith, 153–55, 156, 158; specie, deposit and transportation of, 154, 158, 166–68; accusations against, 155, 156, 158, 165–66, 167–68, 170, 185–88, 190–91; rejects royalist proposal for commercial treaty, 155–56; construction and employment of *Peruviano* as squadron auxiliary, 156–58, 173; safeguards against landing of contraband arms, 159, 161; protects American merchantmen against patriot blockades, 161–63, 170, 178, 181, 183–84; refuses to surrender *Canton* to patriots for alleged violation of blockade, 161–63, 203–4; declares patriot blockades illegal, 162, 172, 175–76; distrust of patriot tribunals, 163, 164–65; denies arms landed at Arica, 165; Spanish officer stowaway on *Franklin*, 169–70; undeclared war with Peruvian Navy, 176–77; successes with royalists, 178, 180–81, 184; hunt for royalist privateer *Quintanilla*, 179–81; dispute with royalists, 179–80; relieved by Hull, 185; backed by administration against critics, 188, 206; court-martial, 191–93, 236. *See also* Blockades, *Franklin*
Stewart, Delia, 150, 152, 169–70, 178, 184, 191, 238
Stewart, Washington, 92, 118

Sucre, General Antonio José de, 174, 176, 194
Surrey, British Merchantman, 126

T

Talcahuano, 7, 21, 29, 31, 33, 46, 50, 51, 55, 60, 105
Tattnall, Lieutenant Josiah, USN, 80, 91, 225
Tea Plant, U.S. merchantman, 143
Telegraph, French merchantman, 161, 163
Tepic, 99
Thais, British merchantman, 118
Thomas, British merchantman, 88–89, 98, 227
Thompson, Smith, U.S. Secretary of the Navy, 70, 144, 150, 230
Torre Tagle, Marquis de, 175, 181
Townsend, Solomon, 35–37
Traveller, U.S. merchantman, 99
"Treaty plan of 1776," U.S. adherence to for neutral rights, 93–94
Treaty of 1795, between U.S. and Spain, 7, 93–94, 203
Trujillo, 98, 175, 181, 183, 184
Tudor, Frederic, 238
Tudor, William, 184, 196, 198, 239
Túmbez, 98, 115
Two Catherines, U.S. merchantman, 45, 46, 50

U

United Provinces of Río de la Plata, 4, 5, 9, 23, 186
United States, USS, flagship of Hull, 181; at Valparaiso, 184; at Callao, 184; kept in Callao-Chorillos area, 197; used to escort merchantman through blockade, 197; British officers entertained aboard on 4th of July in 1824, 198
Upper Peru. *See* Peru

V

Valdez, General Geronimo, 179, 180
Valdivia, Chilean man-of-war (ex-*Esmeralda*), 134–35
Valdivieso, Francisco, 163–65, 185–86, 189, 192
Valparaiso, 5, 12, 13, 20–68 *passim*, 74, 82–102 *passim*, 107, 108, 115–29 *passim*, 138–45 *passim*, 151–85 *passim*, 191, 196
Velos, Spanish man-of-war, 56
Venganza, Spanish man-of-war, 20, 32, 36, 41, 145, 183

W

Ward, Horatio G., 151, 154, 165, 186
Warrior, U.S. merchantman, 118, 128, 146, 158, 228
Water Witch, U.S. merchantman, 157, 161
Wilkes, Midshipman Charles, USN, 175
Williams, S., 178
Wilson, Azariah, Chaplain, USN, 80, 83, 118
Windham, British East Indiaman, 31–32, 33, 34–35, 201
Winifred, U.S. merchantman, 179
Wooster, Captain Charles Whiting, Chilean Navy, 68, 222
Worthington, William G. D., 10, 12, 31, 33, 36, 38, 48–49, 67–68, 78, 228
Wyllie, R. C., 92

Z

Zañartu, Miguel, 31, 49
Zenteno, José Ignacio, 110, 117
Zephyr, U.S. merchantman, 111, 114, 115

www.ingramcontent.com/pod-product-compliance
Lightning Source LLC
Chambersburg PA
CBHW021357290426
44108CB00010B/285